THE UNIVERSITY OF NORTH CAROLINA
SESQUICENTENNIAL PUBLICATIONS

THE CHRONICLES OF
THE SESQUICENTENNIAL

THE UNIVERSITY OF NORTH CAROLINA
SESQUICENTENNIAL PUBLICATIONS

Louis R. Wilson, DIRECTOR

THE CHRONICLES OF THE SESQUICENTENNIAL

THE UNIVERSITY OF NORTH CAROLINA, 1789-1835
A Documentary History

THE CAMPUS OF THE FIRST STATE UNIVERSITY

THE GRADUATE SCHOOL: RESEARCH AND PUBLICATIONS

THE GRADUATE SCHOOL: DISSERTATIONS AND THESES

STUDIES IN SCIENCE

STUDIES IN LANGUAGE AND LITERATURE

A CENTURY OF LEGAL EDUCATION

A STATE UNIVERSITY SURVEYS THE HUMANITIES

SECONDARY EDUCATION IN THE SOUTH

IN SEARCH OF THE REGIONAL BALANCE OF AMERICA

STUDIES IN HISTORY AND POLITICAL SCIENCE

LIBRARY RESOURCES OF THE UNIVERSITY OF NORTH CAROLINA

RESEARCH AND REGIONAL WELFARE

PIONEERING A PEOPLE'S THEATER

UNIVERSITY EXTENSION IN ACTION

BOOKS FROM CHAPEL HILL

THE
CHRONICLES
OF THE
SESQUICENTENNIAL

Edited with a Foreword

BY

LOUIS R. WILSON

DIRECTOR OF THE SESQUICENTENNIAL

CHAPEL HILL
THE UNIVERSITY OF NORTH CAROLINA PRESS
1947

Printed in the United States of America
The William Byrd Press, Inc.
Richmond, Virginia

FOREWORD

THE CELEBRATION of the Sesquicentennial of the University of North Carolina during the period 1939-1946 was one of the most notable events in the one hundred and fifty years of the University's history. Its significance stemmed from several circumstances. First of all, the celebration focussed attention upon the significant relation of the University to the development of higher education in the United States. It brought out clearly the fact that in a very true sense the University was a child of the American Revolution and freedom and as such was the first university founded, supported, and controlled by a state and free from sectarian or other special interests to open its doors to students. Provided for in the state constitution of 1776 when America declared its independence of Great Britain, and chartered by the General Assembly in 1789 upon the adoption of the federal constitution, the University formally opened its doors in 1795 to the first student to enter an American state university. As a result of these measures taken by the founding fathers, the University inaugurated the march, begun in the Southeastern Seaboard in the eighteenth century and extended to the Middle West and the Nation in the nineteenth, of the ever-increasing throng of students to state university campuses. Hinton James, the first matriculate at Chapel Hill, who is reputed to have walked the two hundred miles from his home in Wilmington, and arrived at Chapel Hill on February 12, four weeks after the University was declared formally open, became the first student to enroll in an American state university and thereby contributed to the formation of a pattern of higher education which in the course of a century and a half has become distinctly American in character.

A second aspect of the importance of the celebration is to be seen in the searching self-examination to which the University subjected itself during the sesquicentennial period. From the beginning of the period until the end, the University deeply pondered the problems of a global war that tested anew the foundations of democracy and freedom upon which it was founded and to the defense of which it sent more than 8000 of its sons and daughters. As the new world order succeeds the old, the University, more keenly aware than ever before of its priceless heritage, set itself with renewed and heightened vigor to the search for truth and to the strengthening of freedom and democracy which it was established to promote.

The third element of the importance of the celebration derived from the emphasis which the University placed upon the program of graduate study and research which it projected during the war period for the enrichment of the state, the region, and the Nation, through research and the application of the findings of research to the daily and immediate problems of the civilization of which it is a part. In the first century of its existence, the University successfully passed through its development as a sound American college. In the past fifty years it has made the difficult transition from the status of a college, to which several professional schools had been added, to that of a broadly based, effective university. Today, as the Consolidated University, embracing not only the faculties, libraries, laboratories, and other facilities of the plant at Chapel Hill, but the resources of the plants at Greensboro and Raleigh, looks forward to the next half century, it essays in high spirit the role of a major university devoted anew to the advancement of the frontiers of knowledge and the nurture and enrichment of the human spirit.

A final element of the significance of the ceremonies has grown out of the sense of oneness which the University has felt with the state and people of North Carolina who brought the University into being and have given it their support through the century and a half gone, and of the many expressions of good will and esteem which it received from other institutions throughout the Nation and the scholarly world. The celebration, though carried out during the onset, duration, and ending of World War II, and consequently limited in its public ceremonies by the restrictions of travel imposed by war conditions, was participated in by thousands of citizens of the State and representatives of other colleges, universities, learned societies, and foundations, and the University was the recipient of many expressions of felicitation and commendation from which it will derive strength and courage for the future. Through an extensive series of Sesquicentennial Publications it has also been able to extend the celebration to members of the scholarly world whose participation in the ceremonies was made impossible by reason of the limitations of travel and communication.

The present volume sets forth an account of the celebration from its beginning at Fayetteville, in November, 1939, to its significant and impressive ending in the final Sesquicentennial Convocation at Chapel Hill in April, 1946. It contains the programs of the various events, the addresses of the speakers who participated in the programs, the lists of the recipients of honorary degrees and of the delegates from other institutions, and a record of the other events which were included in the celebration.

Limitations of space make it impossible for me to set down here the names of all those whose aid was generously given the University in carrying the celebration to its conclusion, aid of which the University is deeply appreciative. To Governors Clyde R. Hoey, J. Melville Broughton, and R. Gregg Cherry; to Lieutenant Governors R. L. Harris and L. Y. Ballentine and Speaker Oscar L. Richardson; to the Legislative Commission, the committees from the trustees, the faculty, the alumni, and the students; to the University Marshal and his aids; and to those in charge of the administrative services of the campus whose duties were largely increased by the demands of the celebration, the thanks of the University are especially extended for their assistance in planning and executing the program. To the Carolina Playmakers, the musical organizations of the University, the Departments of Dramatic Art, Music, and Art, and to Mrs. Katherine Pendleton Arrington, President of the North Carolina State Art Society, and Mr. William F. Davidson, Vice-President of M. Knoedler Galleries, Inc., of New York, the University is greatly indebted for the dramatic, musical, and artistic programs which contributed so greatly to the enjoyment of its guests and visitors. The University likewise acknowledges its great appreciation of the gracious hospitality of the hosts and hostesses who generously opened their homes to its guests, and of the substantial assistance of the Alumni Loyalty Fund, the University of North Carolina Press, and other organizations and individuals in financing and otherwise making possible the Sesquicentennial Publications. Special acknowledgment is also made by the University of its indebtedness to the authors and editors of the Sesquicentennial Publications for the preparation of the various volumes, and to Mrs. Agatha Boyd Adams for making the indexes of several of the publications.

LOUIS R. WILSON

Chapel Hill, N. C.
June 15, 1946

CONTENTS

ILLUSTRATIONS

THE CHRONICLES OF
THE SESQUICENTENNIAL

I

PREPARATION AND ADMINISTRATION
OF THE SESQUICENTENNIAL
PROGRAM

THE HISTORIC incidents in the founding of the University of North Carolina, around which the Sesquicentennial ceremonies centered from 1939 to 1946, were the granting of the charter of the University by the General Assembly at Fayetteville, December 11, 1789; the laying of the cornerstone of Old East Building, October 12, 1793; the formal opening of the University, January 15, 1795; the matriculation of the first student, Hinton James, four weeks later, February 12, 1795; and the first Commencement, July 13, 1795.

The celebration of these events on the occasion of their one hundred and fiftieth anniversaries grew logically out of the life and traditions of the University and the practices of other institutions. In 1889 the University celebrated the centennial of the chartering, and in 1925 it celebrated the fiftieth anniversary of its reopening after the Civil War. During the 1920's the University entered upon a new period of expansion and development; in 1931 it had been consolidated with the North Carolina State College of Agriculture and Engineering, at Raleigh, and the North Carolina College for Women, at Greensboro; and in the 1930's it had experienced an increase in enrollment in each of its divisions which called for the serious reconsideration of its entire administrative and educational policies. The depression of the 1930's and the threat of war and its actual coming added their weight to the importance of reviewing the forces and movements which brought the University into being in the difficult years following the American Revolution and attending the adoption of the Federal Constitution. They likewise revealed the necessity for projecting plans for the development of the University in the years to come.

The formal proposal to celebrate the Sesquicentennial was

3

made to the Faculty of the University at Chapel Hill on April 30, 1937, by Dean of Students Francis F. Bradshaw, '16. In the statement which he made to the Faculty he stressed the importance of the role of the University in American higher education as the first of the state-supported universities; the necessity of formulating, as was done in 1920–21, long-range plans for its sound development; and the desirability of securing increased state support and endowment for the enrichment of its educational contribution to the state and the nation. The proposal was heartily accepted by the Faculty, and the appointment of a Faculty Committee on the Sesquicentennial Celebration to work with similar committees from the trustees, alumni, students, and friends in the preparation for celebrating the one hundred and fiftieth anniversary of the founding of the University was unanimously authorized.

On February 8, 1938, after extensive discussion with President F. P. Graham, '09, and others, Dean of Administration R. B. House, '16, appointed the following members of the Faculty Committee on the Sesquicentennial Celebration: Dean Francis F. Bradshaw, '16, Chairman, Professor H. G. Baity, '17, Dr. W. R. Berryhill, '21, and Professors R. E. Coker, '96, W. M. Dey, s.1897–98, A. R. Newsome, '15, Phillips Russell, '04, C. P. Spruill, '20, and Director of the University of North Carolina Press W. T. Couch, '26. Dean House suggested the holding of an early meeting of the Committee to be followed later by a meeting with President Graham, Controller W. D. Carmichael, Jr., '21, and himself, in order that the Administration might participate in the initial discussion of policies and procedures. He enclosed with the notice of appointment of members copies of the statement made to the Faculty by Dean Bradshaw and a quotation from a report by President Graham to the Board of Trustees at Raleigh on January 31, 1938, in which President Graham emphasized the importance of commemorating the fiftieth anniversary of the founding of the North Carolina State College of Agriculture and Engineering (1889) and the Woman's College of the University (1891) as well as the one hundred and fiftieth anniversary of the University at Chapel Hill, and the value of supplementing state support with gifts and endowment.

On Wednesday, March 23, 1938, the Faculty Committee met and indicated the following as probable themes to be emphasized by the University during the celebration:

1. The significance of the beginning here in 1793 of state-supported higher education as a first act of the new democracy.
2. Review of 150 years of growth and work.
3. Contemporary interrelationships of democracy and education.
4. Present American problems and university responsibilities.
5. What is next in this University's work and growth?

It was suggested that departmental discussion might well include these topics as related specifically to the work and interests of the department concerned.

In the autumn of 1938 the heads of departments and schools of the University at Chapel Hill were requested to consider how all parts of the University might participate appropriately in the celebration and to plan for the future development of the University.

Early in 1939 active planning for the celebration of the one hundred and fiftieth anniversaries of the chartering of the University, the laying of the cornerstone of Old East Building, and the opening of the University was begun. The first step was that of eliciting the interest of the state government and the General Assembly in participating in the celebration and securing the appointment of committees representing the state, the Board of Trustees, the alumni, and the students. The General Assembly responded by passing the following joint resolution:

A JOINT RESOLUTION AUTHORIZING THE GOVERNOR OF THE STATE OF NORTH CAROLINA TO APPOINT A COMMISSION TO COOPERATE IN THE SESQUICENTENNIAL CELEBRATION OF THE UNIVERSITY OF NORTH CAROLINA

WHEREAS, the University of North Carolina was chartered by the General Assembly in the year one thousand seven hundred eighty-nine, and

WHEREAS, the cornerstone of the old East Dormitory of the University of North Carolina was laid in the year one thousand seven hundred ninety-three, and

WHEREAS, the University of North Carolina actually opened its doors to students in the year one thousand seven hundred ninety-five, and

WHEREAS, the alumni, trustees, faculty and students of the University of North Carolina are forming plans for the celebration of the one hundred fiftieth anniversary of these three historic events, Now, therefore, Be it Resolved by the Senate, the House of Representatives concurring:

Section 1. That the Governor of the State of North Carolina is hereby empowered and directed to appoint a commission to be composed of seven members to be selected by him for the purpose of assisting and cooperating with the University of North Carolina, its alumni, trustees, faculty and students in the celebration, during the years one thousand nine hundred thirty-nine, one thousand nine hundred forty-three and one thousand nine hundred forty-five, of the one hundred fiftieth anniversary of the founding of the University of North Carolina, of the laying of the cornerstone of the Old East Dormitory of the University, and of the opening of the University.

Sec. 2. That this Resolution shall be in full force and effect from and after its ratification.

In the General Assembly read three times and ratified, this the 3rd day of April, 1939.

In conformity with this joint resolution and the purposes of the University, the following commissions or committees, in addition to the Faculty Committee, were appointed:

Legislative Commission (appointed by Governor Clyde R. Hoey, s.s.l. 1892): Marsden Bellamy, '99, of Wilmington; H. Galt Braxton, of Kinston; Victor S. Bryant,[1] '18, of Durham, Chairman; Gordon Gray, '30, of Winston-Salem; John L. Morehead, s.1911–12, of Charlotte; D. Hiden Ramsey, of Asheville; Capus M. Waynick, s.1907–9, of High Point.

Trustee Committee (appointed by Governor Hoey): Mrs. Kate P. Arrington, of Warrenton; Sam M. Blount, s.1917, of Washington, N. C.; Charles Cannon, of Concord; Mrs. Julius

---

1. Elected Chairman by the Commission at its first meeting.

Cone, of Greensboro; Burton Craige, '97, of Winston-Salem; Josephus Daniels, s.1884–85, of Raleigh; J. C. B. Ehringhaus, '01, of Raleigh; James S. Ficklen, '19, of Greenville; Frank W. Hancock, Jr., s.1912–16, of Oxford; John Sprunt Hill, '89, of Durham; L. P. McLendon, '12, of Greensboro; Kemp B. Nixon, '05, of Lincolnton; John J. Parker, '07, of Charlotte; Thomas J. Pearsall, s.1923–27, of Rocky Mount; Dr. Foy Roberson, s.1901, of Durham; George Stephens, '96, of Asheville; John W. Umstead, '09, of Chapel Hill.

Alumni Committee (appointed by President Charles W. Tillett, '09): Kemp D. Battle, '09, of Rocky Mount, Chairman; Lenoir Chambers, '14, of Norfolk, Va.; Dr. Hubert B. Haywood, '05, of Raleigh; Howard Holderness, '23, of Greensboro; Henry B. Marrow, '12, of Smithfield; Charles G. Rose, '00, of Fayetteville; Lawrence Watt, '26, of Reidsville.

Student Committee (appointed by the President of the Student Body): Donald Bishop, Mitchell Britt, Chauncey Broome, Robert W. Carr, Joseph S. Huske, Jr., Louise Jordan, James M. Joyner, P. Alston Lewis, Mary Wood Winslow.

During the summer of 1939 the various committees developed plans for the celebration of the chartering of the University in connection with the Cape Fear Valley Scottish Festival to be held at Fayetteville, N. C., November 19-24, 1939.

The Festival commemorated the two hundredth anniversary of the settlement of the Scottish Highlanders in the Valley of the Cape Fear; the one hundred and fiftieth anniversary of the ratification of the Federal Constitution, the cession of Tennessee, and the chartering of the University of North Carolina; and anniversaries of the meeting of the North Carolina Grand Lodge of Masons and the organization of the Fayetteville Independent Light Infantry.

World War II Modified Plans

The outbreak of World War II in September, 1939, and the subsequent involvement of the United States in the war, seriously modified the formulation of plans by the University for the Sesquicentennial Celebration. In fact, with the increasing pressure of the war upon every aspect of civilian life, the whole policy of the University concerning the holding of public meetings to which representatives of colleges, universities, learned societies, and other organizations could be invited, had to be constantly revised and restricted. The University plant was largely taken over by the Navy for the training of pre-flight cadets; facilities for entertaining representatives from other institutions were reduced to a minimum; and limitations on gasoline and travel by rail eliminated the possibility of organizing scientific meetings and symposia on a national scale. Consequently, plans for the entire Sesquicentennial period had to be reformulated in accord with the realities of conditions as they varied from time to time. Early in 1943, plans for the celebration of the laying of the cornerstone of Old East Building were announced, and on October 12, 1943, the event was celebrated with addresses by President Graham, of the University, and President Harold W. Dodds, of Princeton University, and a pageant presented by the Carolina Playmakers.

In 1941 and 1942 Professors R. D. W. Connor, '99, and Louis R. Wilson, '99, were added to the Committee, and in the spring of 1943 Professor Wilson was designated Director of the Sesquicentennial Publications of the University. In 1944, Professor Wilson was appointed Director of the Sesquicentennial, and during 1944 Professors S. T. Emory, D. S. Klaiss, E. L. Mackie, '17, W. deB. MacNider, M.D., '03, W. D. Perry, '29, H. K. Russell, Ph.D., '31, Sherman Smith, and Messrs. R. M. Grumman, R. W. Madry, '18, J. M. Saunders, '25, and C. E. Teague, '12, were also added to the Committee. Ceasar Cone, '28, of Greensboro, and Claude W. Rankin, s.1903-5, of Fayetteville, were likewise added to the Alumni Committee in 1944. In the spring of 1945 Dean Bradshaw entered upon educational work in New York City and relinquished his connection with the Committee upon his resignation from the University in December, 1945.

Changes in the Student Committee were also made, since the student body was constantly undergoing change during the war period. Charles Frank Benbow, W. Horace Carter, and Miss Shirley Jane Hartzell attended the meetings of all the committees on May 8, 1944, in the office of the Governor in Raleigh, and in

1945 the following students constituted the committee for the celebration of Hinton James Day: C. F. Benbow, Jr., President of the Student Body, W. T. Crisp, Betty Lou Cypert, Shirley Hartsell, A. A. Hodd, Douglass Hunt, Chairman, Catherine P. Kelly, Lucy Lee Kennedy, Mary C. Marett, Turk Newsome, W. J. Tripp, Jack Vernier, Harvey White, Wynette B. White, Charles Wickenberg, Elizabeth P. Wiggins, Richard B. Willingham.

On May 8, 1944, the Legislative Commission and the committees from the trustees, faculty, alumni, and students met with Governor J. M. Broughton and, after discussion of revised proposals presented by Dean Bradshaw, Chairman of the Committee, and Dr. Wilson, Director of the Sesquicentennial, authorized the Faculty Committee to arrange for celebrations on January 15, 1945, of the formal opening of the University, on February 12, 1945, of the coming of the first student, on June 23, 24, and 25, of the first commencement; to hold special conferences in the spring and summer of 1945 for the consideration of the subjects of research and the contributions of the University to public education; to carry out a program of publication; to hold the final exercises of the celebration on October 12, 1945, in connection with the meeting of the Association of American Universities; and to carry out such other plans as seemed desirable. The group also authorized the Alumni Association to assume responsibility for the solicitation of any funds that might be sought for the University as an anniversary gift.

In accord with the foregoing plans, and in addition to the celebration of the chartering of the University and of the laying of the cornerstone of Old East Building, which had occurred in 1939 and 1943, respectively, the following program was carried out during 1945–46. The formal opening of the University in 1795 was celebrated at a joint session of the General Assembly at Raleigh on the evening of January 15, 1945. Representatives from the alumni and student body participated in a program on February 12, 1945, commemorating the arrival of Hinton James, the first student to enter an American state university. A Conference on Research and Regional Welfare was held May 9, 10, and 11, 1945, to stimulate interest in the promotion of research in the

South. The Baccalaureate Sermon, the Baccalaureate Address, and the rendition of Brahms's *Requiem* by the Department of Music, June 23, 24, and 25, 1945, were designated as features of the sesquicentennial of the first commencement. And on July 27, 1945, at a dinner meeting attended by members of the University Faculty and Summer School and representatives of North Carolina schools, colleges, and universities, an address was delivered by Dr. E. W. Knight, Kenan Professor of Education in the University, reviewing the contribution of the University to public education in North Carolina.

Two other events were included in the program. On October 12 and 13, 1945, the University was host to the Association of American Universities, which held its annual meeting in Durham and Chapel Hill, the session of the Association on the morning of the 12th assuming the form of a special convocation in honor of the founding of the University. On April 11 and 12, 1946, when travel restrictions were lifted and it was possible to extend invitations to representatives from other colleges and universities, learned societies, and educational foundations, the University held a series of concerts, addresses, and exhibits culminating in the final Sesquicentennial Convocation in which the delegates from four hundred other institutions participated and at which thirty-nine honorary degrees were conferred in a colorful and significant ceremonial.

In addition to these events, a series of Sesquicentennial Publications in seventeen volumes representing various phases of the work and history of the University were projected, of which eight were published before June 1, 1946.

Each of these events and publications was planned in extensive detail, and accounts of them, with addresses and other features, are given in succeeding chapters.

II

THE CHARTERING OF THE UNIVERSITY

THE CHARTERING of the University, the first event in the Sesquicentennial Celebration, was commemorated on November 21, 1939, at Fayetteville, N. C., where in December, 1789, provision was made by the General Assembly for the establishment and support of the University. Chapter XX of the Laws of North Carolina, 1789, usually referred to as the Charter of the University, authorized its establishment, and Chapter XXI provided for its support through escheats and moneys due the state.

The specific authorization for the founding and support of the University was contained in the preambles and sections of the two acts as follows:

WHEREAS, in all well regulated governments it is the indispensable duty of every Legislature to consult the happiness of a rising generation, and endeavour to fit them for an honourable discharge of the social duties of life, by paying the strictest attention to their education: And whereas, an university supported by permanent funds and well endowed, would have the most direct tendency to answer the above purpose:

1. Be it therefore enacted by the General Assembly of the State of North Carolina, and it is hereby enacted by the authority of the same, That Samuel Johnston, James Iredell, Charles Johnson, Hugh Williamson, Stephen Cabarrus, Richard Dobbs Spaight, William Blount, Benjamin Williams, John Sitgreaves, Frederick Harget, Robert W. Snead, Archibald Maclaine, Honourable Samuel Ashe, Robert Dixon, Benjamin Smith, Honourable Samuel Spencer, John Hay, James Hogg, Henry William Harrington, William Barry Grove, Reverend Samuel M'Corkle, Adlai Osborne, John Stokes, John Hamilton, Joseph Graham, Honourable John Williams, Thomas Person, Alfred Moore, Alexander Mebane, Joel Lane, Willie Jones, Benjamin Hawkins, John Haywood, Senior, John Macon, William Richardson Davie, Joseph Dixon, William Lenoir, Joseph M'Dowall, James Holland, and William Porter, Esquires, shall be and they are hereby declared to be a body politic and corporate, to be known and

distinguished by the name of The Trustees of the University of North Carolina; and by that name shall have perpetual succession and a common seal; and that they the Trustees and their successors by the name aforesaid, or a majority of them, shall be able and capable in law to take, demand, receive and possess all monies, goods and chattels that shall be given them for the use of the said university, and the same apply according to the will of the donors, and by gift, purchase or devise to take, have, receive, possess, enjoy and retain to them and their successors forever, any lands, rents, tenements and hereditaments, of what kind, nature or quality so ever the same may be, in special trust and confidence that the same or the profits thereof shall be applied to and for the use and purposes of establishing and endowing the said university. (Chapter XX.)

WHEREAS, the General Assembly by their Act, entitled "An Act to establish a University in this state," passed on the eleventh day of December instant, have declared that a University shall be established and erected in this state, which shall be called and known by the name of The University of North Carolina: And whereas, adequate funds will be found to be the means which will most effectually ensure to the state the advantages to be hoped and expected from such an institution:

I. Be it therefore enacted by the General Assembly of the State of North Carolina, and it is hereby enacted by the authority of the same, That a gift of all monies due and owing to the public of North Carolina, either for arrearages under the former or present government, up to the first day of January, one thousand seven hundred and eighty-three, inclusive, (monies or certificates due for confiscated property purchased excepted) shall be and is hereby declared to be fully and absolutely made, for the purpose of erecting the necessary buildings, employing professors and tutors, and carrying into complete effect the act before recited . . .

II. And be it enacted, That all the property that has heretofore or shall hereafter escheat to the state, shall be and hereby is vested in the said Trustees, for the use and benefit of the said University.

III. And be it further enacted by the authority aforesaid, That the lands and other property belonging to the University aforesaid, shall be, and the same is hereby exempt from all kinds of public taxation. (Chapter XXI.)

Following the passage of these acts, and in conformity with them, the cornerstone of Old East Building was laid October 12,

1793; the doors of the University were formally opened January 15, 1795; Hinton James, the first student, was enrolled on February 12, 1795; and the first commencement was held July 13 of the same year.

The ceremonial of the chartering was re-enacted in a pageant *To Make Men Free* written by Beverly and William Peery of the Department of Dramatic Art of the University. The scene of the pageant was the balcony of the Old Market House, situated on Market Square, the original site of the Capitol of North Carolina when the Federal Constitution was adopted and the Charter of the University was granted in 1789.

Three events, each of which had special significance for the state and the University, were featured in the pageant. These were the adoption of the Federal Constitution by the Constitutional Convention of North Carolina; the cession of western lands, which were to become the State of Tennessee, by the General Assembly of North Carolina; and the chartering of the University.

The pageant was presented under the direction of Professors Frederick H. Koch, Director, and John W. Parker, '30, Assistant Director and Business Manager of the Carolina Playmakers of the University. The characters, in the order of their appearance, were: The Historian, Earl Wynn, Assistant Director of the Carolina Playmakers; Governor Samuel Johnston, Clyde R. Hoey, s.s.l. 1899, Governor of North Carolina; James Iredell, I. M. Meekins, Judge of the Federal Court for the Eastern District of North Carolina; General William R. Davie, J. C. B. Ehringhaus, '01, Ex-Governor of North Carolina; General John Sevier, Archibald Henderson, '98, Kenan Professor of Mathematics; Willie Jones, Willie Jones Long, s.1910–12; Timothy Bloodworth, R. B. House, '16, Dean of Administration; Judge Samuel Spencer, Heriot Clarkson, s.l. 1883–84, Associate Justice of the Supreme Court of North Carolina; Colonel John Tipton, A. H. Graham, '12; John G. Blount, W. B. Rodman, '10; other delegates, J. Bayard Clark, s.s.l. 1906; John A. Oates, C. A. McAlister, s.1887–88, Terry A. Lyon, James MacRae, s.1918, Joseph S. Huske, s.1912–15, Thomas H. Sutton, '07, Harry McMullan, '05, W. H. Yarborough, '32; Dr. Samuel McCorkle, Dr. A. R. Mc-

Queen; The President of the University of North Carolina, President Frank P. Graham; A Singing Director; Three Pages; A Military Band.

The pageant was only one of the events of the Fayetteville Historical Celebration, the main event being the presentation, November 20, 21, 22, 23, 24, of *The Highland Call*, a symphonic play by Paul Green, '21, Professor of Dramatic Art at the University and author of the notable pageant *The Lost Colony*. The play, repeated on five successive nights, was presented by a cast of seventy-five or more members of the Carolina Playmakers, students from Flora Macdonald College, and citizens of Fayetteville and neighboring communities. It commemorated the two hundredth anniversary of the coming of the Scottish settlers to North Carolina, the development of the Cape Fear Valley prior to the American Revolution, and the bitter conflict in the region centering around the tragic figure of Flora Macdonald.

Other events which contributed to the colorfulness and impressiveness of the occasion included the skirl of bagpipes, the flash of Scotch plaids, parades, floats, bands, dances, a football game between the freshman teams of Duke University and the University of North Carolina, a meeting of the Grand Lodge of Masons of North Carolina, exercises by soldiers from near-by Fort Bragg, and the presence of representatives of the Scottish clans and of thousands of visitors from within and without the state. All of the activities of the week were carried out under the direction of John A. Oates and Claude W. Rankin, chairmen of the general and local committees of the Fayetteville Celebration, with assistance from the Legislative Commission and the committees from the Board of Trustees, faculty, alumni, and students mentioned in Chapter I, and the officers, directors, and special committees of Fayetteville Historical Celebration, Inc.

Background for that part of the celebration which related to the establishment of the University was drawn not only from the Constitutional Convention held in Fayetteville in 1789, at which North Carolina adopted the Federal Constitution, but also from the Constitutional Convention held previously in 1788 at Hillsboro, which rejected it. The Declaration of Independence in 1776, the Revolutionary War, the Federal Constitutional Convention, and the establishment of the Federal Government set the stage for the entry of the state into the Union and the establishment by it of a university, supported through public funds, which would furnish leadership and direction for state and national development.

Beverly and William Peery, who wrote the script of the pageant *To Make Men Free*, which re-enacted the scenes from the Constitutional Convention and the meeting of the General Assembly, emphasized this relationship between the adoption of the Constitution and the establishment of the University by putting the following words into the mouth of General Davie, Father of the University, as he offered the resolution the passage of which brought the University into being:

"Gentlemen of the Assembly, in that black moment of apparent defeat following Hillsboro, I pledged my heart and hand not to rest until we had established the means of higher education in North Carolina. Our State Constitution, which some of you helped frame at Halifax in 1776, wisely made provision that 'all useful learning shall be duly encouraged and promoted in one or more universities.' For thirteen years the trials of war, the hardships of reconstruction, and the difficulties of establishing our new government have prevented our putting that provision into effect. But the war is now over, the new government established; and we have now taken our place with the larger government. What more fitting time, then, for us to begin the establishment of a great university within our midst? Surely no gentlemen of this Assembly would wish us longer to fail the framers of our State Constitution by refusing to carry out its provisions now that we are able. It lies within your power, gentlemen, to make this day, December 11, 1789, a day that those who shall come after us will not willingly let pass without commemoration. Our children of after times would not condone any further delay.

"Therefore since it is the indispensable duty of every legislature to consult the happiness of a rising generation and to fit them for life by paying the strictest heed to their education, it is with great pleasure that I move, gentlemen of the Assembly, that the University of North Carolina this day be chartered."

III

THE LAYING OF THE CORNERSTONE
OF OLD EAST BUILDING

THE CELEBRATION of the one hundred and fiftieth anniversary of the laying of the cornerstone of Old East Building was held on Tuesday, October 12, 1943, at eleven o'clock, in the campus area between the Old Well and the Davie Poplar. Seats were provided for the Faculty, University Trustees, special guests, students, members of the A.S.T.P., N.R.O.T.C., and V-12 Navy and Marine units, and the general public. A special platform between the Old Well and the Old East Building had been prepared for speakers and members of the various committees responsible for the Celebration. A second smaller platform was provided nearby at the northwest corner of Old East upon which the ceremony of laying the cornerstone was re-enacted.

The academic procession, under the direction of the Faculty Marshall, Dr. W. M. Dey, was led by the University Band. It was followed by the units of the armed services, which were seated before the speakers' platform.

The formal program began at eleven o'clock, Dean of Administration R. B. House presiding.

The Invocation, preceded by the singing of "The Star Spangled Banner," was offered by the Reverend Das Kelley Barnett, pastor of the Chapel Hill Baptist Church.

INVOCATION

Almighty God, Creator of the Universe, the source of our moral and religious ideas, the Father of our spirits, we ask Thy blessing upon this commemorative occasion.

Oh Thou, our help in ages past, we bless Thy name for the providences which have brought us to this hour. We thank Thee for the faith and vision of those who in the long ago laid the cornerstone of this building and saw afar off the possibilities of this day. We remember with gratitude the labor and sacrifice of those who in laboratory and lecture room have brought to fulfillment the dream of the founders.

Endow the administration with wisdom, weave the research and thought of the faculty and students into Thy struggle to bring peace and union to the children of men. Grant that in Thy mercy the University shall ever be the guardian of those ideals by which free men live. And give to us all the power of the disciplined mind and the warmth of the educated heart. Amen.

Dean of Administration R. B. House introduced the Honorable R. L. Harris, Lieutenant Governor of North Carolina, who spoke in the unavoidable absence of Governor J. M. Broughton.

LIEUTENANT GOVERNOR HARRIS

Mr. Chairman, Distinguished Guests, Members of the Faculty, Students, and Other Friends:

It is my happy privilege to bring affectionate greetings from His Excellency the Governor of North Carolina. I join with you in real regret that other plans have prevented his being with us on this Sesquicentennial occasion.

It is altogether fitting and proper to take time out to re-enact some of the high spots of that important and historic event of one hundred and fifty years ago. We should remember that the Declaration was only a little more than seventeen years old, Yorktown was only twelve years in the past, and the Constitution of the United States was less than six years of age.

I consider it a great honor to be permitted to speak for the Commonwealth in acknowledging our obligation to the University of North Carolina for the contributions it has made and is making to the war effort and to the life and happiness of nearly four millions of our fellow citizens. I salute you and bid you God speed as you enter the second half of your second century.

The guest speaker of the Celebration was Dr. Harold W. Dodds, President of Princeton University, who was introduced by Dean House.

DEAN HOUSE

Since the North Carolina Constitution of 1776, which provided for the University of North Carolina, is certainly a close kinsman of the Constitution of Pennsylvania, it is altogether fitting that our speaker on this occasion should be a son of Pennsylvania. Since the University of North Carolina is a spiritual child of Princeton University, it is altogether appropriate that our speaker should also be an alumnus of Princeton and the President of that mother of colleges. Since the University of North Carolina was made possible by the American Revolution in terms of economics, society, and politics, it is in character with the occasion that our speaker should be a distinguished and creative student of economics, government, and political science. And, since the University in all of its purposes has held to the keynote of the scholarly gentleman and the dedicated public servant, we are happy in these days of crowded schedules that this tradition of courtesy and neighborly custom is illustrated in our speaker who for a long time has made a place for us on his busy schedule and has protected it.

I take great pleasure in presenting to you President Harold W. Dodds, of Princeton University.

PRESIDENT DODDS

I am happy to take part in today's exercises—the one hundred and fiftieth anniversary of an historic event in higher education; the laying of the cornerstone of the first building of the first state university to open its doors in America.

I have been purposely precise in what I have just said because I am aware that the University of Georgia contests with the University of North Carolina the claim to being the first state university in this country. This is not the place nor am I the person to attempt to adjudicate these rival claims of many years' standing which will probably be debated for many more to come. But I will be pardoned if I observe that although the University of Georgia, which was founded with the help of Yale men, was chartered first, the University of North Carolina, which was founded with the help of Princeton men, opened first; and that the people of North Carolina in their Revolutionary Constitution of 1776 authorized and enjoined the establishment of a state university nine years before the people of Georgia provided for one in the University of Georgia charter. With all due regard for partial interest, and at the risk of inviting a heavy mail postmarked Georgia and Connecticut, I must say that it seems clear to me that Princeton's North Carolina wins over Yale's Georgia, on the most conservative estimate, by at least a point after touchdown. Both reflected a new and more democratic spirit in education and an avowal of the right of the people to an education stripped of ulterior motives of support of crown or church or rule by a class. I need not labor this point further. Its significance is clear to everyone who thinks a moment about it.

I am proud to join with the University of North Carolina today in praising famous men who on October 12, 1793, laid well and truly the cornerstone of a great educational institution which has earned the honest respect of citizens of this state and of sister institutions throughout the nation.

The cornerstone was laid by William Richardson Davie, a graduate of Princeton, who had been a gallant cavalry officer in the American Revolution, who had assisted Washington and Madison in establishing the American Union, and who was later to be Governor of the State of North Carolina. Davie had more to do with founding the University than merely laying the cornerstone. As one of your historians records it, "He fathered the bill that brought the University into existence. He was its most active trustee in carrying the provisions of the charter into effect. He was a generous contributor to its endowment. He procured its first legislative appropriation. He selected its site. He drafted its plan of study." You call him "The Father of the University" and Princeton proudly exhibits his portrait in its gallery of eminent eighteenth-century graduates along with those of another North Carolinian, Nathaniel Alexander, who became Governor of the state, of James Madison and of Lighthorse Harry Lee, of Virginia, and many other Southern patriots.

The principal address at the cornerstone laying one hundred and fifty years ago was made by Samuel E. McCorkle, who studied at Princeton a college generation before General Davie.

Dr. McCorkle had more to do with the founding of the University of North Carolina than making an address. This is evidenced by the fact that of the seven members of the first class to be graduated, six had been prepared for the infant University at an academy which he conducted.

The first tutor in the University, Charles Wilson Harris, had been first-honor man in the Princeton class of 1792. The first president was likewise a Princetonian, Joseph Caldwell, first-honor man in the class of 1791, who became professor of mathematics in this University at the age of twenty-three and president at the age of thirty-one. Your University existed without a president for the first ten years, its affairs being directed fairly closely by the Board of Trustees through a presiding professor. Evidently conditions did not prove to be of the happiest under this arrangement. In any case after a decade's experience without a president, the office was created with Dr. Caldwell as the first incumbent. Thus it was early demonstrated in North Carolina that university presidents are at least necessary evils. Even if, at times, they are an irritation to the Faculty, an exasperation to the Board of Trustees, and a nuisance to the Alumni, American universities appear to be unable to live without them. From that fact, President Graham, may we both derive encouragement and solace.

I have not stressed North Carolina's natal relations with Princeton to advertise the institution which I have the honor to represent. Rather have I related what is known already to you for the purpose of portraying the broad and harmonious reasons that moved their founders to establish our early institutions of higher education. It is well for us to recall these reasons not merely as a matter of historical interest but because they are as valid and necessary for democracy today as ever.

Let us consider the nature of the colonial college which provided the educational background of those who established your University; for it is clear from the record that they were strongly influenced by their contacts with the then existing colleges in drawing the specification of their new departure, a state institution of higher learning. With one exception, the colonial colleges in America were organized as sectarian institutions by men of strong religious convictions. But these men held that piety alone did not fit one for the ministry. Only when piety and learning were combined in one person was that person equipped to be a shepherd of souls. This linking of piety and education had a peculiar result in America. The power of evangelism drove preachers to become frontier missionaries, and as they went out to preach the gospel they took care to establish schools and colleges where learning had not yet come. Morison and Commager report that Yale alone begat sixteen Congregationalist colleges before 1861, and Princeton, twenty-five Presbyterian ones. A more modern age is apt to cry down the sponsors of these colleges as narrow sectarians. They were sectarians, it is true, but they were more liberal than many would have us believe. For example, none of the colleges founded by them in the middle decades of the eighteenth century imposed religious tests for admission; and this at a time when it was difficult for a non-conformist in England to secure a university education and almost impossible for a Catholic.

The formal affiliation between church and college was bound to weaken as secular knowledge increased. Indeed it is possible to over-emphasize the sectarian nature of the church-related colonial college. For example, Princeton was never formally affiliated with any denomination and existed to train young men for other professions than the ministry. She took great pride in Washington's reference to her as a seminary for statesmen. Service to the state received equal emphasis with service to the church in the minds of the colonial professors and tutors. The origin of the University of North Carolina as the first state university reflects a most modern spirit and an early understanding that learning thrives best when not strangled by sectarian attachments. The modern division of labor which has grown up between church and university does not alter the broad unity of the objectives of both.

Characteristic of these objectives is the preparation of the whole man for service to the state, for the responsibilities of citizenship in a democracy. Thus one colonial college charter expressed its purpose to be "The education of youth in the learned and foreign languages, the useful arts, science and literature . . . that the blessings of liberty may endure."

In 1789 your own charter imposed a similar responsibility upon the government of the state when it asserted that the legislature had the duty "to consult the happiness of a rising generation and endeavor to fit them for an honorable discharge of the social duties of life."

The next year, the Governor of the State of North Carolina, Alexander Martin, expressed in forceful terms what our ancestors had in mind when, of their limited funds, they assessed themselves that their children might receive an education. He said, "This institution [the University of North Carolina] already stamped with importance, having the great cause of humanity for its object, might do honor to this and the neighboring States, had it an adequate support, *where our youth might be instructed in true religion, sound policy and science, and men of ability drawn forth to fill the different departments of government with reputation, or be formed for useful and ornamental members of society in private or professional life.*"

No one today could improve on this concise yet comprehensive definition of the goal of a liberal arts education.

How well the University of North Carolina has fulfilled this purpose is indicated by the long roll of graduates who throughout the years have served as governors of the state, senators of the United States, members of the House of Representatives, judges, legislators, preachers, teachers, and good citizens.

Of all the branches which today comprise a great university, the liberal arts college remains the one charged most heavily with responsibility for maintaining the ideals of the founders. Not that other divisions are unimportant as contributing to preparing the rising generation for an "honorable discharge of the social duties of life." But the college, after all, is the heart of a university—it should be, and usually is, the tie that binds the various rather disparate professional schools together. Its contribution and its outlook should permeate all departments. With the college rests the duty and the opportunity to instruct and promote that understanding of literature, history, science, and government which alone can provide a common basis of thought, a universal discourse, by which people and nations can live in harmony and mutual respect. You cannot organize nations around a new me-

Wootten-Moulton

WILLIAM RICHARDSON DAVIE

Introducer of the act passed by the General Assembly at Fayetteville,
December 11, 1789, providing for the establishment of the University. After
a drawing by Gillis Louis Crétien, an impression of which is in President
Graham's office

THE "STATE HOUSE" AT FAYETTEVILLE

After a sketch made in 1818 by Monsieur Horace Say and presented to the Marquis de la Fayette

PRESIDENT JOSEPH CALDWELL

Professor, 1796; Presiding Professor, 1797-1804; President, 1804-1812, 1816-1835. From a painting by A. Edmonds in President Graham's office

THE LAYING OF THE CORNERSTONE OF
OLD EAST BUILDING

Mural in the Post Office at Chapel Hill, by Dean Cornwell, courtesy of the Section of Fine Arts, Public Building Administration

THE LAYING OF THE CORNERSTONE REENACTED

A scene from a Pageant presented by the Carolina Playmakers, October 12, 1943

Wootten-Moulton

OLD EAST BUILDING

The first State University building erected in the United States

PARTICIPANTS IN THE CELEBRATION OF THE ONE HUNDRED AND FIFTIETH ANNIVERSARY OF THE LAYING OF THE CORNERSTONE OF OLD EAST BUILDING

Left to right: Colonel Preston R. Davie; Professor Wallace E. Caldwell (as William Richardson Davie); Dean of Administration Robert Burton House; President Harold W. Dodds, of Princeton University; President Frank P. Graham

THE CELEBRATION OF THE ONE HUNDRED AND FIFTIETH ANNIVERSARY OF THE OPENING OF THE UNIVERSITY

A scene in the House of Representatives in the Capitol at Raleigh, January 15, 1945, Governor R. Gregg Cherry at the microphone

PARTICIPANTS IN THE CELEBRATION

Left to right, sitting: President Frank P. Graham; the Honorable Josephus Daniels; President Clarence A. Dykstra, of the University of Wisconsin and guest speaker; the Honorable Victor S. Bryant, Chairman of the Legislative Commission; Governor R. Gregg Cherry. Left to right, standing: Representatives Samuel E. Welfare and John W. Umstead; Dr. Louis R. Wilson, Director of the Sesquicentennial; Representative F. E. Wallace; the Honorable Oscar L. Richardson, Speaker of the House of Representatives; Dean of Administration Robert Burton House; Lieutenant Governor L. Y. Ballentine chanical gadget; the gadget makes no appeal to spiritual harmony and may be as useful in war as in peace. But you can organize nations in harmony around ideas. It is this common language of ideas that the college is organized to teach. No other social institution can compensate for the failure of the college to meet this great social need.

The portion of your Charter of 1789 which I quoted a moment ago regarding the duty to *consult the happiness of* a rising generation and to *fit them for the honorable discharge* of their social duties, describes in admirable manner what should be the twofold fruit of a college education.

There are two sides to a college education, and partisans of one are apt to depreciate the other. One is preparation for one's own personal happiness by enlarging one's world of ideas and by developing subjective appreciation of art, literature, history, and science. An education should enable a man to get more fun out of life, by giving him access to the broad empire of the mind where he can find a recuperative release from the restrictions of the work-a-day world. It is the life of the mind and of the soul that sustains one in defeat and gives meaning to victory.

But education misses the mark if it contributes only to one's own pleasure, no matter what level that pleasure attains. The danger is that the intellectual person, concentrating upon the inward look, will yield to the temptation to become merely an observer, good at protesting but poor in constructive attainment. If the educated person is a self-centered person, proud of his inflexible principles, opinionated and introspective, he will seek to avoid the citizen's responsibility for getting things done and to escape his share of the world's work. As Woodrow Wilson once said, "We are not put into this world to sit still and know; we are put here to act." That one's education be used by participation in the affairs of the world about us is as important as the subjective pleasure one can receive from it.

A liberal education should be an education for use. It not only should cultivate a desire in the student to apply his education to the world about him, it should also teach how he can so apply it. It is not enough to teach merely the content of the academic courses. How the student can use what he has learned must be taught also. Classroom training seeks to equip the student with certain techniques for solving problems and arriving at reasoned conclusions. These techniques, which we call the scientific method, strengthen the powers of analysis and synthesis, of weighing evidence and reporting conclusions. The classroom also tries to develop criteria of taste in art and literature, so that the student will come to appreciate beauty at its best, and to establish canons of what is ethically right or wrong for the individual and for society.

Now the subject matter, the methods of analysis and the criteria of judgment with which the classroom deals are equally useful and valid outside the classroom when applied to the actual situations of life. But the student may never become aware of this; he may never bridge the gap between learning about something in an academic way and applying his academic knowledge to the problems of later life. It is the function of the college not only to give him an education and exhort him to use it, but to teach him how to use it effectively. Many a college graduate has never truly realized that there is a blood relationship between the methods and subject matter of scholarship, to which he was exposed as a youth, and the practical job of being a happy and useful citizen. Unless the student is shown the way in college he may never relate what he absorbs from books to the world about him. Failure to do so helps to explain why so many college graduates read so few books.

I have mentioned the need of a broader understanding of the liberal arts as the basis of a common discourse among nations and as an agency of peace. Science and engineering are not enough, important though they be. The problems that divide and keep us apart are human problems which grow out of human emotions and human aspirations. We must come to know ourselves better if the present war is to go down in history as anything other than a link in a chain of wars, each involving greater suffering and devastation than the last.

When the final costs in blood and in supplies are summed up after the war, Americans will find their historic sense of security through geographical isolation profoundly shaken. There are signs that public opinion is moving towards the rejection of "isolationism" as we have heretofore used the term. The resolution passed by the House of Representatives on September 21st is evidence of this fact. While this action affords no ground for complacency, Americans are nevertheless beginning to understand that our freedom from the series of wars that afflicted Europe during the nineteenth century was due more to our geographical position and a delicate balance of power in Europe than to our exceptional virtue as a nation. Within the past quarter-century, two world wars have demonstrated that hereafter we cannot coast along in peace on the assurance that other nations are too busy killing each other to interfere with our vital interests or way of life.

There will be of course those who will argue for a new form of armed isolationism; who will assert that America is big enough and rich enough to "go it alone" in her own military might. This view, I believe, will not prevail, although it will be pressed and it will complicate the issue more than it should. When the folly of such proposals as a "seven-ocean navy" is revealed in terms of economic and social costs and the possible foreign power combinations against us, public opinion will choose, I trust, the path to security which involves our associating ourselves formally with other nations. The issue will then turn on the form that such association should take. Will it be a purely military alliance with England alone, or with England, Russia, China and a restored France? Or will it in addition look also to a supra-national organization for the establishment of collective security through the reign of law among states? The philosophies underlying these two types of organization differ widely, and it is important to understand how they differ.

There is a growing body of opinion which believes that neither military isolation nor military alliance along the familiar lines of balance of power will give us security against future wars of annihilation. This school holds that unless we organize for peace we shall not have peace; that the sentiment for peace must be embodied in an international political institution or else the talk of peace remains vain and empty.

Let us understand clearly that an alliance for more military defense is not an organization pointed to peace. It is merely a device by which each contracting nation seeks to improve its own position in wars to come. Its purpose is to prevent defeat in the next war by putting a nation in an advantageous power position to meet war when it comes. The psychology behind a military alliance is a war psychology, not a peace psychology. If peace exists for a time under the balance of power system, it does so merely as a by-product of preparation for war.

Therefore, while believing heartily in the importance of the allied nations remaining associated after the war, the tie that binds must be more than one of military advantage; it must include a common desire to substitute international collaboration and the reign of law for the right of any state to unlimited use of force in its relations with other states. This aspiration towards international collaboration must not be left suspended in the air on pious hopes for peace, without the support of strong sustaining girders. It must be brought down to earth and planted on a foundation of an international organization which will implement the desire for peace in a practical way. At best any workable organization for collaboration among nations must be simple and limited at the start. It will have to grow naturally on the basis of experience, and not artifically from beautiful but extravagant blueprints which rely on ingenious political gadgets. Given the right start it will develop naturally as it succeeds in the primary duties assigned to it.

When we return to ways of peace, we must be prepared for heavier civic responsibilities than have been customary in the past. Democracy will be on trial then as always; the strain of reconstruction may test it as never before in our history. It cannot survive in a world of nations primed for war. Unless we can lay the specter of new and more terrible wars in the future, we shall not be able to establish an environment friendly to the solution of domestic problems or to realize our full possibilities for economic prosperity and human advancement. If at the end of this war we have to begin to prepare for the next; if we must continue to divert a large proportion of our national wealth and energy to war purposes; if we must militarize our national behavior to assure military security, we shall defeat the way of life we are now fighting to preserve. Those who will win this war in their own sweat and blood can see to it that this does not occur.

It is a trite and threadbare statement that colleges and universities exist to supply leadership. Much claptrap has been talked by educators, including college presidents, about training leaders. The literature of every endowment campaign carries some appealing note about how dear old Siwash turns out leaders. Nevertheless, the fact is that programs of social action do not bubble up of themselves from undifferentiated mobs. Programs have to be made; they are conceived by the few and accepted by the many. Democracy cannot lift its mass weight by its own bootstraps. It needs leaders who can raise us to heights we should not otherwise attain, but they must be responsible leaders, not bosses. The problem of democracy thus resolves itself into the age-old problem of leadership, and by leadership I do not mean merely the services of the selected few who can achieve national prominence and newspaper headlines, important though they be. Democracy cannot dispense with distinguished men but it will not be saved by reliance on Napoleonic personalities. It must have community leaders, neighborhood leaders, as well. Every man—he may be the keeper of a crossroads country store—whom his neighbors trust and follow is a leader.

The agency at hand best fitted to infuse into society a constant leaven of leadership, motivated by an understanding of science, history, and the arts, is the American college. Without men in posts of leadership, sensitive to the values of those subjects, our free society as we know it will crumble. True, there are many such who have never had the opportunity of a college education, but the country cannot rely upon a casual supply of broadly educated people. It must act positively to develop them, and one of the chief instrumentalities at hand is the non-vocational college.

And now I return to the point at which I began. We need our colleges today for the same reasons which moved their founders to set them up many decades ago. As a people we require knowledge as never before. We need science as never before; we need to know more about economics and government than ever before. But knowledge is not enough. Of what avail is it, if we lack the will and the wisdom to apply it? During the last twenty-five years, the leaders of the nations knew more about economics and political science than they were able to put into practice. The egregious errors of the nations of the world over the past generation have been due to their unwillingness and lack of courage to apply the knowledge they possessed. We all lacked the will because we had dismissed as secondary those human values which distinguish men from beasts.

In its respect for human values, in its determination not to be beguiled into philosophies of crass materialism, in its insistence that learning must be free and untrammeled that the blessings of liberty may endure, the University of North Carolina has become eminent among the universities of the land. The one hundred and fiftieth anniversary of the laying of the cornerstone of her first building falls amidst the disturbances and ravages of war. When the war is over and the evil thing we are fighting has been destroyed, she will go on to greater fame in harmony with her long history.

In closing may I quote from a recent address by Mr. John G. Winant, our Ambassador at the Court of St. James: "We must be great of purpose or we cannot survive. We are fighting to win a second chance to make the greatest of traditions come true. Do not let us ever talk as if we were fighting to substitute something else for that tradition; because there is nothing to substitute. Either we go ahead, perfecting the political and moral system we have inherited, or we let the system perish and the world revert to barbarism."

These words might well be accepted as the platform for the future of the University of North Carolina. May her President, Trustees and Faculty go ahead perfecting the magnificent tradition they have inherited. May she always remain humble before that tradition, true to the ideals of her founders.

President Dodd's address was followed by that of President Frank Porter Graham.

President Graham

We are deeply appreciative of the presence and noble message of the President of Princeton University.

One hundred and fifty years ago today General William R. Davie, a soldier of the American Revolution, a framer of the Constitution of the United States, son of Princeton University and father of the University of North Carolina, as grandmaster of the State Masonic Order, laid the cornerstone of Old East, the first building of the first existing state university to open its doors in America. It is timely that as sons and daughters of alma mater, here and on all the embattled fronts of freedom, we recall her memorable beginnings. It is fitting that we renew ourselves in her historic traditions, co-terminous with the free traditions of this Republic. It is imperative in her cause that we repledge ourselves to her great hopes as boundless as the humane hopes of mankind.

It is also pardonable, at the outset, on such a historic anniversary to consider comparatively, for the sake of accuracy, but not invidiously for the sake of vainglory, the ages of the members of that large and growing society composed, as suggested by Dean House, exclusively of the universities which claim to be the first state university. Our own former President Harry W. Chase once bore from Chapel Hill to Athens the fellow-greetings of the first state university in North Carolina to the first state university in Georgia. Another former president also in good humor once remarked that he had held to the loyal idea that his university was the oldest state university until he was, I am sure, with amused unconcern, put in his time and place behind state universities which opened after his alma mater. This tendency of colleges and universities to give their oldest possible ages, and sometimes over, raises a question as to the long accepted idea of their feminine gender.

It has been said that Virginia, in whose behalf at times have been appropriated our own Roanoke Island, Virginia Dare, and the finest North Carolina tobaccos, also claimed the first state university; but not so. Virginia, mother of North Carolina, mother of the founders of the Republic, mother of presidents and commonwealths, does not claim the motherhood of the first state university. Virginia prefers the fatherhood of Jefferson to the motherhood of the first state university. It is understandingly sufficient that the first and only university founded by Thomas Jefferson was the University of Virginia, chartered in 1819 and opened in 1825. The major prophet of human liberty was so busy founding our nation and our democracy, that, in the providence of history, William R. Davie and his co-founders, largely sons of Princeton, led the way in founding the first existing state university.

The University of Pennsylvania, founded in the mid-eighteenth century as America's first private non-sectarian university, became, as a significant episode of the Revolutionary insurgence against Toryism and as a factional political maneuver against sectarian encroachments, for ten years a state university, from 1779 to 1789. However, the dispossessed trustees vigorously maintained that the state had violated the obligations of the original charter. In 1789 the legislature restored the University, under the original charters of 1753 and 1755, to its former status as an independent non-sectarian university. On such an independent foundation, with features of a public nature lately supplemented with public grants but without assumption of public control, the University of Pennsylvania became one of America's foremost universities, but was not founded as, is not, and does not wish to be a state university.

It can with some justification be suggested that, in the comparative terms of early and adequate financial support, the University of Michigan was the first really state supported university. Also, it can be held that the University of Wisconsin was the first university to make the whole people the democratic responsibility and concern of the whole university. North Carolina was first in the Southern States to follow in the democratic train of Wisconsin. It remained for a son and former president of the University of North Carolina nearly three decades ago to make the most profound, comprehensive, and eloquent interpretation of university extension as an organic part of the democratic function of an American state university as he sought to make the campus of the University "coextensive with the boundaries of the commonwealth." Michigan, earliest in adequate state support, and Wisconsin, first in the democratic function of manifold state-wide services, did not open as colleges until well on in the nineteenth century. The way for Michigan and Wisconsin and all the other useful and great state universities, from Virginia to California and from Texas to Minnesota, was prepared by the pioneer universities of North Carolina, Georgia, and South Carolina, three neighbors in the Revolutionary South, and by the University of Vermont.

The University of North Carolina had its first foundation in the Revolutionary State Constitution, adopted at Halifax in 1776, which enjoined that "all useful learning shall be duly encouraged and promoted in one or more universities;" was chartered by the legislature at Fayetteville in 1789; had the cornerstone of its first building laid in Chapel Hill, October 12, 1793, long known as University Day; and was opened as the University of North Carolina with extensive lands, one building, and the beginning of another, a faculty and students in 1795. The University of Georgia had no foundation in the State Revolutionary Constitution of 1777, was chartered in 1785, had its site selected in 1801, and opened as Franklin College in 1801. Without a provision in the Revolutionary Constitution of South Carolina, the South Carolina College was chartered in 1801 and opened in 1805. The University of Georgia was closed for a few years during the Civil War and the University of North Carolina for a few years during Reconstruction. Both soon reopened. The sons of the University of Georgia, as of yore always foremost in her history, became a factor in making Georgia the Empire State of the South and gave most eloquent voice to the unconquerable spirit of the risen South and our reunited country. The University of North Carolina, through her sons, from the beginning basically a part of the history and development of the State, its government, internal improvements, public schools, economic, civic, educational and religious life in the ante-bellum South, was on the eve of the Civil War one of the largest American universities, and became in the later nineteenth and early twentieth century the source of a public educational crusade which marked a turning point in the history of North Carolina and the South. The University of South Carolina, center of historic struggles for intellectual freedom before the Civil War, and though seated in the burned Confederate City of Columbia, refused to close its doors and has had an unbroken life of service from its opening in 1805 to this hour. The University of Vermont had a constitutional basis in the Vermont Constitution of 1777 which provided that "one university in this state ought to be established by direction of the general assembly," was chartered in 1791, and opened with a president and four students in 1801. The University of Vermont, closed briefly in the War of 1812, was consolidated with the new Land Grant College in 1865, and is the pioneer state institution of higher learning in all New England.

As we look back through the old records we find that the only state university in existence in America the last five years of the eighteenth century was the University of North Carolina in Chapel Hill. Georgia had been chartered earlier but did not come into being until 1801. By the charter or license test Henrico College was the first American college because it was licensed by the crown and ordained in the Instructions of the London Company to Governor Yeardley of Virginia in 1618. Yet Harvard is universally acknowledged to be the oldest American college or university. Henrico College, though licensed by the crown, was never born. Neither a royal license nor a charter is a certificate of birth but a certificate of the right to be born. In the Revolutionary Constitution North Carolina, in 1776, as had Pennsylvania, and as Vermont was to do in 1777, provided the right and enjoined the duty of the state to give birth to a university. If the test is a piece of paper, then an injunction in the constitution is a more fundamental provision than a royal license or a statutory charter. If the test is the implementation of the piece of paper, then the real implementation is in the land, buildings, faculty and students of the corporate university. The real date of birth is neither the date of the constitutional injunction nor the date of the legislative charter but the date when the University came into being with lands, buildings, faculty and students as a going university, breathing, living, teaching the youth, and serving the people of the commonwealth. The University of North Carolina, which opened and received its first freshmen in 1795, graduated its first seniors in 1798, three years before the next state university was to admit its first freshmen. A traveller in America in 1795 would have found no site, no buildings, no faculty or students of any other state university. He would have found all at Chapel Hill in the winter and spring of 1795. It was to be six years before the next two state universities, and ten years before the fourth state university, opened their doors.

Thirty years were to pass after the opening of the first state university before the fifth state university opened in the Virginia hills. From their rugged side there had earlier come down a stalwart and fiery-haired young man, with a free mind and humane spirit, to take up his life-long struggle for American democracy and human liberty. As one of the crowning acts of his far-visioned life he founded the University of Virginia. This founding of a state university was in part a keeping of the oath he had sworn on the altar of Almighty God, pledging his eternal hostility to every form of tyranny over the mind of man. It was, in part, keeping faith with the great declaration of the rights of self government of men endowed by their creator with the unalienable rights of life, liberty, and the pursuit of happiness. In these ideas and events he became the major prophet of public education in a democracy and of a public university in the commonwealth. He is still the spiritual voice and champion of the American Revolution as the most decisive event in the march of the people's revolution around the earth, embracing in the course of its democratic movements the English Revolution of the seventeenth century, the American and French Revolutions of the eighteenth century, the European and Latin American Revolutions of the nineteenth century, and the Chinese and Russian Revolutions of the twentieth century.

THE UNIVERSITY—A FOCUS OF THE PEOPLES' REVOLUTION AND THE COUNTER REVOLUTION

Our own world revolutionary period is marked by the countermarch of the Fascist Revolution around the earth, seeking to reverse the course of some two thousand years of civilization, to reverse the course of some three hundred years of expanding democracy, to impose the totalitarian tyranny over the mind of man, to subjugate the free institutions of the people, and, with crushing force, supplant the ideals and humane ways of peace with the ideals and ruthless ways of war. The University of North Carolina, on this anniversary day, in a comradeship in arms for the freedom of the human mind and the moral autonomy of the human spirit, pledges anew the people's university in the people's war for the people's freedom and the people's peace.

The university is one of the free institutions at stake in this global war. For the Nazi state Hitler had to strike down the freedom of the church and parliament, the freedom of men to organize in business corporations, agricultural co-operative societies, and labor unions, the freedom of the press, radio, school, and university. Next to religion with its basic conception of one God and one human family, of all men as brothers and sons of God, the university, by its very nature, as the keeper of both the noblest past and the most youthful hopes, as the treasure house of the human spirit and an outpost of the free mind, is the most strategic source of the democratic civilization which Nazism would strike down. Nazism and free universities cannot endure together. If Nazism prevails, then falls the university as the center of the great heritage of liberal learning, of the zestful inquiry of the free mind for new knowledge, of a living democracy of youth struggling for self mastery and self government, the most hopeful source of the unceasing quest of the human spirit for a free and better world.

In Revolutionary America Princeton University, refusing the detachment of its classic shades, was at the forefront of American colleges in active participation in the Revolutionary movement. John Witherspoon, the president of Princeton, was one of the makers of the American Revolution. The sons of Princeton went into the American upcountry and set the forests afire. Davie, McCorkle, Waightstill Avery, and the Caldwells were all sons of Princeton, all champions of the Revolution and of useful learning in a university of North Carolina.

THE UNIVERSITY OF THE PEOPLE

The University, which they founded as a stronghold of humane civilization, is by heritage deeply in this global war. The people's university, as an outpost of the people's revolution, is in the middle of this world struggle. The people's university is an epitome of the people's revolution. Once our universities were chartered by the king, now by the people; once were supported mainly by devoted sects, private gifts and endowments, now in addition by all the people; once provided curricula only for a few learned professions, now increasingly for all professions, vocations, and human needs as deep as life and as wide as the world; once served mainly the privileged classes, now increasingly all groups and all people as the source, purpose, and life of both the university and the commonwealth. Today the University at Chapel Hill, consolidated with the Woman's College in Greensboro and the land grant State College in Raleigh, and in co-operation with the North Carolina College for Negroes in Durham, is more widely and deeply the university of the people of North Carolina.

The fiftieth anniversaries of the North Carolina State College of Agriculture and Engineering and the Woman's College have already been commemorated in memorable exercises celebrating the founding, history, traditions, life, and manifold services of these noble institutions. Their stirring stories are still fresh and vivid in the grateful hearts and minds of the people of the state which they so greatly served in their distinguished ways, coordinated now in a three-fold agency expressive of the integrated will and devoted to the vigorous and various life of the people, all out to win the war.

The co-operation of the University of the people with the good neighbor Duke University and with all the colleges and schools of the region, has laid here the foundations for a high adventure in the advance of a great region. For the three-fold University we propose in time an annual appropriation twice the present appropriation and an endowment to yield an income equivalent to the doubled appropriation as the broader foundation of the consolidated greater University needed to develop integrated, victorious, youthful personalities and to make a more productive, beautiful, and noble state in serving the basic needs and high hopes of all the people. This high service of our democracy and the vision of the fathers in laying the foundations in a wilderness of the first university of the people will yet inspire a great people and generous benefactors to provide the resources for creative co-operation in building on these foundations one of the great university centers of the world.

THE UNIVERSITY IN THE WAR

Such hopes and plans depend upon the winning of the war. All colleges and universities by reason of their nature, their heritage and hopes, by their commitments to civilization are in this war of the self-defense of civilization. If the people's revolution is overthrown by the fascist counter-revolution, then the people's university goes down with the freedom of the people. It was but a confession of the faith of the University that twenty months before Pearl Harbor the first university of the people by authority of a unanimous and prophetic resolution of the Board of Trustees offered all its resources to the War and Navy Departments for the defense of those things for which the nation and the University have stood since the great commitment of 1776. Compulsory physical education was inaugurated for all students, and the civil aeronautical program was enlarged. The University Inter-American Institute was established here as a part of the good-neighbor policy. When the war came, scientific and social scientific research for defense was speeded up in laboratories and libraries. The University curriculum was readjusted. The Extension Division in co-operation with the School of Commerce and other departments enlarged its war training program. The Institute of Government became an adjunct of the Federal civilian war services. The University Press projected timely publications. The Director of the Institute for Research in Social Science became the Southern leader for improvement in tense inter-racial relations on the basis of essential justice. The Student Institute of Human Relations, the Student Political Union, and the Student International Relations Club provided lively discussions on the issues of the war and post-war plans. The business organization creatively reorganized its structure for sudden loads, heavy strains, and an expanded plant. University schools and departments co-operated with the Government and the armed services in dramatic, recreational, and physical education programs. The College for War Training was set up for the development, clearance, and administration of the war activities of the University. The liberal and fine arts made their special contributions. Professors went into every field of the national service. Students lately exercising their freedom to discuss every old and new idea rushed off as volunteers in defense of this freedom. The Student Volunteer Training Corps was quickly formed. The Library organized a War Information Center for the campus and the state. The Naval R. O. T. C. was soon a regular part of the college. One of the four naval pre-flight schools was on the unanimous recommendation of two survey committees established here to train annually some seven thousand of the picked youth of Eastern America for combat in the air on all the fronts of freedom.

It was appropriate that the University became a center for the Naval R. O. T. C., the Navy Pre-Flight School, and V-12 sailors and marines, not only for educational reasons, but also because of historic Naval associations. In one sense the American Navy was born in North Carolina. On the banks of the Albemarle in historic Edenton lived and worked Joseph Hewes, signer of the Declaration of Independence, first chairman of the Naval Affairs Committee of the Revolutionary Continental Congress, promoter of the first American Navy, and patron and champion of John Paul Jones. North Carolina gave to the nation five secretaries of the Navy, four of whom were alumni of this University. A son of this University, James K. Polk, as President of the United States founded the Naval Academy and carried through a policy which placed the expanding nation on the Pacific Ocean. Another son of this University, as Secretary of the Navy, projected the expedition of Commodore Perry across the Pacific which opened Japan to the world with far repercussions in this hour. Another son and trustee of the University, Josephus Daniels, here today, most distinguished living North Carolinian, and one of the greatest secretaries of the Navy, secured from Congress the authorization of the largest Navy in time of peace and led the American Navy victoriously through the First World War.

The University, we are happy to say, was also chosen by the Army to train advanced college students in the basic medical sciences, also those proficient in mathematics and physics, and those most advanced in languages, regional geography, and social science. We look to our Pre-Meteorology, Army Medical and Area and Language students to uphold the best traditions of the University and the Army, not only in their studies here, but also as they go to their high responsibilities in the uttermost parts of the earth.

We express for the University gratitude to all the students in the V-12 under Captain Popham, in the Pre-Flight School under Commander Graff, the Marines of V-12 immediately under Captain Marshall, and in the Army Specialist Training Program under Lieutenant Horton, to all our students from whatever school and college, men and women, undergraduate, graduate, and professional, in whatever service, civilian, Naval and Military, for their work, spirit, and co-operation now in one student body, as one team working to win the war and rebuild the peace of the world. Thousands of you will soon join the four thousand two hundred alumni for more than a year in the fighting services and many hundreds of alumnae in the Wacs, the Waves, the Spars, the Hospital Corps, the Red Cross, the war industries, the vital social services, and all the basic work of women in total war. Of the alumni at the fighting fronts thirty-seven have been killed, twenty-one are still missing, twelve are prisoners of war, and fifty-six have been decorated for bravery in action. They have kept faith with the highest traditions of their University and their country.

THE PEOPLE'S FREEDOM

We need on this occasion of rededication to remind ourselves that to win the war and no more would be both to lose the civilization the war was fought to save and to betray the valiant dead who died for the people's freedom and the people's peace. The people's freedom means the political and civil liberties of Jefferson, the human emancipation of Lincoln, and the four freedoms of Roosevelt. The freedom of the peoples includes the freedom of autonomous nations to provide for all their citizens, freedom of person, speech, assembly, worship, and equal educational opportunity; protection of property; equal freedom to vote, to work, to organize business enterprise, agricultural co-operation and industrial collective bargaining, and to broaden the foundations of economic security in order to raise the level of human life, liberty, and the pursuit of happiness everywhere in our one world.

THE PEOPLE'S PEACE

In this one world the gigantic industrial framework of concrete highways, steel railroads, oil pipelines, telegraph and telephone lines, high tension powerlines across continents, cable lines underseas, ocean lanes, shiplines, airways and wave lengths, has encompassed the earth and tied the nations together for destruction or for co-operation. This dynamic mechanical framework catches up wars and depressions everywhere and enmeshes peoples everywhere. It may serve the course of tyranny and the destruction of civilization or it may serve the cause of justice and the advance of civilization. Coal, iron, oil, rubber, and all the far-flung economic resources of land and water, field and mine, as the stakes of the struggle for power, can divide and destroy civilization or as the cores of interdependent creative co-operation unite the nations for the production of abundance and freedom everywhere. A spiritual voice calls across two thousand years not to crucify mankind on the cross of a third world war. The ten million soldier dead of the First World War and the uncounted dead of the Second World War call to us from Russia, China, Britain, and all the seas and continents not again to pass them by in unholy isolation.

We hear above the tumult of the years the voice of Princeton's greatest, and one of the greatest Americans, Woodrow Wilson, sounding again his prophetic warning that America's refusal to join in the international enforcement of peace would "break the heart of the world" and bring on another world war. For America a second time to fail to rise to the responsibility of her power and the opportunity of her greatness would be to trade and trifle in the temple of the world's heroic dead. Americans who came from all the lands to make of the American dream one nation of freedom and justice for all citizens now, with their great allies, fight in all lands to make of the human dream one world of freedom and justice for all peoples. Twice in one generation America has joined in an allied organization for war against militaristic aggressors. America must not again fail to join an association of nations for the organization and enforcement of peace.

William R. Davie, in the shade of these ancient trees on this beautiful hill one hundred fifty years ago, laid the cornerstone of the first existing state university to open its doors in the new world. Today Adolf Hitler seeks to destroy, in the old world and the new, everything for which the University stands. The father of our University helped the father of our country to found the United States. Today thousands of the sons of this University have offered their lives to help our present great President to make the United States of America a cornerstone of the United Nations to include in God's good time all peoples in the world neighborhood of human brotherhood. On this day of commemoration and dedication we pledge anew the people's university in the people's war for the people's freedom and the people's peace.

The address by President Graham was followed by the singing of the University Hymn.

UNIVERSITY HYMN

Dear University!
Thy sons right loyally
    Thy praises sing.
For thee, our Mother dear,
May every coming year
Fresh-crowned with joy appear,
    Fresh honors bring.

Heaven blessed the genial ray
Of that October day,
    When at thy shrine,
Under the poplar shade,
Their vows our fathers paid,
Thy cornerstone they laid
    With rites divine.

Fair may thy hours roll on,
As numbering one by one,
   Thy tuneful bell
Now rings for duties done,
Now calls for honors won,
Or, for a comrade gone,
   Tolls out a knell.

O Thou! whose promise nerved
Our fathers when they served
   For Liberty
Still be their children's God,
Still with Thy staff and rod
Show us the path they trod,
   The path to Thee.
                    —Mrs. Cornelia Phillips Spencer

In accord with a custom of long standing in the observance of University Day, the audience read responsively "In Praise of Famous Men" and stood in silence in memory of Alumni who had died since October 12, 1942.

RESPONSIVE READING

LEADER:
   Let us now praise famous men,
   And our Fathers that begat us.
ASSEMBLY:
   The Lord hath wrought great glory by them,
   Through His great power from the beginning,
   Such as did bear rule in their kingdoms,
   Men renowned for their power,
   Giving counsel by their understanding,
   And declaring prophecies. . . .
LEADER:
   All these were honoured in their generations,
   And were the glory of their times.

      .   .   .   .

LEADER AND ASSEMBLY:
   Their seed shall remain for ever,
   And their glory shall not be blotted out.

Their bodies are buried in peace,
But their name liveth for evermore.

From the *Apocrypha*.

The exercises were concluded with the presentation of "A Dramatic Episode of the Laying of the Cornerstone of Old East Building," written by Ruth Oncley and produced by the Carolina Playmakers, assisted by members of the Hillsboro, Pittsboro, and University Lodges, A. F. and A. M., and by the University Department of Music. The leading roles of the pageant were played by Dr. Wallace E. Caldwell, as General William R. Davie; Joseph Salek, as the Reverend Samuel E. McCorkle; Tom Avera, as Historian; Robert Burrows, as James Patterson, Contractor; W. M. Pugh, as Senior Grand Warden; and Henry West, as Junior Grand Warden. Other members of the cast were J. O. Aguiar, M. W. Henry, Sherman Lazarus, Anne Osterhout, Mildred Monks, Margaret Suttle, and Libby Johnson. Professor J. E. Toms directed the Chorus.

A DRAMATIC EPISODE OF THE LAYING
OF THE CORNERSTONE OF
OLD EAST BUILDING

A chorus begins to sing:

> Oh God, our help in ages past,
> Our hope for years to come,
> Our shelter from the stormy blast,
> And our eternal home.

As the chorus finishes the verse, the Historian, *dressed in academic robes, takes his place at the microphone at one side of the platform. The chorus hums the hymn softly as he begins to speak.*

HISTORIAN

Let me guide your imaginations back to the Chapel Hill of one hundred and fifty years ago. There were none of the shaded walks and stately buildings which surround us now—only a tiny community situated at the crossing of the two main roads through our state. Over these roads, daily, passed wagons carrying supplies of molasses and sugar, tobacco, grain, iron and flint and powder, and ribbons and combs and trinkets. These wagons also brought the news of the outside world to Chapel Hill, then known as the Hill of New Hope Chapel—that Washington had accepted a second term of presidency—that the King and Queen of France had been guillotined—that a Yankee school master, named Eli Whitney, had invented a device for picking the seeds out of cotton. To this little settlement, far remote from the political and business world, it must have seemed strange indeed that a *university* was to be founded there—amid the quiet, glorious woods and hills, where squirrels and deer joined with the hospitable farmers and tradesmen to watch with interest and some awe the laborers already at work on the clearing of the grounds.

In the spring of 1793, the newly formed Building Committee of the University of North Carolina drew up a contract for the making of 350,000 bricks for one hundred and forty dollars. On

July 19, they contracted with James Patterson of Chatham County for erecting a two-storied brick building, 97 feet and 7 inches by 40 feet and 1½ inches—the cost, $5,000. The building was to contain sixteen rooms and four passages for the accommodation of fifty students, and was to be completed by November 1, 1794.

On the tenth of August, the committee met in Chapel Hill to mark off the sites for the buildings, "together with the necessary quantity of land for offices, avenues and ornamental grounds." And on October 12, 1793—one hundred and fifty years ago today—the cornerstone of that first building—known to us as Old East—was laid.

Here the chorus sings the first verse of The Builder:

> I am the builder of castle and hall,
> And I lay the stone in the temple wall;
> I lay the stone and I raise the tower,
> And mine is the glory of strength and power,
> For I am the builder,
> Oh hear me sing
> The song of the sledge as its echoes ring!
> I am the builder,—who walks with me
> The glory of cities upraised shall see,
> And the towers that rise
> To the arch of the skies,
> For I am the builder, come walk with me!

During the song the procession begins from the Playmakers Theatre. When the chorus has finished the verse, the Historian *speaks again. The procession is now in sight of the audience.*

HISTORIAN

This October the twelfth is indeed one which will long be remembered, as the group of Trustees and other notable men of the state, along with various people of the community, makes its way along the narrow road, which will be known to future generations as Cameron Avenue. They march with stately tread, reminding us of their seven years' struggle for independence. They march solemnly and proudly—fully aware of their responsibility as leaders of the new University.

By this time, Davie, *first in the procession, is approaching the platform.*

First in the procession is the tall, commanding figure of William R. Davie, truly an extraordinary man—officer in the Revolution, lawyer, orator, politician, and, above all, educator. He wears the Grand Master's insignia of the Masonic Fraternity, and it is he who has been chosen to lay the cornerstone.

Samuel Eusebius McCorkle, one of the most noted orators of his day, follows next in line. Dr. McCorkle is the only preacher and teacher in the group of Trustees of the University, all chosen because of their integrity and qualities of leadership, and to him falls the high honor of speaking at the dedication of the cornerstone.

Following him is James Patterson, the contractor for the building, who walks with due awareness of his important contribution to the cause of education in the state.

Then come the others—some of them Trustees and officials of the state; some, local men and women who feel proud of the honor bestowed on their small settlement. They mount the platform—(*The action of the characters on the stage is simultaneous with the words of the* Historian.)—a silence falls over the gathering—Davie steps forward—it is a great moment for all of us—now and always.

The Historian *steps back as* Davie *speaks.*

Davie

We are gathered here for an auspicious occasion—to dedicate the first building of the University of North Carolina.

Brother Senior Grand Warden, what is the proper jewel of your office?

Senior Grand Warden

The level.

Davie

What is its masonic use?

SENIOR GRAND WARDEN

Morally, it reminds us of equality and its use is to lay horizontals.

DAVIE

Apply the implement of your office to the foundation stone, and make report.

The SENIOR GRAND WARDEN *does this and then replies.*

SENIOR GRAND WARDEN

Most Worshipful Grand Master, I find the stone to be level. The craftsmen have performed their duty.

DAVIE

Brother Junior Grand Warden, What is the proper jewel of your office?

JUNIOR GRAND WARDEN

The plumb.

DAVIE

What is its masonic use?

JUNIOR GRAND WARDEN

Morally, it teaches rectitude of conduct, and we use it to try perpendiculars.

DAVIE

Apply the implement of your office to the several edges of the foundation stone, and make report.

This is complied with.

JUNIOR GRAND WARDEN

Most Worshipful Grand Master, I find the stone is plumb. The craftsmen have performed their duty.

DAVIE *dips his trowel, which is handed him by* PATTERSON, *in the mortar and applies it to the cornerstone.*

DAVIE

This cornerstone has been tested by the proper implements of masonry. I find that the craftsmen have skillfully and faithfully performed their duty, and I do declare the stone to be well-formed, true and trusty, and correctly laid.

On this foundation the University desires to rest the enlightenment of the people, their instruction not alone in secular learning, but in religious truth, leading up to and sustaining liberty by demanding and shaping beneficent laws under which wealth may be accumulated and individual happiness and national glory be secured, all sanctified by the blessings of God; these are the objects, these are the methods, these are the good rewards of the University—to these ends I dedicate the University of North Carolina.

Here the chorus swells again into the music of The Builder—*the second verse:*

> I am the Builder of forest and glade,
> I am the Hand that has hewn and made
> The peak of the mountain, the caves of the sea,
> I am the Maker of worlds that be,
> Yes, I am the Builder of suns and seas,
> The Master of human destinies.
> I am the Builder, who walks with Me,
> The glory of souls risen up shall see,
> And I build with the soul
> That is clean and whole,
> For I am the Builder, come walk with Me!

As the chorus finishes, the HISTORIAN *speaks again.*

HISTORIAN

William Richardson Davie is affectionately called the "Father of our University." Dr. Samuel McCorkle is one of the best friends it may ever hope to have—he has worked for it, begged for it, preached for it. It is fitting that he should pronounce its benediction.

The HISTORIAN *steps back, and* DR. McCORKLE *comes forward.*

DR. McCORKLE

Knowledge is wealth—it is glory—whether among philosophers, ministers of state or religion, or among the great mass of the people. Britons glory in the name of Newton, and have honored him with a place among the sepulchers of their kings. Americans glory in the name of Franklin, and every nation boasts of her great men who has them. Though many a potentially great man has been born and buried among our unlettered men, *if* we cannot educate them, we cannot realize their greatness. Knowledge is liberty and law. When the clouds of ignorance have been dispelled by the radiance of knowledge, power trembles, but the authority of the laws remains inviolable.

Here we have founded a university—to instruct and teach our youth so that they may have the fullest possible knowledge, and so gain the fullest measure of happiness. May this hill be for religion as the ancient Hill of Zion; and for literature and the Muses, may it surpass the ancient Parnassus! We this day enjoy seeing the cornerstone of the University, its material and architect for the building, and we hope ere long to see its stately walls and spire ascending to their summit.

We pray, our God, that our University will ever grow, and that it will ever hold fast to Thy truths and Thy laws. Watch over it that it may prosper in Thy sight.

The chorus sings softly the last verse of the University Hymn:

> O Thou! whose promise nerved
> Our fathers when they served
> For Liberty
> Still be their children's God,
> Still with Thy staff and rod
> Show us the path they trod,
> The path to Thee.

Then the organ bursts into a modulation, leading into Hark the Sound of Tarheel Voices, *as the cast leaves the stage. The chorus and the audience join in the singing of the college song, and the pageant and the ceremonies of the day, except the review of the armed services, at 2:30 in Kenan Stadium, and the exhibit of University Portraits in Person Art Gallery, end.*

EXHIBIT OF UNIVERSITY PORTRAITS

In 1942, Dr. Arthur E. Bye, of Philadelphia, official restorer of oil portraits of Princeton University, began the work of restoring the portraits belonging to the University and to the Dialetic and Philanthropic Literary Societies. On October 12, 1943, a hundred or more of the portraits of distinguished alumni and others associated in various ways with the history of the University and of North Carolina were placed on exhibit in Person Hall Art Gallery. The story of his work, and of his impressions of the portraits, a number of which he considered exceptionally notable, is related in the following pages by Dr. Bye:

PORTRAITS INTRODUCE RESTORER TO UNIVERSITY*

The restoration of the portraits at Chapel Hill has been for me a surprising and exhilarating experience;—surprising because of the discovery of neglected (if not buried) treasure;—exhilarating because of the acquaintanceships made with distinguished men who made North Carolina history.

Coming from another part of the country, I can, with little effort, look upon the collection here almost as a Philistine—but an open-minded Philistine, if you please, conscious of my ignorance of your traditions, and willing to learn. In other words, I didn't know Dobbin from Ruffin, nor Murphey from Calvin McNair.

You can imagine, therefore, the thrill, while restoring the fading features of such a man as, shall I say Paul C. Cameron, to learn that he was the only man in the Carolinas to remain wealthy after the War between the States!

As I grew to know these casualties from the past, brought to me literally on stretchers, torn and wounded, but yet alive, made immortal by the brush of Peale, or Sully, Harding or Garl Browne, I grew to revere them, as men of ennobling influence, whose lives still touch upon our own. And it has been inspiring to me to work in the halls of the historic Debating Societies, first in the Dialectic Senate, and later in the Philanthropic Assembly,

---

*From *The Alumni Review*, December, 1943.

49

where most of the portraits once hung. Here, as boys, the men whose portraits I was called upon to restore, once stood upon the rostra, made their first speeches, made history in fact, and thus prepared, went forth to public life. For this is what they did. Was it not in great part due to the training in these societies that such a man as James Cochran Dobbin was able in the short span of his life of forty-three years, to achieve such eminence in his state, that four years before his death, twenty-one years after graduating, he was called by President Pierce to be Secretary of the Navy, and in that short time revived the Navy which was termed the "Rip van Winkle of our National defenses" and made it a vital force?

It was fitting that their portraits should hang here; impressive that their faces should look down upon the present generation; to work here made me feel like a North Carolinian myself. Yes, gradually I came to learn that Davie, whose portrait was on my operating table, connoted the Davie Poplar; Cameron, the main artery of life in Chapel Hill, at least of the campus; Morehead, the graceful bell tower whose chimes enchanted me the first day of my arrival; and Caldwell, the foundation of the University itself. The names of these one hundred men were on every hand; at chapel I found them in Memorial Hall; when I crossed a street I found them on the curbs; nearly every building I entered seemed to have the name of Swain or Murphey, Hill or Kenan, over the door.

And it was not merely this contact with the personalities of those portrayed which made my work a thrilling experience, but the acquaintance I made with some artists I did not know before.

Perhaps North Carolinians themselves do not know how many excellent artists are represented in this collection—some of them of acknowledged eminence, others not, but deserving it. Those known as old masters are Charles Willson Peale and Thomas Sully, represented by two portraits; William Dunlap, Chester Harding, Henry Inman, Eastman Johnson, and William Garl Browne, this latter artist represented by at least seventeen examples, while there are several outstanding portraits of anonymous authorship. Among these latter are the portraits of Thomas Ruffin, and Bishop Otey.

I am often asked which do I think is the best portrait in the collection? It is always difficult to answer such a question; when I am asked, "Who is the greatest artist who ever lived?" I refuse to answer. Even for experts it is a matter of personal interpretation. But in the limited field of the pictures at Chapel Hill, and confining myself to the artists of the past, I do not mind suggesting that the portrait of James Cochran Dobbin by Eastman Johnson is, perhaps, the best, although the portrait of John C. Calhoun is a close rival.

How do we judge what is good in a picture? I say it is a matter of interpretation. But we look for certain things. Back of every fine picture there is an artist, a man, who has been deeply, profoundly moved by some experience. This experience may be the perception of beauty, or of character, and the greater he himself is as a man, and as a craftsman (for both insight and skill are needed), the more powerful are his feelings, the more he is stirred to express himself to others, that others may share the experience which so inflamed him. To put it another way, the artist, no matter what kind, is one who sees what the rest of us do not see, and who wishes to share his visions with us, that we may appreciate and understand them. There are mediocre artists who are not so different from the rest of us, who do not have the insight, or do not have much to give us. These we pass by. So I put inspiration first, and craftsmanship second, yet I admire craftsmanship intensely, for without it, the artist has no way of interpreting himself; the more skillful he is, the better, or the clearer, is his interpretation.

In the portrait of James Cochran Dobbin, 1814-1857, we find that keen perception of greatness, that emotion which was stirred by the individuality of the subject. The artist, Eastman Johnson, has made us share with him the experience which moved him so profoundly when he studied the face of that frail lovable man of whom it was said, "He was of great vision and an able executive as well." James Dobbin lives upon the canvas; although pathetically infirm of body, a virile spirit shines out from his face, radiating the fire within. That I can write thus about him is a proof of the skill of the artist, for you see he has made me share his privilege of knowing Dobbin. And that skill is also shown in painting the dying man (for it was painted in 1856 hardly a year before his death) in a fur-trimmed gown and great flowing tie. This was picturesque and I have no doubt it was true to life.

This is one of those rare instances where the impact of a fine spirit upon an equally fine artist produced a work of art.

Eastman Johnson is best known for his genre pictures—that is, scenes of American life, such as "My Old Kentucky Home," "Crack the Whip," "Corn Husking," etc.; but actually he was one of the best interpreters of character as a portraitist that America in the nineteenth century produced. In my opinion this is Eastman Johnson's masterpiece.

The portrait of John C. Calhoun, 1782-1850, evokes equal enthusiasm. Painted about 1820, it shows us the South Carolinian statesman much younger than in most portraits, and more handsome. He, also, is alive; his forceful personality, and determined, quarrelsome character show in his face. Yet, there is humour, that saving grace, and a joyousness which makes us believe he loved life in and for itself. Technically, too, this is masterly, for there is a third dimension to that massive head, form under the well modeled flesh, and a rare combination of breadth with delicacy of detail as shown in the treatment of the hair. Chester Harding was a prolific portraitist. Like many of the great English painters, he was largely self-taught, and, therefore, truly American.

Other outstanding portraits which I would like to mention are those of Thomas Ruffin, William Richardson Davie, Rev. Francis L. Hawks, Benjamin Franklin, Dr. Jesse Graves, Abram Rencher, Bishop Otey, Richmond M. Pearson, James Mebane, and David L. Swain.

Ruffin's portrait is interesting both for the subject and the artist. Thomas Ruffin, who was born in 1787 and died in 1870, was one of the most remarkable men of the state. He was Chief Justice of North Carolina in 1833-1852, during which period "he established a reputation, as a jurist, extending wherever English law is known," ranking with John Marshall as an authority on constitutional law. His biographers state he was a man of austere appearance, but of a fiery nature which he held in restraint. I think you see this in his portrait. It is strange we do not know the artist. He was a good one, for, in spite of certain defects, a little stiffness, and laboriousness of handling, the force of the man's character—his intellect—his robust countenance—is well interpreted. There is life, not only in the eyes, but in the color, the glowing flesh tones, the brilliant white of the cravat. The technique is unusual, not that of any identified artist of the time; so there is here a field of research for someone who wishes to discover other portraits by the same hand, some of which might fortunately be signed.

The profile portrait of William Richardson Davie (1756-1820) was painted by one of the most celebrated artists of our early history. Luckily we have ample evidence that it was from the brush of Charles Willson Peale, enlarged from an engraving by Gilles Louis Crétien (Paris 1800), an impression of which the University also owns. I regard Peale as our first truly great American painter, for he was born here, in Maryland, lived all his life here, and died in Philadelphia. While practically all his contemporaries went to England, either to study or to remain and practice, Peale stayed here, and his own art, sound, sincere and unaffected, was characteristic of our temperament.

Davie was a courtly gentleman, an aristocrat, as Peale has represented him to be. It is curious that the portrait, in this respect, seems so representative of the early character of the University. Davie stamped an aristocratic exclusiveness upon it which lasted until the great commoner David Swain opened its doors to the whole people of the state. It is fortunate that the virtual founder of the University, who was also a General in the Revolutionary War, and one of the earliest governors of the state, should be so well represented in the collection.

The portrait of the Rev. Francis L. Hawks (1798-1850) is interesting, historically, because of the correspondence in regard to it, wherein Hawks, writing from Philadelphia, very modestly accepts the honour of being asked to sit for his portrait, and recommends that Inman, of that city, be the painter. Hawks is remembered chiefly as the historian of North Carolina. Henry Inman, as Hawks suggested, was—in fact—one of the best portraitists of his time and painted many celebrated men—John Marshall, the Chief Justice, for example. But, unfortunately, our portrait was one of the most badly damaged of the collection, having suffered from lack of varnish. Painted thickly, it cracked, and in spite of restoration, cracks still show. However, there is great spirituality in the face, and, in its essential character as a portrait of a lovable man, is well preserved.

The University is fortunate in possessing the panel portrait of Franklin, which is important in portraying that many-sided genius in advanced age, by an artist who knew him in life. William Dunlap was the author of the first history of art in America, a work he entitled *A History of the Arts of Design in the U. S. A.* The portrait is dated New York 1826, long after Franklin's death, but it must have been executed from a study which Dunlap had previously made. On a panel, and unframed, it had become badly warped, and somewhat cracked, but not irreparably.

The portrait of Dr. Jesse Graves was painted by himself, when a student in Paris in 1845. In its forceful design, severely correct draughtsmanship and emphasis on line, it shows the influence of the great French classicist Ingres, who was supreme in the art world of Europe at that time. It seems that Graves gave up art for medicine; consequently it is not strange that an artist so capable as this portrait represents him to have been, should not be better known. He is not mentioned in the encyclopaedias of American artists.

I mention the portrait of Abram Rencher because it is signed by an able artist, J. M. Stanley, 1857, who is not very well known. There is a great deal of sureness in his brushwork, drawing that shows a thoroughly trained hand, and that quality I always admire, interpretation without slavish imitation.

The portrait of the Rt. Rev. James Harvey Otey (1800-1863) somewhat fascinates me. In spite of his office, even in spite of the fact that he was first Episcopal Bishop of Tennessee, I cannot help feeling that here is a reincarnation of a neolithic Druid. Certainly the artist, whoever he was, and we do not know, was impressed by his wizard-like character; he painted what a true artist should, what he saw, and felt, not necessarily what Otey's parishioners would like to admire. So let us forget that this man with a thick heavy mouth, and serpent-like eyes was a bishop, and regard the portrait as a rather daring work of art. (A portrait of Otey reproduced in Appleton's *Biographical Encyclopedia* presents him in quite a different aspect.)

I now come to the portrait of Chief Justice Richmond M. Pearson, which is listed, but not signed, as by William Garl Browne. It does not seem to be by Browne, but by an equally good painter, whom I wish we knew. Remarkable, it seems to me, is the serious, thoughtful countenance of the eminent judge. There is an easy naturalism in his pose, a breadth and freedom in its execution which suggest a skillful hand.

Before I discuss the portraits by William Garl Browne I wish to answer a question which I know is being asked by those familiar with the University collection: "Why haven't I placed the portraits of President Polk and his Secretary of the Navy, John Young Mason, by Thomas Sully, among the best?" These are undoubtedly valuable pictures; that the University should have an alumnus to become President of the United States, and another to become Secretary of the Navy as well as Minister to France, is something to be proud of, and their portraits should be prized, while Thomas Sully was one of the most eminent portraitists of the nineteenth century. But, unfortunately, these are not striking examples of Sully's best style. Sully was at the height of his powers the first twenty years of his career—that is, from about 1807-1827. These were painted in 1847 when Sully had fallen into a facile mannerism, a sort of lethargy, out of which it took a beautiful woman to arouse him. Thus the portraits of Polk and Mason leave us disappointed.

I know, too, that lovers of North Carolina history would like me to mention the portraits of Judge Gaston, the Rev. Elisha Mitchell, and the Hon. William R. King. Historically, like the two just mentioned, these are of great interest, for each one of these men has left his mark upon the state—yes, even upon the country. After Mitchell, the mountain, highest east of the Rockies, was named; King, a Senator from Alabama, was Minister Plenipotentiary to France, and elected Vice President of the United States, an office he never filled because of his sudden death; Gaston, 1778-1844, was so efficient and popular a judge that the Constitution of the state, which allowed only Protestants to hold office, was changed so that he could serve on the Supreme Court of the state. But Judge Gaston's portrait is a poor copy, by Bogle after George Cook; that of Elisha Mitchell is the work of a man more distinguished as an engraver than as a portraitist in oil—Nathaniel Jocelyn—and while in many ways charming, lacks the force and grandeur with which the subject should have impressed the artist; the third, that of King, which is an original by George Cook, by no means approaches the quality of the portrait of President Hooper of Wake Forest painted by the same hand. This latter is really from a technical standpoint, of exquisite quality. Cook, who was born in Maryland, 1793, studied abroad, where, as we can see, he acquired a facility with the brush second to none in this country.

I, myself, find several early anonymous portraits delightfully quaint as examples of the so-called "primitive" manner,—for example, the portraits of William Miller and John Owen, among the earliest in the collection. That of Miller has a colonial building with a cupola in the background which some North Carolina historian might identify. (My guess is that it is the Court House at Edenton, the oldest Courthouse still standing in North Carolina.)* Delightful also is the little portrait of Henry Clay, said to be by an artist named Moeller.

But with the collection of sixteen or seventeen (one is in doubt) by William Garl Browne, we come to the most noteworthy group belonging to the University, in fact—a collection which alone makes North Carolina unique. Up until now William Garl Browne has remained practically unknown. The only one of his works I had come across before coming to Chapel Hill was a portrait in the Union League of Philadelphia. This interested me, but though I did everything possible to trace him, I could learn nothing. Either he was too modest to gain national recognition, or our historians have been too obtuse. Yet he worked in Virginia, especially in Richmond, and the Carolinas for fifty years, executing over two thousand portraits, nearly one a week—a prodigious feat. He should be ranked high as one of the most skillful artists of his period. He was the Sully of the South. His life and works are being published at the present moment, so I will not attempt to repeat or even to summarize what will soon appear in print, except to note that he was born in England, came

---

*It was not the Court House.—Ed.

to Richmond somewhere around 1840, when he was still young enough to develop into a thoroughly American painter with an individual style, easily recognizable. He painted not only the eminent men of the South—giving them an air of distinction, but women and children with elegance and charm. The portrait of Mrs. John S. Henderson of Salisbury, now hanging in the home of her daughter, Mrs. Lyman Cotten of Chapel Hill, painted as late at the 1880's, shows him, like Sully, to have preserved in his portraits of women, his colorful style long after it had declined in his portraiture of men.

I believe that his biographer agrees with me that the portrait of James Mebane is his masterpiece. Mebane is of particular interest to North Carolinians as the first President of the Dialectic Society; he later acquired a wide reputation in the politics of the state. Painted in 1850, Mebane's portrait belongs to Browne's early period before he achieved too much facility and fell under the influence of the academicism of the late nineteenth century. His early work, as shown in this portrait, is rich in color. Browne loved red chairs and curtains, and accessories such as tables, columns, or shelves of books. For he believed, and I think he was right, that to place a man amid his surroundings, as, let us say, in the case of a judge—his law library; or in the case of a public official—against the imposing background of a public building, suggested by marble columns, added to his characterization, or, at least, to the interest of the canvas, which was first and foremost with him at the time. These accessories made the canvas decorative.

James Mebane is seated naturally, if carelessly, in his great red chair, seriously thoughtful. The figure is well and evenly lighted, so that the cut of the clothes, even to creases and folds, forms a pattern, even though they are black. The garments are not just one plain black area as in so many portraits. Technically the painting has been done somewhat laboriously, conscientiously so; this in itself, as with primitive painting, is what we admire; but above all, we feel that the artist has grasped the bigness of the man, and expressed something which no camera, or no other agency than paint, could do.

The portrait of David Lowry Swain, I feel, is of the same

character. Notice how painstakingly and honestly the hands are executed; this is rare in American portraiture, even at the present day. One of the visitors to my studio, upon seeing this picture for the first time, exclaimed: "How like Lincoln it is!" And President Swain was like Lincoln; he arose from the same background, and remained the plain rugged, honest, thoughtful and deep-seeing man. The famous portrait of Lincoln by Carpenter is like this in many respects.

David Lowry Swain, 1801-1868, was, when elected in 1832, the youngest Governor of North Carolina. At the close of his term of office he was made President of this University and remained so for thirty-three years. During the War between the States and the Reconstruction, he was adviser to Governors Vance and Worth, and at the end of the war adviser on reconstruction to President Andrew Johnson. It was said that he was so wise in council that he was kept close to men in public life who constantly sought his advice. This sagacity, this integrity, we find in Browne's impressive portrait.

The portraits of William A. Graham, Willie Person Mangum and James Phillips belong to his next period. Graham, whose dates are 1804-1875, was United States Senator, Governor of North Carolina, and Secretary of the Navy under Fillmore; it was he, when Secretary of the Navy, who sent Perry to Japan! Mangum, 1792-1861, was also a United States Senator, a Judge, and honored with the degree of LL.D from this University. Phillips, who was born in England in 1792, was professor of mathematics at Chapel Hill most of his career, which was ended by his death in 1867.

In these portraits we find men of distinction—jurists, statesmen, churchmen. It is appropriate that they are given dignity, with even an air of grandeur, in their portraits. But we find less sincerity than in the earlier portraits; they are being turned out in a mold. Perhaps the artist felt this, himself, or realized the need for a change in style, for subsequently he abandoned to a great extent the accessories of the background, forsook, in fact, the decorative and official manner, and substituted for it a greater naturalism. From 1870 on, we find on Browne's canvases a general grey tonality, with plain backgrounds, against which he emphasizes a lifelikeness which is at times almost startling.

Browne by this time had attained such facility that he could dash off portraits as easily as any Frenchman of his day. There is a strong analogy between such portraits as, let us say, those of Robert R. Bridgers (1881) or John Motley Morehead (1882) or Bartholomew F. Moore, and the work of the Frenchman Fantin-Latour, whose portraits are so imitative of reality that one can mistake them for the living subjects. The result of this tendency was for Browne to lose that inestimable interpretive quality we admire in his early work. Many of his later portraits are merely photographic.

I have confined myself in this article to the painters of the past. There are many portraits in the University collection by living artists, which are interesting chiefly for their subjects. A few, and I regret to say, only a few. are, from my point of view, notable for their excellence as works of art. These latter, like the best ones of the past, should be used as examples of the importance of selecting only the most accomplished artists to paint the portraits of those now living, who are today giving distinction and renown to the University.

IV

THE OPENING OF THE UNIVERSITY

THE ONE hundred and fiftieth anniversary of the opening of the University, the third major event in the series of Sesquicentennial ceremonies, was celebrated in an impressive meeting in Raleigh in the Hall of the House of Representatives before a joint session of the General Assembly at 8:30 P.M. on January 15, 1945. Lieutenant Governor L. Y. Ballentine, President of the Senate, and Speaker Oscar L. Richardson were the presiding officers, and Victor S. Bryant, chairman of the Legislative Commission on the Sesquicentennial, directed the program of the occasion. In addition to the speakers participating in the ceremonies, the meeting was attended by members of the Legislative Commission on the Sesquicentennial, the Director of the Sesquicentennial, committees representing the trustees, faculty, alumni, and students, and Deans of Administration and the Administrative Council of the three branches of the University, and by the public.

Following recognition by President Ballentine, Mr. Bryant spoke.

MR. BRYANT

May I express to you the appreciation of the University of North Carolina Sesquicentennial Legislative Commission for holding this joint session of the General Assembly. In doing so you not only pay tribute to the University itself, but to those General Assemblies of the past whose unforgettable farsightedness made the University of North Carolina a reality.

The date of January 15th is an important one in University history. It was one hundred and fifty years ago today that the University first opened its doors. Dr. Kemp P. Battle in his *History of the University* says: "The morning of the 15th of January, 1795, opened with a cold, drizzling rain. As the sighing of the watery wind whistled through the leafless branches of tall oaks and hickories, and the Davie poplar, then in vigorous youth, all that met the eyes of Governor Richard Dobbs Speight, state officials, trustees, and other distinguished visitors, were a two-storied brick building, the unpainted wooden house of the presiding professor, the avenue between them filled with stumps of recently felled trees, a pile of yellowish red clay dug out for the foundation of the chapel, or Person Hall, a pile of lumber collected for building Steward's Hall, a Scotch-Irish preacher professor, and not one student."

The presiding professor experienced whatever comfort he could find in solitude until February 12, the date on which the first student entered the University. His name was Hinton James. We are told he had walked to Chapel Hill from his home in Wilmington, though I believe it possible that he did some hitch-hiking. Before the term was over a number of other students arrived and took up their studies, mostly of a classical and mathematical nature.

A Trustees' Visiting Committee soon visited the University. For the most part they were pleased, but, as I believe is customary, drew some criticism upon their heads by finding a few things not entirely to their liking. They stated that the conduct of the students was good, although they cautiously added the refrigerating words "everything considered."

The actual opening of the University, however, was only the ripening into fruition of plans conceived and fought out years before. Nineteen years before, the groundwork had been laid at the Halifax Convention, which in December, 1776, met to adopt a constitution for the new free State of North Carolina. The background of this convention is most significant. The year before, in 1775, the famous shots had been heard at Concord. The Mecklenburg Resolutions of May 31st had been passed, the Battle of Bunker Hill had been fought. In the early part of 1776 in our own state the British nose had been bloodied at Moore's Creek. In Philadelphia the Declaration of Independence had been signed in July. By August, however, General Washington had been driven from New York, retreating toward Philadelphia. Defiance gave way to fearsome doubts while dismay and consternation seized many Americans. It was in this same month of December, 1776, that Thomas Paine wrote, "These are the times that try men's souls."

North Carolina then had a population of barely two hundred thousand inhabitants, most of them widely scattered and poorly armed. We had thrown down the gauntlet to a mighty nation with a tradition of invincibility. Within the century England had broken the power of Louis the Great of France; with characteristic thoroughness had crushed the Pretender and his followers at Culloden; had sent General Wolfe to storm the heights of Quebec; and had firmly secured the mastery of the seas.

With no organized militia, and lacking in all of the sinews of war, courage alone excepted, and with our own people sadly divided, North Carolinians were fighting a life and death struggle. The members of the Halifax Constitutional Convention themselves did not know whether they were meeting as patriots or as traitors. Thus, they set about the task of framing a constitution with a resoluteness summoned from realms beyond those of pure logic. These men were wholly devoted to the public good. In the discharge of their duties they now seem to have recognized and come squarely to grips with the challenge of an unborn posterity. The constitution which they finally gave the state in December, 1776, was so warily and wisely drawn that it stood for over half a century without change.

I do not know whether the idea was sponsored by the Scotch-Irish influence of the Mecklenburg delegation, as many think, and as all Mecklenburgers admit, or whether it developed from the solicitude of the entire group for the enlightenment and education of future generations, but in Section 41 of the new constitution we find these golden words: "A school, or schools, shall be established by the Legislature for the convenient instruction of youth, with such salaries to the masters, paid by the public, as may enable them to instruct at low prices; and all useful learning shall be duly encouraged and promoted in one or more universities." This was democracy in theory. It typified the spirit which has led impartial historians in writing of the period to describe North Carolina as democratic in comparison with other southern states.

This was high ground. The seed of public education had been

planted. The nurture of the seed, however, had to await the sunshine of a more convenient season, and its growth had to await the return of peace. There was yet to be experienced the desolation and despair of Valley Forge. The battles of King's Mountain and Guilford Court House still had to be fought, and, finally, Yorktown was not to come until 1781.

For thirteen years after the Halifax Constitutional Convention a state university was an idealization with no counterpart in reality. Then in 1789 the Constitutional Convention of North Carolina, convening in a momentous session at Fayetteville, voted on November 21 to enter the Union, and on December 11, the General Assembly of North Carolina, also meeting in Fayetteville, granted a charter to the University of North Carolina. Under its terms the University could not be built within five miles of the state's seat of government or of a place of holding courts. I do not know whether the Assembly had in mind the protection of the courts or of the students. I suspect the students' welfare was uppermost.

The bill chartering the University carried no appropriation. Having served with much pleasure as a member of the Finance and Appropriation Committees with so many of you, and with our present Governor, and having heard the well-known legislative observation, "This bill will not cost the State a penny. It is a good bill and ought to pass," I can well believe that this familiar legislative technique must have been employed at that time.

Had the bill carried an outright appropriation I believe its passage would have been doubtful. I hasten to add this is no reflection upon the members of that Assembly. It must be remembered that there was then no General Fund surplus, and about the only approved types of expenditures were the defense of the state from its foes, the punishment of crime, and the payment of meager salaries to the few state employees. The charter did, however, give the University the right to receive donations, as well as escheats and unclaimed land grants. Thus, as Dr. Battle said, a number of revolutionary veterans in uncoffined graves became the unintentional benefactors of the University.

Still running true to approved and skilled procedure, the bill chartering the University having been safely passed, another bill was offered at the session of 1791 to provide financial assistance. On December 29 in the House and December 30 in the Senate, the Assembly voted to loan £5,000 to the new University to be used in erecting buildings. The vote in favor of the loan in the House, then called the House of Commons, was 57 to 53, and in the Senate, now sometimes known as the House of Lords, 28 to 21. Some years later the loan was made a gift. A site was chosen, and buildings which I have described were erected. Then, on January 15, 1795, the first state university in America was formally opened.

I am happy to say that many subsequent legislatures, including recent ones, have been liberal with the University. Their generosity has been bread cast upon the waters.

We have seen that the University was conceived for the purpose of encouraging and promoting useful learning for the people of North Carolina. True to the concept of its origin, the University has done just this. For a hundred and fifty years its campus has been "the dwelling place of dynamic democracy and a citadel against the forces of intolerance and bigotry." Opposed by secularism, sectionalism, and at one time by the belief that a university should not be supported by tax money, it has more than held its ground. It has, and this is said without belittling or discounting the brilliant and useful records of other institutions of learning in this state, led and moulded the thought of the people of North Carolina. On its campus freedom of thought has not been circumscribed. Not content with merely teaching useful learning, it has dared challenge its students to extend the boundaries of human knowledge. It has promoted the critical examination of the evidential bases of knowledge, the correction of error, verification of data, and the discovery of new truth as the verifiable way of progress in education, industry, society, and government. Through all of this, sight has never been lost of the fact that the University of North Carolina belongs to the people of North Carolina, and in its democratic idealism it is the University of the people.

The reality of this democracy was typified by an incident which I witnessed almost thirty years ago. My father and I were sitting under the shade of one of the magnificent oaks near the well in front of the South Building at Chapel Hill one Sunday afternoon. We saw a little fellow about six or seven years old wearing the remnants of a cotton shirt, patched and re-patched many times. His trousers, faded by many washings, were held in place by a piece of twine strung over one of his shoulders. He was barefooted, and was carrying a gallon water jug. He went to the well, and, having pumped the jug full, took the familiar tin dipper off the top of the pump and drank until his thirst was satisfied. He picked up his jug and trudged off home. A few moments later an automobile—a large one for that day—drove up and stopped at the well. The Governor of North Carolina alighted. Governor Bickett went to the pump, and took the same dipper off the top of the pump and drank until his thirst was satisfied. He got back into his automobile and started off to Raleigh to the executive mansion. I shall never forget my father's remark: "My son," said he, "that is the democratic way of life they teach at Chapel Hill."

I am not irreverent when I say that the waters from the wells of wisdom at Chapel Hill have meant in an intellectual way to the people of North Carolina what the waters of the Samaritan well, hallowed by the lowly Nazarene of the first century, have meant in a spiritual way to people everywhere.

I do not claim that the vision of the founders has yet been realized. The goal has not been reached. The increasing complexity of state life, the need for practical education of our boys when they return from overseas, the greater need for research, the education of unborn generations, all come under the head of unfinished business for the University. I do claim, however, that since the University opened one hundred and fifty years ago today, its influence for good has gone to every section of North Carolina, and even beyond its boundaries.

Since the days of Hinton James, lads have come to Chapel Hill from every section of North Carolina. It has been the meeting place of many elements—seafaring lads from the homes of simple fishermen on the outer banks, speaking a difficult dialect for the rugged mountaineers from cabins back in the coves and on the ridges of the Great Smokies; sons of wealthy planters from the

Albemarle; blue bloods from the Cape Fear region; boys from cotton and tobacco farms in the Piedmont; descendants of the Scotch-Irish of Mecklenburg, and of the Scotch Highlanders of the sandhill and long-leaf pine sections; a Quaker from Alamance or Guilford, a Moravian from Forsyth; eager self-help students from every section, and a host of others—all have come together at Chapel Hill, rubbed shoulders, exchanged ideas, learned to tolerate different viewpoints, and to respect the rights of others.

Their maturing minds have been enriched by wholesome contacts with intellectual nobility. To mention only a few: the Battles, the Mannings, the two Grahams, including our present President, Dr. Winston, Dr. Alderman, President Venable, Dean Stacy, President Chase, Dr. Mangum, Dr. MacNider, Professor Horace Williams, Dr. Archibald Henderson, and many others.

Influenced by all of these contacts they have gone back to their homes in every village and section of North Carolina, carrying with them something of the essence of Chapel Hill—yes, something of the very heart and essence of North Carolina itself.

It is no accident that North Carolinians have hastened forward to clash with the aggressor powers, and have acquitted themselves with honor on the field of battle. The University has stood for these things. Then, too, after some unpleasant experiences with fire in 1861 to 1865, in which our section was burned out without fire insurance, we Southerners have had the feeling that we wanted the war fought elsewhere.

It is no accident that North Carolina has had good government, untarnished by suggestion of fraud or bribery. It is no accident that North Carolinia has had a fine public school system, and has been noted for its progressiveness. It is no accident that North Carolina has been blessed with a line of good governors, including the present incumbent. These are not mere coincidences. They are the natural fruits sprung from the seed planted more than a hundred and fifty years ago.

The University has prospered because it has supplied the vital human need for enlightenment. It will endure because its precepts hold that democracy and freedom under the law are fundamentals which must be preserved at any cost.

At the conclusion of his address, Mr. Bryant introduced His Excellency R. Gregg Cherry, Governor of North Carolina and President *ex officio* of the Board of Trustees of the University.

GOVERNOR CHERRY

Mr. President, Mr. Speaker, and Members of the Joint Session of the General Assembly, Distinguished Guests, Ladies and Gentlemen:

In celebrating the one hundred and fiftieth anniversary of the opening of the oldest state university, it is fitting that we turn back to see briefly what happened on that earlier occasion. Today it is a far cry from that date a century and a half ago, and the state and its people have come a long way since January 15, 1795. At that time, North Carolina had only recently emerged from the long struggle for independence, and still more recently the state had entered the Federal Union under the Constitution. The scattered population totaled less than one-ninth what it is today, there was no city nor even any large town in the state, and travel and transportation were slow and difficult. The site of the State Capital at Raleigh had been selected less than three years before, the first State House here had not yet been completed, and indeed the legislature was holding its first session in Raleigh at the very time when the University was formally opened at Chapel Hill.

The site of the University had been chosen the same year the site of the Capital had been agreed upon, and the two were some thirty miles apart. The cornerstone of the first building at the University, Old East, had been laid in 1793 and the village of Chapel Hill had been hewn out of the forest, but stumps yet stood in the midst of what were called streets. In January, 1795, the one University building stood surrounded by the pile of red mud which had been excavated for its foundation, and the only other structure yet erected was the house of the presiding professor. It was indeed a small beginning in an isolated community.

On that day, coming from the new and raw village of Raleigh, with its unfinished State Capitol, to the new and muddy village of Chapel Hill, with its one unfinished University building, were Governor Richard Dobbs Spaight and a group of prominent state officials, together with members of the General Assembly. The day was cold and rainy, the wind whistled through the bare trees, and the distinguished Assembly shivered as they proceeded with the exercises. The building, though not yet complete, was declared ready to receive students, and the Governor then issued a statement inviting the youth of the state to enter the institution. As yet there were no students, and the first one did not acually arrive until February 12, nearly a month later. By the end of the term the number had increased to forty-one, and during the next term to nearly one hundred.

Small though these beginnings were, they represent a significant and distinctly American development. Prior to the Revolution nearly all of the institutions for higher learning in the thirteen colonies had been denominational: Harvard, Puritan in background; William and Mary, Anglican; and most of the others under the control of one religious group or another. After independence had been won, however, the states determined to set up their own public institutions for higher learning—not for any limited group, not for any special class, but for the people as a whole. This was a long step in the direction of democracy, of granting equal opportunity to all, regardless of wealth, creed, or social standing. It was a fruition of the doctrine of the rights of man, which had been a rallying cry of the colonists in their long struggle for independence. And be it ever remembered that of all these institutions, the first to open its doors was the University of North Carolina!

Later other states followed North Carolina's example. Most of the original thirteen states established universities, and as one western commonwealth after another was admitted to the Union, a new state university was set up. Thus the march of the pioneer westward was marked by a parallel march of the state-supported university. Indeed, it was in the areas beyond the Alleghany Mountains that these institutions came to enjoy their greatest popular support and largest growth, and we think of them in particular in connection with the states of the Middle West and Far West. Today, all but a very few of the states of the Union, from Atlantic to Pacific and from Canada to Mexico, maintain these institutions.

There had been nothing quite like this in the Old World. In Britain, the universities functioned largely for the benefit of the upper classes—were in the main gentlemen's institutions—and on the continent of Europe, while this had been true to a lesser degree, there was nevertheless no institution designed to educate all the people, regardless of economic condition, social status, or religious creed. Here in America, on the other hand, the university operated on the theory that all the people are entitled to an education and that it is the duty of the state to provide for this.

In the beginning, it is true, the theory was not fully carried out in practice. At first the state universities were hardly more than liberal arts colleges, and they did not include the various professional and graduate schools which we know today, they did not admit women, they were small and supported in only meagre fashion, and they were in no position to conduct advanced research. And yet the foundation was there. All that was needed was to build upon that foundation.

From such small and limited beginnings, the state university in America has expanded and developed in many ways to meet the growing needs of democracy. As the American people broke away from the earlier concept of a society controlled and dominated by the upper classes, they came more and more to believe in the rights of the common man and in the equality of all. As tax-supported public grammar and high schools were established in one state after another, the state university came to be looked upon, not as something superimposed upon a group of privately supported academies and other private institutions, but rather as the capstone of the entire public educational system, which extends from the first grade all the way up through the university. It came to be, indeed, the crowning glory of the American system of public education.

Under this new and broadened concept, the state universities have constantly extended their functions and have come to render new services. From mere liberal arts colleges they have expanded into institutions with many and varied functions. Women have been admitted, divisions for professional and other specialized training have been set up, graduate schools have been established, extension divisions have been created, and publications have been issued in a variety of scientific and cultural fields. Thus the American state university has come to accept an ever broadening responsibility in order to meet the needs of a democratic commonwealth. Today, its varied functions include teaching and training the citizenship of the state, conserving knowledge and ideas, discovering new knowledge through research, publishing the results of investigation and interpreting them to the public and serving the state through extension courses, institutes, libraries, laboratories, and the work of experts on its staff.

The part which the state university has played in the growth of the American nation and the development of the American way of life is shown in bold relief when we look at conditions in certain foreign countries. In the nations which are dominated by dictators, where liberty and the rights of the individual have been stamped out, the universities have been closed or their function has been limited to little more than the dissemination of propaganda. There can be no objective and unbiased search for truth, nor is it permitted to teach the truth. Rather, the universities have been taken over to serve merely for the promulgation of party doctrine. In our own country, on the other hand, the universities yet remain as beacons of light for the discovery and teaching of truth. There are no restrictions or limitations on research and the quest for knowledge, for it is the conviction of Americans that there is nothing to fear from knowledge and truth. If "the truth shall make men free," then indeed the American state university is in the vanguard of the march toward freedom. For the future of American institutions and of the democratic way of life rest upon an educated and informed citizenry, prepared and unafraid to meet any and all the problems and issues which the future may hold.

In the growth and development of these typical and basic American institutions, our own State University has been at the very forefront. During the first few decades of its history, it grew into a useful liberal arts college, the natural sciences received emphasis, and later it was drawn into closer contact with the state at large, with its chief purpose the training of men for public service. Just before the War between the States, the enrollment reached a peak of 456, and the "alumni included one

President of the United States, one Vice-President, seven Cabinet Officials, ten United States Senators, forty-one Representatives in Congress, fifteen State Governors, and many State Judges and Legislators." From 1814, when a University alumnus first became Governor, until the present time, twenty-six of forty-four Governors of North Carolina have studied at the University.

During the War between the States, the University remained open, though most of its faculty and students joined the Confederate armies. But Reconstruction closed its doors, and they were not reopened until 1875. Since that date, the institution has seen its period of greatest growth and expansion, and each of the seven presidents has made a distinct contribution. The consolidation of the three schools at Raleigh, Greensboro, and Chapel Hill into the greater University of North Carolina has made possible increased services in many fields. At the outbreak of World War II, the regular enrollment at Chapel Hill had reached 4,406; at Raleigh 2,572; and at Greensboro 2,260—a total of 9,238 students.

We may be proud that our University today, in a series of surveys and rankings by outsiders, is rated as one of the leading state universities in the nation. It stands high in graduate work in the ranking of the institutions in the South and in the nation. In a national foundation's survey of achievements in the natural sciences, the University stood first in the South. In surveys conducted by experts of the United States Navy regarding the best locations for Pre-Flight Schools, Chapel Hill was adjudged to be among the first, not only in the South, but also in the East.

State College has received similar recognition. In the past ten years, it has come to be ranked first in the South in its agricultural program. Its School of Engineering includes no less than four departments which have recently been placed on the approved list by the Engineering Society for Professional Development, and the national society of Sigma Xi, which is installed only at institutions which can qualify for excellence of graduate research, has now been installed at the College. The Textile School is easily the best in the South and is on the way to becoming the best in the nation.

Likewise, the Woman's College since consolidation has shown

rapid advancement. General standards of academic work and scholarship have been raised, chapters of the national society of Phi Beta Kappa and of five other national honor societies have been installed, and the College has been placed on the approved list of the Association of American Universities. These are but a few of the many instances which might be given to show the ranking of the Consolidated University among the educational institutions of the nation.

Today, the University is not merely a *college*, as it was in the beginning, but it includes many divisions and branches, and it is equipped and prepared to train men and women in a wide variety of fields—in law, in education, in medicine, in public health, in commerce and industry, in engineering, in agriculture, in the fine arts, in the natural sciences, in home economics, in government, in library science, in journalism, in pharmacy, and in many other professions and activities. Such training affects and benefits, not merely the individuals who happen to attend the University, but the daily life and well-being of the entire state and every citizen thereof.

In the present world conflict, the University, along with other institutions of higher learning, is playing a major role. Its full facilities have been placed at the disposal of the armed forces, and both the Navy and Army have maintained on the campuses a variety of units. Thousands of former students and members of the staff are in the armed forces, serving the nation in every part of the world.

When the war has ended, when Hitler and Tojo and their fanatical cohorts have been crushed, more than three hundred thousand young men and women will return to our state to pursue again the paths of peace. Many of them who have had their education interrupted, will wish to take up again where they had left off. Others will need specialized training to equip them for what each of them will want—a job. It will be the duty of the state to provide in every way possible for these men and women who have served us so well, and we ought to make—and in so far as it is in my power we will make—that provision fully and generously.

In meeting this problem, we will expect to use to the fullest the facilities of our State University, with its physical, intellectual, moral, and spiritual equipment for the training of men and women. Every war veteran who so desires—and there will be many thousands of them—can find here the opportunity to equip or re-equip himself as a peace-time citizen of the state. For this purpose, and for preparing the University to serve in every way in the growth and development which the state may expect after the war, we pledge and give our full support.

And so today, on the one hundred and fiftieth anniversary of the opening of the oldest state university, we are proud of the record of service which the University of North Carolina has made to the state and its people. The past one hundred and fifty years have seen tremendous growth and achievement. We are confident that in the future our University will go forward to even loftier heights of service in the building of a greater and a better North Carolina.

The address of Governor Cherry was followed by that of President Graham in which many examples of specific service to the state were cited.

President Graham

During its one hundred and fiftieth anniversary any university, however inadequate and despite all its failures and frustrations, has the sesquicentennial duty, by illustration and suggestion, to report something of its story and services to the state which sustains it as a source both of historic pride in its own child and of the democratic opportunity of the people it was created to serve.

The University of North Carolina was conceived as a fundamental institution of an original American state by a provision in the state constitution adopted by the convention of the people at Halifax in 1776. A child of revolution and democracy, the University thus had its origin in the beginnings of this Republic in the birth year of the American Revolution. The Revolution, which gave birth to the self-government of the people, gave birth to the University of the people as necessary to self-government. In the very first hazardous year of the Revolution the people of North Carolina foretold the still prophetic idea that government of the people, by the people, and for the people could not endure without education of the people, by the people, and for the people.

The University was chartered by the state legislature in Fayetteville in 1789 in the month and in the city in which the convention of the people ratified the Constitution of the United States with its inclusion of the Bill of Rights. The charter of the United States which had preceded the charter of the University gave it the enduring strength of the nation and the intellectual freedom and moral responsibility of the Bill of Rights. By the Bill of Rights, freedom of research, teaching, and publication are thus an organic and historic part of the freedom and purpose for which both the University and the Republic were founded. These charters of the state and nation unite the history of the University, North Carolina, and the United States as chapters in the rise of human freedom, as sharers in the great traditions and treasures of the human spirit, and as present participants in the struggle of the people for responsible and just self-government through universal and thorough self-enlightenment.

The cornerstone of the first building was laid in Chapel Hill October 12, 1793, by General William Richardson Davie, Grand Master of the Masonic Order, later Governor, formerly a bold cavalry officer of many Revolutionary battles and, in a dark time, the resourceful quartermaster general who made possible Green's masterly delaying tactics across North Carolina which helped to prepare the way for Yorktown. Long champion of the founding of the University and of the first legislative grant of state funds, this son of Princeton is traditionally remembered as the father of the University of North Carolina.

The University was formally opened January 15, 1795, one hundred and fifty years ago today, the first existing state university to open its doors in America. Our State University opened its doors more than six years before the next state university opened its doors. Our University had graduated its first seniors in 1798, three years before the next state university had admitted its first freshmen. The first student to enter the University was Hinton James of Wilmington, February 12, 1795, a forerunner of scores of thousands of alumni whose lives and services are a vital part of the history of our state and nation.

Because of her early responsibility and long history, it is only natural that it was through her teachings and the efforts of her sons, that there were born at Chapel Hill the North Carolina pioneer movements for the development of railroads, agriculture, industry, public schools, good roads, public health, public libraries, public welfare, historical collections, the liberal arts and sciences, folk plays, scientific, humanistic, and social research and publications, and the general state-wide extension of the services of the University for the building of an economically more productive, imaginatively more creative, and spiritually nobler North Carolina. We will not stop now to call the roll of the alumni of the University at Chapel Hill who have been President and Vice-President of the United States, Secretary of State, Secretary of War, Attorney General, Secretary of the Interior, and Secretaries of the Navy, ambassadors, senators, congressmen, federal judges, chief justices of the state supreme court, governors, legislators, promoters of agriculture, dairying and forestry, mining and fisheries, founders and builders of great industries, railroads, banks, insurance companies, and hospitals, leaders of labor, leaders of political parties, and insurgent revolts of the people against privilege and vested power, publishers and editors, scientists, historians, artists, novelists, painters, poets and playwrights, physicians, teachers, bishops of the church, ministers of religion, and champions of the intellectual and spiritual freedom and of the moral and social welfare of mankind. Out of the past we will call the names of three governors, sons of the University, who, at historic moments, standing where the roads of destiny crossed, chose the high road for a greater state: Morehead, who built railroads to join East and West and promote the development of agriculture and industry; Vance, the war governor and tribune of the people; and Aycock, the educational governor, who led the great crusade for universal education and declared in the teeth of prejudice and fear that the state must educate equally all her children, white and colored.

The University has made enduring contributions in developing the pioneers indispensable to the decisive forward movements in the common life of the state—men and women willing boldly to step out in the lonely front and take a beating for a cause later to be the triumph of the people. In one hundred and fifty years their names, on monument and shrines and in the hearts of the people have become legion, one of the great honor rolls of any American state—in public schools, Murphey, Yancey, Wiley, Alderman, McIver, McLean, and Allen; in public highways, Alexander, Holmes, Pratt, Berry, and Page; in public health, Wood and Lewis; in public welfare and public libraries, individuals still among the living; in industry, agriculture, commerce and finance, science, literature, the arts, public service, and religion, names eminent in history and in contemporary America.

In higher education the records show that one of the founding fathers and an original trustee of the University of North Carolina later went over the mountains and founded Blount College, which has since become the University of Tennessee; that the alumnus who later became Vice-President of the United States was a prime mover in the founding of the University of Alabama; that the two chief founders of the University of the South at Sewanee were graduates of the University; that sons of the University were co-founders of Wake Forest College, Davidson College, Peace Junior College, North Carolina State College, the Woman's College, East Carolina Teachers College, and Appalachian State Teachers College, and in Durham donated the land for Trinity College which today is the campus of the Woman's College of Duke University.

Sons and daughters of the University have also been presidents of all these colleges save one and, in addition, of the Greensboro College for Women, Saint Mary's Junior College, Chowan College, Mitchell College, Gardner-Webb, and Converse, and many other colleges and universities outside North Carolina including Tulane University, the University of Texas, and the University of Virginia.

The great common law chief justice before the Civil War, Richmond M. Pearson, and the great social-minded chief justice, since the Civil War, Walter Clark, were alumni of the University. The present chief justice and all the six associate justices of the North Carolina Supreme Court, and the pre-eminent senior judge of all the Circuit Courts in the United States are also alumni. Of the recent legions of distinguished alumni we shall note among them only those who hold a national first place: two of the last three presidents of the American Bankers Association; a National Commander of the American Legion; the national leader of the Democratic Women of America; first archivist of the United States; two Pulitzer Prize winners; the founder and director of the Town Hall of the Air; the director of the international health program of the Rockefeller Foundation; the chairman of the National Board Advisory to the Director of War Mobilization and Reconversion.

In the present Faculty at Chapel Hill are professors who have been or are national presidents of twenty-five American scientific, learned, and professional societies and associations.

In addition to the many on leave in the fighting forces or in naval and military research is a young man who did much of the basic financial thinking for the United Nations at Dumbarton Oaks and another even younger man who prepares the expert reports on oil for the guidance and decisions of the combined Allied Chiefs of Staff.

In national and international affairs an alumnus is one of six special assistants to the President of the United States and his father is the University's fifth and America's greatest Secretary of the Navy, perennial tribune of the people, ambassador of inter-American goodwill and the international organization of peace. He brings to mind two other alumni. One was Secretary of the Navy who, a decade before the Civil War, projected the expedition of Commodore Perry which opened up the island outposts of Asia to the western world with far reverberations in this hour. The other was the first honor man in his class and President of the United States, who, by the reannexation of Texas and the reoccupation of Oregon, extended the national domain from the boundaries of the Louisiana Territory to the shores of the Pacific. James K. Polk also founded the United States Naval Academy, whose graduates today make safe the oceans from America to the beachheads of Europe and to the island gateways of Japan.

With the momentum of its great traditions, this old University is carrying on and is renewing its youth as witnessed by the national surveys which placed it first in the Southeast in the social sciences, in the basic sciences, in folk plays, historical, literary, and economic publications, in physical education, and in the number of departments qualified to give the Ph.D. degree. By heritage and outlook, Chapel Hill has become the Southeastern center of public health, interracial, industrial, and international relations. The traditions of a great past and the resiliency of a vigorous youth are combined in the efforts of the University for the winning of the war. Up from the past come the spirit of the soldiers of the Revolution who founded the University, and the heroism of her sons who fell on battlefields in larger proportion than from any other university in either side of the war which for four terrible years broke the Union of states. We see General Pettigrew, first honor man of his class, leader of heroic assaults in Pickett's charge at Gettysburg, later fall mortally wounded guarding the retreat of Lee as he revealed his moral grandeur in defeat. Left high up on the heights at Gettysburg was another brilliant young alumnus and commander of a regiment who, as he lay dying among his comrade dead, dipped his finger in his own fast-running blood and wrote on the back of an old envelope, "Tell my father that I died with my face to the foe." We see sons of the University in the First World War stand and fall by the side of the American field officer who, when ordered to retreat from a hopeless road down which the Germans moved in massive final spear-pointed thrust at the gallant but tired heart of France, replied, "Retreat, hell! We have just got here!" They are still there, buried where they fell to turn the tides of war. Today the sons of the University in comrade spirit with gallant youth on all the fronts of freedom from Budapest to Luzon and Bastiogne are giving their all that their University, their country, and all people everywhere may be free.

Today, the sons and daughters of the University celebrate, in comrade spirit, the historic significance of all three institutions of the Consolidated University. In 1938 and in 1942 respectively were celebrated the fiftieth anniversary of the founding of the North Carolina State College and the Woman's College of the University of North Carolina. On those occasions were reviewed the memorable histories, the enduring values, and manifold services of those noble institutions. We only note in addition at this time that the North Carolina State College has become the acknowledged leader in agricultural research, teaching, extension, and publication in the entire South. In the fields of the science of soils, experimental statistics, textile and Diesel engineering, North Carolina State has moved to the forefront in America. Five departments of engineering within the decade were placed on the approved list. The Woman's College has won the installation of a chapter of the national honor society of Phi Beta Kappa, five other national honor societies, and a place on the approved list of the Association of American Universities.

All three in recent years have had their largest enrollments, largest appropriations, highest national standing, and have advanced in the democratic structure, function, and values of faculty and student self-government.

Our dream is that State College, the Woman's College, and the University at Chapel Hill for their high purposes and functions shall be equal in standards, salaries, equipment, and faculty, and second to none in the nation.

By the continued co-ordination and integration of these three historic and increasingly useful institutions and by co-operation with all our colleges, schools, and agencies of the people's life and by co-operation with the neighbor University, North Carolina can seize the opportunity to build one of the greatest of the American commonwealths by building one of the great intellectual and spiritual centers of the world.

As we stand here in the critical vantage time of January, 1945, and look back through the history of our people we see that the history of the University for one hundred and fifty years has been a continuous part of the history of North Carolina. As we stand here in this historic and strategic capital city and look in all directions across the length and breath of the state we see that the life and service of the manifold Consolidated University reaches into every county, town, and community in North Carolina and into every part of the world where tens of thousands of the men and women of our three institutions serve and fight for the cause of human freedom.

The look backward through one hundred and fifty years, in

which the University has been a creative part and the look across the world at war, in which over 20,000 youth in the uniform of our country have been trained in her halls, move us, gathered in this historic General Assembly, to look forward to the grim days ahead, the most terrible in responsibilities and the most hopeful in opportunities which have ever come to any generation. These days of commemoration by your participation have become days of rededication of the people of North Carolina to the winning of the war, to the advancement of the state and the nation in the rebuilding of a broken world toward the organization of freedom and justice, peace and plenty, we pray God, in a world neighborhood of human brotherhood.

Dean R. B. House then presented the guest speaker of the Celebration the subject of whose address was "The State University."

DEAN HOUSE

Our guest speaker is Dr. Clarence Addison Dykstra, President of the University of Wisconsin and Provost-Elect of the University of California at Los Angeles, an expert in education, government, and city management in theory and practice. He was born in Ohio, educated in Kansas and Illinois. He has taught in and run every type of American school from private academy to university in the South, the Mid-West, and the Far-West. He has run everything about a modern city from the water department to its whole government, in Cincinnati, Chicago, and Los Angeles. He has looked into and advised on state government and national government in employment, fiscal affairs, public works, taxation, and the functions of state and federal governments. He has been president of the International Association of City Managers, Director of Selective Service of the United States, and chairman of the National Defense Mediation Board. And all the while, he has taught and written, and has lectured in every American state. It would be impossible to find a man who has absorbed and digested more of America, American education, American government, and American business. He carries the feeling of democracy in his heart, his brain, and his finger tips.

President Dykstra

Today is a significant date in the history of American education for it marks the one hundred and fiftieth anniversary of the day that the public officials and citizens of North Carolina formally opened our first state university to students of the Commonwealth. We must assume that transportation was meager or that news traveled slowly, for the first student did not arrive until February 12. The important item to remember, however, is not that he did not enroll on January 15, *but that he came* and that he was the first of the millions who have been coming to state universities ever since. It is worthy of note also that there were men in North Carolina as early as 1776, when the Constitution was adopted, who looked forward to an institution of higher learning in the state and who a few years later were bold enough to launch one with a financial backlog made up of some claims on a few sheriffs and other public officers, some escheats, some unclaimed land warrants, a few small gifts, and a loan from the state. From such humble beginnings has come the modern University of North Carolina, one of the most significant among state universities and a bold bearer of the twin torches of freedom and truth. Your sister institutions of the other American states greet you today with warmth and affection; they glory in your history and in your long record of service; they salute you for your many demonstrations that freedom of thought and of teaching are more important in the life of an educational institution than appropriations and that truth can live and thrive more vigorously in poverty than in trammeled affluence. You have not bent the knee that "thrift may follow fawning."

We at Wisconsin have a unique reason for pride in your University for you do us the honor of declaring that we have pioneered in ways in which you emulate us. We at Wisconsin were naturally pleased when on October 12, 1943, at the exercises commemorating the laying of the cornerstone of "Old East" your distinguished president said, "It can be held that the University of Wisconsin was the first university *to make the whole people* the democratic responsibility and concern of the whole university. North Carolina," said he, "was first in the Southern States to follow in the democratic train of Wisconsin." It is this conception of the work of a university which North Carolina has emphasized in recent years and for which your president praises as a pioneer, your neighbor in the old Northwest Territory, which I have the honor to represent.

These state university neighbors of yours out in the West trace their origin to the Northwest Ordinance of 1787 passed by the Congress of the Confederation. Among other things this document said quite pointedly, "religion, morality and knowledge being necessary to good government and the happiness of mankind, schools and the means of education shall be forever encouraged." This declaration was followed soon after by the adopted Congressional policy of making grants of land for the use of future public institutions of learning in the new territories of the continent. Within fifteen years, and not long after this University opened its doors, the first of these Western schools was established in the wilderness at Athens, Ohio, out of the proceeds of the sale of public lands. In other words, your example and state action became the pattern for a national policy of public support for certain types of institutions of higher learning. State constitutions, one after another, chartered or made provision for state universities almost universally.

What was the meaning of this significant departure from the traditional method of college establishment in the United States? Put in briefest form, it meant that the people were asking for their own schools and colleges—institutions somewhat different from the ones they knew and representing the democratic aspirations of men who were beginning to take over their own governance. Something new was going on in America, something momentous, something definitely a break with the past. A new society was rising in this new land and it wanted an education suited to its needs. It asked for the free mind, for free inquiry into the secrets of nature, for an examination of human institutions, social establishments, and the processes of government. It sensed that education and free government were closely related. Here was an answer to Hamilton's allegation that "the people, sir, is a great beast." Here was an expression of faith in the common man; here was belief in equal opportunity made manifest in educational terms, the chance for individual development.

Today we celebrate one hundred and fifty years of dedication to this idea of a people's university. One after another the American states and commonwealths have followed the pattern with varying degrees of fidelity. Some of these state institutions have lived and labored for more than a century; many are tremendous establishments with magnificent physical plants, distinguished faculties, and many thousands of students pursuing hundreds of courses of study. The history of the people's institution and its contribution to the larger life of our citizens is the answer to those who predicted that the masses, as they were called, would not support consistently the cause of higher education. Other prophets announced that such institutions would lack the basic integrity required of "the higher learning," that they would become the cat's-paws and playthings of the politicians and special groups and interests, that they would yield principle for prosperity.

It was inevitable, of course, that state universities would become involved in social and political controversies from time to time if they were to be people's institutions. Democratic procedures and democratic management are always in danger and they naturally are subject to certain risks. Modern democracies in our own generation have discovered over and over again that political seas can be rough and waves can be high. It was too much to hope, therefore, that the course of public education would always be smooth. It has not been, and our universities from time to time in state after state have had difficult sailing. Democratic institutions inevitably have had to suffer the growing pains which attend the growing up of democracy. There is even now a bitter conflict going on in the affairs of the university of our largest state. Such controversies reflect the fundamental danger to which sound public administration, educational, fiscal, social, and what not, is exposed in popular government when sudden desire or various types of pressure can be translated into action at the ballot box or in the attitude and actions of public officials. It cannot be maintained, however, that other types of government run no risks or show greater stability. Universities have been destroyed and books burned and professors ill-treated in countries in which the democratic idea has no standing whatsoever. Let us not be discouraged or down-hearted, therefore, because here and there on occasions our state universities have been involved in evils to which the democratic flesh is heir. Let us take pride in the fact that for more than one hundred years all over this land these state universities have somehow or other weathered the gales and held their course and in so doing have played a larger part in the life of the people than universities anywhere else on earth. The very source of some of our difficulties constitutes in the long run our strength—the power of the democratic idea. The ideals of our people are fundamentally sound and we should never forget that we have the opportunity and the obligation to affect these ideals and popular aspirations. Long ago James Bryce pointed out that the public university must "serve the time without yielding to it." This is both a challenge and the great opportunity for constructive democratic service.

There will come times, then, when those who are in responsible charge of public education must stand fast for the things that are true and honorable and righteous and in the long-time public interest; when group pressures must be withstood; when political expediency or even attempted political manipulation must be checkmated; when an all-out stand for the freedoms which inherently characterize universities must be made even if individuals are sacrificed in the process.

Such occasions there will be; such incidents are inevitable in democratic societies, which perforce share human weaknesses. The people make mistakes and allow their representatives to make them. They take foolish and precipitate action; they miss the road and do violence to their own traditions and even their best interests. But it must be remembered that in the long run they recognize mistakes, they do rediscover the main highway, and they do recover their balance. And so, if there is evidence now and again of what we call political interference with public education, we can only say that this will at times be the way of human beings who run their own concerns. It is a price we pay for the opportunity of self-government; and who will say it is not worth the price even while we try to make such occasions as infrequent as possible? Time is on the side of freedom; universities are timeless and ageless institutions. They have outlived and will outlive those who, through the generations, have attempted to shackle them and curb their freedom to teach. History teaches us that whenever there is power of any kind, political, economic, ecclesiastical, or military, there will always be temptation to use it—sometimes for motives that do not square with our highest ideals. This is one of the tendencies in human beings which a sounder education may eventually help to discourage. It is the solemn obligation of public education to raise not only the standards of scholarship but also those of citizenship and public aciton. Our universities, then, must first of all be true to themselves.

The times saddle another obligation upon our state universities and colleges—the cherishing and furthering of other freedoms besides that which we usually call academic freedom. These freedoms flow also from our Revolutionary heritage which emphasizes "life, liberty, and the pursuit of happiness." We are even now engaged in a great war which is testing the democratic principle as it has never been tried before. We shall win the war; our universities have given themselves wholeheartedly to assure the victory. When victory comes we face the herculean task of establishing the oldest hope, but as yet the newest and greatest of all freedoms—freedom from war. Freedom from war would bring with it the greatest revolution in history, freedom of peoples the world over to determine their destinies emancipated from the agelong fear of attack and aggression from the powerful of the earth. It would mean opportunity to use wealth, labor, and intelligence for the solution of domestic problems which face all peoples everywhere.

We must commit ourselves to this, the boldest undertaking which mankind has yet conceived, the complete abolition of war as an instrument of national policy. No generation has had such a challenging demonstration of the fact that war has become so impersonal, so inhuman, and so devastating on such a gigantic scale that civilized man can no longer tolerate it. To continue to entertain the idea that war is still inevitable in the face of what the world has experienced in recent years is defeatism. To allow any nation or any people to initiate or undertake any act of military aggression from this time forth would be treason to mankind. This must be the last war between nations, and we the people of the most powerful country on earth can do nothing less at this time than so to help organize the peace that freedom from war will be established as an inalienable right the world over.

There are many, and some in our universities, who will say that this freedom cannot possibly be assured. Let us remember that there were many not so long since who were certain that democracies did not cherish their freedoms sufficiently to protect them against the aggressors—to safeguard them by the use of force. Let us also remember that there were those in 1787 who predicted that the union of thirteen states could not last and that jealousy and suspicion would wreck the new union of sovereign states. These prognosticators were wrong; the democracies created the united nations and are putting down the aggressors; the thirteen states are now forty-eight and more united than at any time in their history.

What we face at the moment is the invention of a method which can prevent aggression and war. What we desperately need is an educational program which will create a climate in which the will to peace may thrive. Fortunately, we now have a working hypothesis which we call the United Nations joined together in a common purpose to put down aggressors. What we must develop is some continuing organization of nations or, better yet, of peoples united to prevent future aggressions. Out of such cooperation can come further constructive common programs and action. This idea is not so much more impossible than was the common action of 1776 and 1787. In those day Thomas Paine wrote, "These proceedings may at first appear strange and difficult; but, like other steps which we have already passed over, will in a little time become familiar and agreeable."

There are always difficulties of many kinds in getting used to new ideas. We must recognize of course that our notions of national sovereignty, of neutrality and balance of power have a powerful hold on many. It is hard to give them up. But it is just this problem of getting acceptance for new ideas which our universities have faced from the beginning. And it is in this province of ideas involving peace that universities now and in the near future can serve their generation powerfully and constructively.

This is not the place, nor is there the time, to discuss the problem of a world organization which might plan a constructive peace. It is the time and place, however, to call upon public universities to dedicate themselves to an educational and action program which will serve the needs of a post-war world as they have so wholeheartedly and effectively served the cause of the United Nations in time of war. This would be a supreme and priceless public service.

From the beginning these universities of ours have believed in the admonition to "prove all things." Translated out of the King James' version, the meaning is "probe all things"—inquire, test, dissect, analyze, discover the facts, find the truth. And the purpose of the inquiry and the findings? To let the people know in the hope that out of the knowing might come wise action. There can be no question but that our founders who were setting up an experiment in self-government believed that the experiment would fail unless the people had wide opportunity for educating themselves, and that a fundamental purpose of public education was the development of intelligent citizens.

This objective is even more important now than it was a century ago, as citizenship takes on heavier and wider obligations with the passing years. So many more things are tinged with the public interest, as public policy and public action take on new forms and greater responsibilities. The times call for a public participation in the affairs of families, communities, industry, business, and agriculture such as the fathers never dreamed of. The state is no longer neutral—the umpire among men. It is a positive force in our lives. It takes an active interest, for instance, in inspecting and safeguarding the purity of the food we eat, the milk our children drink, and the quality of water we use, in sanitation and public health, in public and industrial safety, in transportation, in the conservation of natural resources, in flood control, in reclamation, in soil erosion and forests, in employment, unemployment, and the conditions of labor, in old age and retirement systems, in housing, in the prevention of exploitation and monopoly, in credit and investments, in trade controls and tariffs, in experimentation and scientific endeavor, just to mention a few peace-time activities of a modern government. In time of war, of course, its activities widen to embrace almost all of our interests. Such functioning of our public enterprise requires a vast personnel in public employment and the means of training this administrative force. We must add, therefore, to the obligation of educating for citizenship in our schools, the training of public servants who day by day will carry on the public functions entrusted to them with intelligence, competence, and loyalty to the general welfare. We must also help to educate the great mass of our citizenship to an understanding of the place of social instruments in the life of modern men—to a belief that politics and public life can be fine and wholesome, and should be made so—to the idea that a politician should be a student and practitioner of public affairs rather than a partisan rounding up votes for a special interest.

One of the great contributions of the public university in its comparatively short life is to be found in its insistence that science may be applied to practical situations to the advantage of the whole people. For the first time in history these public institutions showed that men may actually possess the earth and so use, or work with, natural forces that human life can be made happier and more wholesome. The application of science and the scientific method to agriculture has so transformed production in a few decades that today our country, with a smaller agricultural population than ever before, is able to feed 130,-000,000 Americans and scores of millions of allies besides. The work done in university laboratories and the trained men sent from our campuses have in a very real degree helped to make possible the miracle of industrial production which is bringing victory to the arms of the United Nations. This great wealth of production now and in the future must be married to a miracle of distribution. The machine we have created must be made a beneficent force for all. Here is the challenge for those who study man in organized society—our social scientists. Here is another frontier to explore as we move into a post-war world; it is a frontier of abundance which can, if properly understood and its implication mastered, bring new freedoms and new opportunities to add to those we now guard and fight for.

Today we pay tribute to the idea of the university publicly conceived and sustained. That idea born here on this ground has given universities to most of our states. "From these universities," said the Wisconsin historian, Frederick J. Turner, "shaped under pioneer ideals have come the fuller recognition of scientific studies and especially those of applied science devoted to the conquest of nature; the breaking down of the traditional required curriculum, the union of vocational and college work in the same institution; the development of agriculture and engineering colleges and business courses; the training of lawyers, administrators, public men and journalists—all under the ideal of service to democracy rather than of individual advancement alone." Turner did well in reading the history of state universities to point up the fundamental concept of education and service in the public interest as supplementary to the idea of education of the private person for the competitive life. Such a concept joins hands with the philosophy embodied in the Federal Constitution that governments are human associations to further the general welfare, among other things. More and more the democratic impulse in modern life emphasizes the desire of the many for those opportunities and freedoms which once were the prerogatives of the few. In a very real sense these universities have contributed to the creation of the desire and to its gradual fulfillment. Freedom of opportunity in education, the spread of the knowledge of science, training of the boy born on the wrong side of the tracks for positions of responsibility, the making of two blades of grass grow where only one grew, the making of abundance out of scarcity, practical service to the state in a thousand ways, all of these things have contributed to the general welfare and the possibilities of the abundant life. This they have done by the democratic method of attacking specific problems, one at a time, and finding solutions; by training men in all fields to help agriculture, industry, business, and society in general to identify needs and human possibilities and do something about them. They have joined together thought and action, scholarship and performance. They have been both lighthouse and service station.

Today these institutions find themselves confronting increasingly complex and baffling problems and on a widening front. Their obligations multiply. Not only must they devise educational programs which will better fit the world into which we are moving, but they must attack difficulties and help to find solutions in fields which are for the present at least highly controversial. We live in a world which has the knowledge and power to produce wealth on a scale undreamed of a century ago, and to promote the general health and welfare in a fashion never before possible. None the less we have in our own time wrought death and destruction on a scale never before known. Something is wrong that needs correction. We have witnessed the utterly strange spectacle of nations preparing for and waging war instigated in some part by the desire to exorcise the curse of unemployment. There are individuals and groups in all countries today who fear to see the war's end because they have a suspicion that it will mean the end of prosperity for them. We can only hope that these are an insignificant minority among us. The point should be clear, however. We have full employment—in fact we clamor for more labor power in time of war. In peace time we and other nations have bread lines with millions desperately asking for work. No expenditure is too great in time of war. We pinch the pennies between wars. In a recent book Carl Becker, of Cornell, puts it this way, "We seem to live in a world in which the easiest way to abolish one wrong—unemployment and want —is to practice on a grand scale another wrong—war. It is surely a curiously ordered world in which we can abolish one serious evil only by creating another and worse one." . . . "The dismaying thing is that both of these evils seem to be worse than they ever were. Never before, or not for two hundred years, have unemployment and want, during so long a time, in so many countries with every means of creating wealth in abundance, reached the proportion of a major social disaster. Never before has war been so nearly 'global' or 'total,' so ruthlessly brutal and disastrous as to threaten the destruction of civilization." * What we need to discover is why, when we know enough to abolish both evils, war and unemployment, these evils are becoming worse instead of better.

*How New Will the Better World Be? (Alfred A. Knopf, 1944), p. 8.

Perhaps such a discovery will consist simply in disclosing the fact and the implications of the technological age. The fact of the machine driven by non-human energy is clear and accepted. We understand or at least accept mass production. What we have not accepted are the implications of mass production—that income and purchasing power must be widely distributed in a constant flow if the machine is not to run down; that the business cycle must be controlled and regulated; that money is a token to be used in barter; that spending is as important as saving in an economic system; that production is for use; that men will not be satisfied with a price system that from time to time stops the machine to effect a scarcity of goods or plows under corn, cotton, or pigs to protect a seller's market. If the machine requires war to keep it running, it were better to smash the machine as workmen tried to do in those early days of the industrial revolution. There is no natural or mechanical reason that the machine cannot produce abundantly in time of peace—only certain economic orthodoxies which humans have crystallized while they labored in an age of scarcity. Our possibilities are those which are bound up with production abundance; our habits and our dogmas are those derived from the age of hand work and therefore scarcity. Our social scientists must catch up with the engineer and the industrial technician and devise an economy which will take advantage of the machine's possibilities for human welfare or the machine will wreck civilization. This will doubtless mean some social control of our economy. What we in this country hope for is an economy which will provide in the largest possible measure for individual opportunity with the least necessary social action.

This day calls out to the university for leadership and leading on this broad economic front. Only in the university are we far enough removed from the market place and the competitions of day to day business operations to take the long objective view which, originating in the most careful and disinterested research, can be made, through educational processes, the common possession and directive for all of us. We need today knowledge about our economic machine, how it works and how it affects us all. We are, by and large, a nation of economic illiterates.

Scholarship, to which we pay homage in the university, has social implications. Often it is true that scholarship is concealed where only the sequestered scholar can find it. But it has another hiding place—the living concourse of mankind. And there only that scholar can find it who is able to recognize truth in its living form. In the public university we have a place for that scholar who works in the marts of trade and in industrial establishments, with labor and the consumer, to find that delicate system of equilibrium which will assure plenty in time of peace as well as in time of war. His findings ought to have as ready acceptance as those of the discoverer or inventor or what are called the natural scientists. And so I say to the university today that another immediate obligation to contribute to human welfare lies in a solution of the distributive difficulties which engulf us, as decades ago the problem to which we gave attention was in the field of production. We must work the same wonders in distribution that we have in production.

Reference has been made today to the ideas out of which the modern state university has been made and to some of the current obligations which such state institutions face—guardianship of the freedoms that are inherent in the university idea, the promotion of a climate in which the will to peace will have a chance, the century-old responsibility for the education of citizens and public servants, the study of the implications of our technological age to our economic enterprise, a search for a solution to the problem of unemployment, and the prosecution of our general services to the state in the public interest. There remains also the continuing original and eternal obligation of the state university because it is a university—the holding high of the ideals of sound learning in all realms, the conserving and disseminating of the best thought and experience of the race, the exploring of widening horizons of knowledge in all directions, the cultivating of freedom and the liberty of the human spirit to the end that we shall have in this country as many truly educated men and women as is possible. We shall need them all in order to insure the perpetuation of the things we hold dear and to build the world of the future—a decent, reasonable world in which all peoples can live at peace and in harmony with those ideas which we project in that moment when we express our highest spiritual yearnings.

> Ye that have faith to look with fearless eyes
> Beyond the tragedy of a world at strife,
> And trust that out of the night and death shall rise
> The dawn of ampler life;
> Rejoice, whatever anguish rend your heart,
> That God has given you for a priceless dower,
> To live in these great times and have your part
> In Freedom's crowning hour;
> That you may tell your sons who see the light
> High in the heavens—their heritage to take—
> "I saw the powers of Darkness put to flight
> I saw the morning break." *

The official authorization for the holding of the joint session of the General Assembly was the passage by the Senate and House of the following joint resolution on January 5, 1945:

A JOINT RESOLUTION INVITING HIS EXCELLENCY,
THE GOVERNOR OF NORTH CAROLINA, PRESIDENT CLARENCE A.
DYKSTRA, AND OTHERS TO ADDRESS A JOINT SESSION
OF THE GENERAL ASSEMBLY

WHEREAS, by act of the General Assembly of North Carolina passed at the session of 1789 the University of North Carolina was incorporated;

And WHEREAS, pursuant thereto said University was formally opened on the 15th day of January, 1795;

And WHEREAS, by act of the Governor of the State of North Carolina a legislative commission composed of Mr. Victor S. Bryant of Durham as Chairman and Messrs. Marsden Bellamy, H. Galt Braxton, Gordon Gray, John L. Morehead, D. Hiden Ramsey and Capus M. Waynick was appointed to make preparations for the observance of the sesquicentennial anniversary of the founding of the University of North Carolina;

*Sir Gwen Seaman (1861-1936).

And WHEREAS, said commission has requested His Excellency, the Governor of North Carolina, Honorable R. Gregg Cherry, and President Clarence A. Dykstra of the University of Wisconsin to make addresses at exercises on said occasion;

And WHEREAS, it is considered fitting and the General Assembly of North Carolina desires that these exercises be held in the Hall of the House of Representatives at a joint session thereof;

Now, Therefore, Be It Resolved by the House of Representatives, the Senate concurring:

Section 1. That His Excellency, the Governor of North Carolina, Honorable R. Gregg Cherry, President Clarence A. Dykstra, President Frank P. Graham, Dean R. B. House, and Mr. Victor S. Bryant, Chairman, be invited to address the joint session of the General Assembly in the Hall of the House at eight o'clock P.M. on Monday, the fifteenth day of January, 1945, and further that the other members of the Commission be invited to attend these exercises.

Section 2. That a committee of two from the Senate be appointed by the Lieutenant Governor and a committee of three from the House be appointed by the Speaker to extend invitations to each of the above to appear before the joint session of the General Assembly at that time.

Section 3. That this resolution shall be in full force and effect from and after its ratification.

The resolution was introduced in the Senate by Senators Claude Curry, of Durham, and Archie Gay, of Jackson, and in the House by Representatives John W. Umstead, of Chapel Hill, and W. F. Taylor, of Goldsboro. The resolution was ratified January 5, 1945, and Messrs. Curry and Gay, of the Senate, and Umstead, Taylor, and Wallace, of the House, served as a special committee on arrangements.

The addresses were recorded by W.P.T.F. of Raleigh, of the National Broadcasting Company, and the address by Governor Cherry was broadcast Tuesday morning, January 16, at 9:45. All of the addresses were heard from recordings in Chapel Hill by the students, faculty, and members of the community on Monday, January 29, at 4 P.M. in Gerrard Hall.

As a souvenir of the Celebration, the Alumni of the University presented to those in attendance a handsomely designed, eight-page-with-cover booklet entitled *Proudly We Hail!* The statement of greeting and the text of the booklet follows:

THE
34,432 LIVING ALUMNI
JOIN THE GENERAL ASSEMBLY
IN THEIR TRIBUTE TO THE
UNIVERSITY OF NORTH CAROLINA
ON THE 150TH ANNIVERSARY
OF ITS OPENING DAY
JANUARY 15, 1795

January 15, 1795 . . . one hundred and fifty years ago today . . . the people of North Carolina, acting through their Governor and their Legislature, opened the doors of their University—the first state university in the Americas. . . . North Carolina, first in many things since the First Colony in 1585, was again a pioneer. . . .

Nineteen years before, in 1776, the Halifax Convention framed a Constitution which provided "that all useful learning shall be duly encouraged and promoted in one or more universities."

Our forebears recognized the great interdependence between free government and education. They wanted their own university . . . a university *of* the people . . . a university *for* the people. . . . They were determined to build a great commonwealth and they wanted a university that would serve its needs . . . a university that would, at all times, "serve the time without yielding to it."

Proudly we hail this University today. It has never failed the commonwealth. For a century and a half the University has served the people of North Carolina . . . in time of peace and in time of war.

And at this serious hour the panorama of the past flashes back through every war that America has ever fought.

"Going to War" is a 150-year-old story for the University of North Carolina. Actually, no University students fought in the Revolution—for the University was a child of the Revolution.

The institution was founded by returning Revolutionary heroes . . . veterans coming home to build a great state. . . .

In the War of 1812, University men stood with Andrew Jackson at New Orleans. . . .

In the Civil War every man in the senior class of 1860 who was able to bear arms rushed to the front; one out of every four of them was killed on the fields of battle. . . . It has been said that no university on either side of the conflict gave a higher percentage of its sons to the armies than did the University of North Carolina. In all, 2,285 sons of Chapel Hill fought in the Civil War . . . and the Gold Star Roll of University alumni *killed* reached 308.

In the War with Spain, again young men from the classrooms in Chapel Hill, in high spirits, joined the colors and took their battle stations at the fighting fronts—on land and at sea.

The First World War took 2,250 of the University's sons off to Plattsburgh and Oglethorpe and then on to France. . . . Forty-one of them never came back.

Now, in the Global War, the figures are even more heartbreaking. 7,888 alumni of the University are "somewhere in the fighting forces." Already 145 are known to have died in line of duty . . . 45 more are listed as "missing" . . . 37 are known to be prisoners of war. . . . One University alumnus has been awarded, posthumously, the Congressional Medal of Honor; 241 alumni have received medals for distinguished service. . . .

Twenty months before Pearl Harbor, the Trustees of the Consolidated University offered its complete resources—the Woman's College, State College, and the University in Chapel Hill—to the Federal Government. When war struck, the peaceful old Chapel Hill campus over-night became a war camp. Over 20,000 "war-time alumni" have been trained in Chapel Hill in the Naval ROTC, the great Navy Pre-Flight Program, the Navy V-12; Army Air Corps, ASTP, and Army and Navy Medical Programs. And the record is not yet complete!

The war-time has been served but not yielded to! Despite the sunrise to sunset concentration on the work to be done, planes overhead, and the "hup-two-three-four" underfoot, the spirit of Chapel Hill is unchanged. Despite its big war job, Chapel Hill has maintained the essentials of a great University—a peace-loving University, a peace-building University. Many messages from alumni at the far corners of the earth have come back to Chapel Hill expressing gratitude and admiration for this achievement. And these letters say that the things for which the University lives are the very things for which men are willing to die.

Already the young alumni—veterans of this war—are beginning to come back to Chapel Hill. Reconversion is a tough process; but they make it—and they make great citizens. After all, the University has lived through five reconversions—or four reconversions and one Reconstruction.

Over eighty veterans of this war have resumed or started their studies in Chapel Hill. Many in hospitals today have made application to enter at the beginning of the next term. Again the University is doing its utmost to serve the peace-time—to meet the needs of every citizen in North Carolina who comes to it.

On January 15, 1945, the doors of the University—after a hundred and fifty years—stand wide-open, welcoming the people of the state to come and make even greater use of all that they have put there over a century and a half, in spiritual and cultural and scientific resources.

The first hundred and fifty years have been memorable; yet we believe that the past is but the *prologue* to coming generations of greater achievement as our University provides the leadership in the building of a healthier, and wealthier, and happier North Carolina.

WILLIAM B. UMSTEAD
President of the Alumni Association of the University of North Carolina

V

HINTON JAMES DAY

FEBRUARY 12, 1795, shares with October 12, 1793, the distinction of being one of the major firsts in the history of state-supported higher education in the United States. Whereas the cornerstone of the first state university building was laid on October 12, 1793, on February 12, 1795, Hinton James, from Wilmington, N. C., was the first student to enroll in an American state university. On that cold, rainy February day, James became the first of the hundreds of thousands of students, who, in the one hundred and fifty years have, in increasing numbers, taken up their studies upon state university campuses from the eastern seaboard to the Pacific.

In recognition of the significance of the event, the University has designated February 12 Hinton James Day and set it apart as the day in the Sesquicentennial Celebration featuring student and alumni activities.

The program of the occasion was, accordingly, arranged for the participation of the students and alumni through a committee consisting of Douglass Hunt, Chairman, C. F. Benbow, Jr., President of the Student Body, W. T. Crisp, Betty Lou Cypert, Shirley Hartsell, A. A. Hood, Catherine P. Kelly, Lucy Lee Kennedy, Mary C. Marett, Turk Newsome, W. J. Tripp, Jack Vernier, Harvey White, Wynette B. White, Charles Wickenberg, Elizabeth P. Wiggins, and Richard B. Willingham representing the students, and William B. Umstead, President, and J. Maryon Saunders, Secretary, representing the General Alumni Association.

The exercises assumed the form of a general convocation of the University, with academic procession, and were held in Memorial Hall at 11:15 on the morning of the 12th with Dean of Administration R. B. House, presiding. Following the singing of the "Star Spangled Banner," led by the University Band, the invocation was offered by the Reverend Henry G. Ruark, pastor of the Methodist Church of Chapel Hill.

INVOCATION

Eternal God, giver of all wisdom and spiritual grace, create in us here that sense of reverence which will see in the heritage we now treasure the working of Thy providence. We are conscious that other men have labored, and we are entered into their labors. We thank Thee for the vision which led our fathers to establish this University for the enlightenment of the people. We are grateful for those teachers and leaders who here, with patience and courage, have sought and taught the truth. We thank Thee for those, who, in each generation, have come to this place and from it have carried into the life of our commonwealth both knowledge and devotion to the people's welfare. For all the influences for good which have come out of this institution we give Thee praise.

Save us now from pride and complacency. Make us ever aware that the adventure is only begun, that we yet do see but fragments and segments of Thy boundless truth. Build up in us the faith that the truth, because it is Thine, is good. And so let this be a rededication of ourselves to the purpose that here, in the future as in the past, men may seek without fear or hindrance; to the end that Thy ways may be more fully known and Thy will increasingly become our law. Amen.

Before beginning his address, "The Significance of the Day— A Historical Introduction," President Graham introduced Hinton James III, of the North Carolina State Department of Conservation, who had been present at the celebration of the Centennial of the University in 1889, and whose son, Hinton James IV, was absent in the armed services in France. For the second time, Mr. James stood upon the platform as the direct descendant and representative of the first student and in himself gave vivid and dramatic evidence of the continuity of the influence of the University through the fifteen decades of its service to the State and Nation.

HINTON JAMES III

Fifty years ago at the Centennial Celebration I stood on this platform, a whiteheaded little shaver, representing the first student of this great University.

Today I find myself here again, whiteheaded, but a regular shaver now.

I wish it were possible for the first student to be represented more worthily by my only son, Hinton James, the fourth; however, he is on the fields of France in the service of his country.

I trust that not only he but all of our boys will be returned to us long before we celebrate our two hundredth anniversary.

I believe all of you would like to join me in the thought expressed in a prayer which is repeated in unison every Sabbath morning in my home church:

> O God of Love, O King of Peace,
> Make wars throughout the world to cease.
> The wrath of sinful man restrain,
> Give Peace, O God, Give Peace again.

Following the address of Hinton James, President Graham spoke.

PRESIDENT GRAHAM

The establishment of the University was enjoined by a provision in the Revolutionary Constitution adopted by the convention of the people at Halifax in 1776, was chartered by the legislature at Fayetteville in 1789, had the cornerstone of its first building laid in Chapel Hill, October 12, 1793, and was formally opened January 15, 1795. At the formal opening there assembled the Governor of the State, members of the Legislature, members of the Board of Trustees, and the Presiding Professor. But no student. The stage was set, the curtain rose, but the Prince of Denmark did not appear.

The teacher, the campus, and the building were all there for the formal opening, but what it was all about was not here. The dream of a twentieth-century high-standard college registrar was achieved by this late eighteenth-century university struggling to be born—conditions for entrance so difficult as to admit no students! The difficulties of communication and transportation were, however, valiantly surmounted on February 12, 1795, when Hinton James of New Hanover arrived to be the first student to enter an existing state university, the first of 44,802 to enter this institution, and the first of many hundreds of thousands who have since streamed through these universities of the people, by the people, and for the people, to become bulwarks of government of the people, by the people, and for the people for which died Abraham Lincoln, one of the greatest men in all history, who was born 136 years ago today.

Hinton James came from historic New Hanover into this up-country in which the Regulators before the Revolution had petitioned for more freedom and equality of opportunity and in which the little village of Chapel Hill was to become the cross-roads of the ideas, religions, sections, factions, work, hopes, and dreams of the people. From the first students and all their diversi-ties there slowly developed a unifying devotion to their University and a common dedication to their commonwealth, which for one hundred and fifty years has run like a golden thread through the texture of that great family of people called North Carolina.

Hinton James was a young man of high faith who overcame more than slow communication and difficult transportation. He was casting his lot in Chapel Hill with something new under the sun. It was almost nineteen years since the convention of the people of Pennsylvania and North Carolina had made consti-tutional provisions for a university. It had been only six years since the University of Pennsylvania, chartered in 1753 as America's first private, non-sectarian university, had renounced the maneuver which, in violation of its charter, had made it an unwilling state institution for ten years. The University of Pennsylvania even for that brief decade was not in foundation, purpose, and spirit a state university and has developed its his-tory and traditions and its present life and functions as a great non-sectarian, privately endowed, and independent university. The University of Georgia, which was not provided for in the Revolutionary Constitution of 1776 but which was chartered by the legislature of 1785, was not yet established. No building, campus, faculty, and students were then all assembled to give life to any state university in America when Hinton James left his home in New Hanover County in the winter of 1795 for the new University of North Carolina. When he arrived February 12, 1795, campus and building, faculty and student were all assembled at Chapel Hill and nowhere else in America for six years yet to come. In Chapel Hill was first to be tried out in enduring form this new venture of a people's university as the enduring basis of a people's government.

The traditional and acceptable thing for a young Carolinian of means and credentials to do then was to go to one of the old true and tried establishments such as Princeton, Pennsylvania, and William and Mary, or even to far-away New England. To go to this new kind of institution struggling to be born in the up-country woods was more than an act of curiosity. A person's family and birthplace, always, and often his church are chosen for him. For Hinton James it was not only an act of choice, but also a venture in faith to choose his alma mater and link his life with the unproved experiment of a state university. There was then no University of North Carolina tradition in his family to send him to Chapel Hill. There was no history of this institution to appeal to his own sense of historic pride. There were no alumni to tell him of the precious values and spirit of the University of North Carolina. The venturesomeness and imagination of the youth himself were greater than any of these as they urged him over the rough road to the new university which had been opened near a chapel on the hill in the woods of Orange.

This first student was an all-round student. He was an honor student, especially proficient in the sciences. As a result of a secession from the Dialectic Society, led by Maurice Moore in July, 1795, he was, along with seventeen other students, a charter member of the Concord, soon to become the Philanthropic Debating and Literary Society. He took a stand against the evils of militarism, and he wrote an essay on the values of the sun. In the first session the student body increased to forty-one and in the next session to over one hundred. Thus Hinton James received the developmental values of a real student body. He celebrated July 4, 1798, along with six other students in good standing by passing his final examination for graduation from the University of North Carolina. He was an engineer who worked for the improvement of navigation in the river below

Wilmington and was for a term the mayor of Wilmington. Born in 1776, in the year the University was first conceived in the womb of the mother commonwealth, he died in 1843 and was buried near the old home place in that part of New Hanover which is now Pender County. The records of the North Carolina General Assembly have a contemporary sound in the vote of Representative Hinton James in 1807 for a resolution in favor of a third term for Thomas Jefferson as President of the United States. Hinton James was not only our first student, but also foretold the carry-over of campus citizenship into the honorable public service which has since distinguished the sons and daughters, the Faculty and Trustees of the University of North Carolina.

Since its foundation, the Trustees have been the historic source and guardian of its freedom and democratic responsibility of the state for the University and especially so after it became state policy for the legislature to elect the members of the Board increasingly from all sections of the state and all groups of the people. In the traditions of our people the legislature has the responsibility (1) of making fair and adequate provision for all divisions of the University of North Carolina; (2) of electing the best and most representative citizens of our state to the Board of Trustees; and (3) of protecting the responsible freedom and function of the Board in the development of a great three-fold University of the people for the training of youth in all fields, for the service of every human need, and for the development of all the natural resources and all the physical, intellectual, and spiritual capacities of a great people.

The central Library, under the care and guidance of the Faculty, has been and is the repository of the great intellectual and spiritual treasures of the race, the precious legacies of humane learning, and the master creations of the human spirit in all ages. The Faculty, with laboratories of the most modern scientific equipment, carrels for inquiry and reflection, and institutes for research and service, is the finder of new truth and the interpreter of old and new learning to the students, to their fellows, and to the people. The Faculties of our three institutions of the one University have created and determined the place of the University, the distinction of its work, and the value of its services to the state and nation. It is the responsibility of the administration, with the Board of Trustees, to guard the freedom and advance the opportunities of the Faculty in its teaching of students, in its research and publication that more of truth may be found and that truth, goodness, and beauty may increasingly prevail in our state and in our one world.

The students themselves have developed a campus life, a freedom and responsibility of their own whose rootage is deep in the soil of this place and in the subsoil of one hundred and fifty years of history and tradition. From the beginning of what was almost exclusively faculty government of student affairs there evolved slowly on the campus an increasing measure of student self-government through the early participation of the Di and Phi Societies in the self-control and discipline of students, through the later rise of the academic classes, professional schools, and fraternities as sources of student government, and today through the organization of the whole student body as the broad base and main source of student self-government with its political parties, campaigns, voting booths and ballot boxes, general elections, student legislature, dormitory councils, inter-fraternity council, student audit board, uncensored student publications, and personal freedom with responsibility for honesty, decency, and fair play under a code of honor administered by the Student Honor Council. One of the most developmental and enduring lessons this University has to teach is vital experience in real freedom and democracy through actual experience in the spirit, processes, responsibilities, and values of democracy.

It is our faith that there is no freer, more responsible, or more developmental student self-government anywhere than the campus democracy grown here in the one hundred and fifty years since Hinton James became the beginning of student life at the University of North Carolina. The message of this century and a half to us in this complex world of strain and struggle is that liberty requires responsibility and that rights require duties, and that the risks of freedom require the protection of a simple respect for sobriety and human decency, rigorous thoroughness and honesty in scholarship, and a vigorous sense of honor in all relations. The intellectual freedom of the University carries with it an insistent responsibility to develop the generous capacities and instant power of concentration, logical organization of information and ideas, accuracy and clearness of thought and statement. Student freedom demands intelligence in the management of the body as an instrument of the mind and the temple of the spirit. The more robust the body, the more intent the mind; the more profound the spiritual resource, the higher the personal life and the wider and more lasting its influence. Something happens here when hills, skies, forests, and youth get together. Sunset behind the hills, skyline above the forest, song and story, picture and play, prayer and aspiration are stuff out of which the human spirit builds the nobler mansions of the soul and releases the spirit of youth to have a creative participation in his own education. Here in the woods of Orange, teachers and trees, buildings and traditions, library and laboratories, within walls of ancient stone, in response to great human needs in North Carolina and beyond, have, with the voices of one hundred and fifty years, called to youth to be intelligent, adventurous, and courageous in their struggles and hopes of the American dream to make the world a freer and fairer place for all people as brothers of men and sons of God.

Hinton James came to the University out of the era of the American Revolution and the federal organization of the United States. He and scores of thousands who came after him had the responsibility of building our state, our union of states, and our national democracy. Thousands of students will soon be coming to us out of this era of world revolution and the federal organization of the United Nations. Theirs will be the responsibility of building a fairer state, nation, and union of nations into a federated commonwealth of the free peoples of the world. Hinton James was a student pioneer in helping to build the first university of the people. After him came pioneers in building railroads, farms, industries, schools, roads, and welfare.

Pioneers are today stirring the state, east and west, to upbuild the health of all the people. From the tidewater sandbanks and the remotest mountain coves and from all parts of North Carolina the people are calling for more doctors, more hospitals, and more adequate medical care. No pioneer who ever stood with axe and rifle along the frontier of the unconquered wilderness ever faced an adventure more thrilling than that which calls this morning to you students of this pioneer University as you stand with inquiring minds along the frontiers of the vast wilderness of our yet unmastered civilization. Stout be your hearts as you go forth on the rough roads to win this global war for human freedom. May you in your day play your adventurous part in the building of new and nobler institutions of the people; an economic society in which every human being will have the free and fair opportunity to earn a decent living; and an international society of nations for the organization of liberty, justice, and peace in the world.

Douglass Hunt, Chairman of the Student Committee on the Sesquicentennial, spoke impressively concerning the kind of university the students hoped to see the University become in the future. He stressed the importance of good teaching, of sound investigation, in which many students should be involved, of the building up of a great library for the conservation of knowledge and the support of teaching and investigation, and of the training of students in the fine art of democratic, self-government.

DOUGLASS HUNT

One hundred and fifty years ago today an educational miracle occurred when, on a February morning, the first student entered the first state university in the nation. That miracle makes it all too easy for us who love the University to celebrate this anniversary with such paeans of praise that the whole occasion is made to look somewhat ridiculous. Fortunately, our estimate of the University's worth has been measured in praise it has earned. Nonetheless, on an occasion of this sort, it is not altogether bad for someone to regard the whole affiair with a slightly critical eye.

We are, today, reviewing the University's history. But, if Hinton James Day is to be more than an occasion for self-congratulation, we need quite humbly to re-examine that history, to re-think it, and more than that, to re-vitalize it. We can re-tell our exploits and boast about them, but they have merit in our time only as a key to the present and a guide for the future.

Speaking as a student on this day when old and new students join in honoring the University, I should like to measure what we have in terms of what we can have. To make that comparison we need an adequate standard for measuring the kind of university we want and can have; and to set up that standard we must examine the functions which a great university performs for the people it serves. I should like to suggest that those functions are at least fivefold.

It seems more obvious upon examination than we like to think upon casual reflection that a university's most important function is teaching. Teaching involves two or three general methods the first of which is classroom instruction. It seems almost too trite to say that great teaching requires great teachers. But that fact needs to pervade all our minds: you can oust a teacher for anything: for being a "red," for being too old, for having a wrong-shaped nose—although at this University teachers have the personal guarantee of a great president standing between them and their persecutors. Nonetheless, except for that guarantee, you can fire a teacher on any trumped-up charge—as the Rainey tragedy, where a similar guarantor was removed, demonstrates—but you can't fire a teacher for bad teaching.

Why should not this University pioneer in developing techniques which would assure that the men who teach are qualified to teach? Why should the University of North Carolina be content to measure its teachers' worth only in terms of their scholarly pursuits? Perhaps that is stating the issue a little too strongly; yet one cannot escape the conclusion that however fortunate we may have been in the number of great teachers who have given life and meaning to this University, our methods of securing those men have in no way assured us that they are as able to teach as they are to pursue scholarly inquiry. Certainly before a man becomes a professor of any rank he should be qualified to teach; either that, or he should have the equally important rank of research professor. Is it not time we realized that some men have natural aptitudes for specialization in one or the other fields, and that many do not have them in both?

Such judgments of human capacities as those entailed in choosing effective teachers are difficult. Yet, we cannot escape the necessity for making them.

When these ablest teachers have been chosen, we should not be afraid to give them every opportunity not only to work with advanced students, but with freshmen as well. The kind of teaching students respond to in their first year may well determine the kind of students they are to be throughout their college careers.

Another of the methods of teaching in a great university involves the use of the student as a scholar in partnership with his teachers. Whatever his academic interest he should have the invigorating experience of working with his teachers on the exciting problems of new research: the past, thought dead until that moment comes, will take on new meaning—it will be seen as the matrix of the present, without which our time and problems are meaningless. And this experience in research that is new ought not to be denied the undergraduate if he is to have his most intense curiosity stimulated.

The idea of scholarly partnership accents another truism: great teachers and great books cannot guarantee a great university without great students. This very day illustrates that fact: the University opened on January 15, 1795, but it was not until Hinton James arrived on February 12, that the University could undertake its real work. Should not the University of North Carolina open a new way as it has so many times in the past? Why should not its post-war planning stimulate reciprocity— the basis of this scholarly partnership—by soliciting student reaction to curriculum through an advisory group which could work closely with the faculty, not in a spirit of presumption, but in a spirit of co-operative good will?

The third method of teaching—one which this University seems to exploit more, perhaps, than the others—is to make demands on the student's development, both individual and social, through student self-government founded on the honor system of student responsibility. I suspect we all sense how hard it was during the one-hundred-and-fifty-year development of student government to remember the foundation in responsibility and honor which alone makes it possible. On this Hinton James Day do we not all need to remember something of the story of the hundred and fifty years of hard work and tough-minded thinking which made possible the system of student self-government we now enjoy? The honor system is never safely our own. It can be lost by any generation of students —any year, any month, any day. Students themselves have to make it work. Students remember, or it is forgotten, that each new student generation must learn the honor system all over again. And upperclass students, grown weary of fighting for honor and a system in which the only cure for the most violent disasters is more honor, need constantly to re-think it, re-learn it, and re-dedicate themselves to it. The very best in the University's heritage deserves the best in us all.

We students know that our teachers find it painful to stand aside and watch us make mistakes: there is always some irate critic of the University to complain that it is blissfully and captiously allowing the young people of the state to go straight to the Devil. We all know, however, that that criticism, coupled with the mistakes we make, is the price we pay to produce men whose training in freedom made them responsible citizens: men like James K. Polk, Edward Kidder Graham, Horace Williams, and Josephus Daniels. And we students believe the University still wants to produce them.

Never forgetting that teaching constitutes the University's most important function, we cannot, in measuring this University against the one we should all like to have, overlook its other important functions. It is astonishing how long we managed to consider ourselves a competent University with a library whose chief boast lay in the fact that it was not smaller than most of the others in the impoverished South. Not until fairly recent times did the University recognize its obligation by moving to make the University Library supplement the work of its distinguished professors. The fact that the University Library now has its basement filled with boxes of materials for which there is no room in the stacks is not nearly so significant as the fact that we are now ignoring an opportunity to establish in this region what could conceivably be one of the greatest university library centers in the nation. It is fairly obvious that the State of North Carolina will not in the foreseeable future be able to pay for the establishment of such a center. Consider these facts about our present facilities:

Among forty institutions in the South the University of North Carolina has, within the last twelve years, dropped from second to fifth place in the amount spent for books; from second to eighth place in the number of volumes added annually; from first to fifth place in the amount of salaries paid the staff. Among forty-eight institutions of higher learning in the nation, North Carolina has dropped in the same period from fourteenth to twenty-eighth place in the amount spent for books; from fourteenth to twenty-eighth place in the number of volumes added annually; and from nineteenth to thirtieth place in the amount of salaries paid the staff. The reason is plain. In 1929, for example, the state appropriated $33,600 for books. In 1943 it appropriated $22,400—a cut of $11,200. President Graham, asking for funds to buy books, has set $100,000 as the goal. This year, for the first time since the depression, the appropriation for books exceeds the 1929 level. It totals $35,500. Thanks to supplementary monies in the form of gifts, trust funds, and departmental funds, the Library will be able to spend approximately $47,700 for books. It is good that the legislature has increased the appropriation. But so long as the Library must rely on gifts for its support, so long as it cannot depend on the state for subsistence funds; just so long will it continue to lose ground, just so long will the University suffer.

These facts do not, however, add up to a hopeless picture when we suddenly discover that we have been overlooking the most important fact of all and realize that the path for development is already being blazed. For some years the Library of this University and that at Duke have co-operated closely in making their volumes available to the faculties and students of both campuses. More than that, they have developed a program of co-operation which largely eliminates duplication of expensive titles and they have exchanged sets of author cards so that each library knows what materials the other contains. If this program is continued and extended to include other North Carolina libraries it will be possible to build up a library center which would enrich both universities and the universities and colleges of the region as a whole. Admitting that there are manifold difficulties to overcome in developing such a program, we should continue to work toward it as a goal which determination will enable us to achieve. In any case, we shall not be able to co-operate fully with Duke if we expect her to carry most of the burden. This Library must be able to do its full part. Only the State of North Carolina can make that possible.

The University's function to conserve knowledge implies its equally important function to discover new knowledge. The nation itself is indebted to its universities for the work they have done in research, research carried on both by the staff of the universities and by their students. There are six universities in the nation each of which spend over $2,000,000 annually on research. Fourteen spend over $1,000,000 a year. The Consolidated University of North Carolina, ranking forty-eighth in a list of one hundred and nineteen institutions published in the 1938 report of the National Resources Committee, spent between $250,000 and $300,000—an amount which has, however, been increased since that time. But money for research alone is not enough. We need to go out of our way to recognize research and the men who engage in it. This University could well be the Southern center for research. There was a day when that was very nearly true. It ought to be true again.

Another measure of the University's work in research may be found in the number of fields in which it is able to give Ph.D. degrees. We are proud, and rightly so, that the University of North Carolina is qualified to give Ph.D. degrees in more subjects than any other university "south of the Potomac and east of the Mississippi." On the other hand, if we are to remind ourselves that we have not yet achieved our goal, we must remember that such a figure by no means tells the whole story: true, this University has been adjudged competent to give Ph.D. degrees in nine fields: but the major universities of the land can give Ph.D.'s in from thirty to thirty-five fields.

Nor should we limit ourselves to talking of the number of degrees we can give: we ought to remember how many we do give.

In the three years from 1934 to 1937 the National Resources Committee report showed that North Carolina ranked thirty-first in a list of eighty-six in the number of Ph.D. degrees given. The top three universities in the nation gave 601, 488, and 413, respectively. North Carolina gave 64, ranking behind both Duke and Virginia. In the fifteen years, 1930 through 1944, North Carolina gave a total of 381 such degrees, an average of 27 a year. In the three-year period cited above at least one of the universities mentioned averaged 200 Ph.D. degrees a year, while the lowest of the top three averaged 137 a year. In that three-year period North Carolina averaged 21 a year. Allowing for manifest improvements since that time, we still have a long way to go.

Having done its part to conserve knowledge, to teach, and to increase the world's store of knowledge, the University has the obligation of publishing the results of its investigation and research. Even now most of the scientific and scholarly journals of the University are operating on a very limited financial basis. Much of the money for their support and for the support of the University Press has come from gifts and foundation grants, but such funds should constitute a supplement, not the bulk of the investment. The University Press has maintained a publishing program of exceptional excellence in the face of obstacles which would have stymied a less able and determined organization. Both the *Nation* and the *New Republic* in their lists of the best books of 1944, ranked the University of North Carolina Press third in the nation in the number of worthwhile books published. But, the record could be better if more money was available. The plain fact is that the Press does not have sufficient funds to enable it to seek authors and manuscripts which will insure constant first-rank distinction. The state alone is properly able to provide such support.

All of the functions of the University might be summarized in the phrase "service to the people," but that phrase has a more specific meaning in the five-fold plan of the University which we share as our hope for the future. The University of North Carolina needs to continue its work of making available to all the people of the state its libraries, laboratories, and staff. It needs to redouble its efforts in a fight which must be won anew with each passing day. Already it is branching out into radio, in the fields of journalism, and foreign affairs. But the radio could be used as a University instrument of service which would set alight the conscience of North Carolina from the Lost Colony at Manteo to the Mozart Festival in Asheville. And the state government itself ought to have the resources of the University at its disposal. The face of North Carolina could be changed if the State Planning Board here at the University, for instance, were given free rein to search out ways to utilize the natural, industrial, scientific, and cultural resources of the state. Such a program would involve the use of every department in the Consolidated University and in the state government, together with the best efforts of all the people of the state translating their hopes into fact.

We can never escape the fact that this education which we call the keystone of our democratic process is first and foremost a process of discovery and growth. There is nothing static about democracy. The University, if it is to remain what it has so long been, the keystone of our democratic faith and the vigilant guardian of the people's liberty, must also grow. If it does grow, it will aid in the solution of the problems which the state must solve if it is to have the benefit of the population it now raises and contributes to other parts of the nation, if it is to offer a real incentive for Tar Heels to return here and make their homes after the war is over.

The University can never give its full measure of service to the people until the state feels impelled to make that service possible. For a century and a half the University has consistently fought for growth, until on this February 12, it can boast three educational contributions. It has fought for a free faculty bound by its conscience to teach the truth. It has fought for student self-government so that students may learn responsibility by living creatively. It has grown from one male student at Chapel Hill in 1795 to nearly nine thousand men and women students in Raleigh, Chapel Hill, and Greensboro in 1945. And, with all its diversity of populations and curricula, it is one University, with one policy of service. It can continue to be of service if the state makes it possible. Since the benefits of that service accrue to the state, can there be any hesitancy?

The state has nowhere more profitably invested its funds than in the Consolidated University. And the state owes a debt to the University. It can discharge that debt by guaranteeing the whole Consolidated University stability independent of the uncertainty of biennial legislative attitudes. There should be a base to build on, a base below which the state should guarantee the University will never be allowed to fall.

All of us who realize the worth of the Consolidated University must fight for her. Let us remember that. Let us who love the University resolve to be frank about her weaknesses. Let us struggle to make her stronger. Let us subject ourselves to inward scrutiny that we may be worthy for the contest. Let us give our best effort—the strength and vigor of our bodies, our time and energy, and the best of our minds—that we may preserve the University enlightened and vigorous. We shall then know that another generation may have the opportunity to pursue happiness and search out truth.

William B. Umstead, of the Class of 1916 and President of the General Alumni Association, which celebrated its Centennial in 1944, spoke in behalf of the Alumni of the University. Introduced by his classmate, Dean House, he spoke as follows:

WILLIAM B. UMSTEAD

Colonial Carolina must have been by nature one of the choicest spots of the new world. Imagination is kindled by thoughts of the pristine beauty and grandeur of its towering peaks, rolling hills, fertile plains, and sweeping shores. But it was nonetheless a far cry from the Commonwealth that we know, love, and enjoy today. Many of the things long since classified as necessities of life were then unknown, and the comforts and conveniences now so casually enjoyed had not been thought of. One hundred and seventy years ago few roads broke the magnificence of the forest, and these were little better than trails. Generally, rivers could be crossed only at great hardship and risk. Means of even most urgent communications were slow and uncertain. Housing was of necessity limited and crude. Travel and transportation were slow and risky. Assembly was difficult. The exposure, risks, and dangers of the frontier had not disappeared. Though the region was lavishly endowed by nature, the practical circumstances of life in colonial Carolina were so rugged that the weak had to grow strong or perish.

Under such circumstances we would expect to find the citizenry, consisting of about three hundred thousand, giving all of their time and attention to meeting and mastering the practical and difficult problems of life from day to day. But such was not the case. Our great forbears must have been dreaming of the future state of which we are so proud today, when, despite all the difficulties by which life was then beset, they found time to consider and the means collectively to express their conviction as to the part education should play in the future of the Commonwealth by the clear declaration in the Constitution of 1776 that "All useful learning shall be duly encouraged and promoted in one or more Universities."

The ensuing dozen years were filled with important events that had come now to have world-wide significance. The Revolutionary War was fought, peace was made, and the Constitution of the United States was proposed, debated, and ratified. North Carolina, after much consideration and some hesitation, joined the other states by ratification on November 21, 1789.

But these important and stirring events were not permitted long to obscure the declaration of 1776. Twenty days after ratification of the Constitution of the United States the legislature in session at Fayetteville on December 11, 1789, chartered the State University, declaring in the Act,

> In all well regulated Governments it is the indispensable Duty of every Legislature to consult the Happiness of a rising Generation, and to endeavor to fit them for an honorable Discharge of the Social Duties of Life, by paying the strictest attention to their Education.

Ten days later an Act was passed providing for the erection of buildings and the support of the University. The Board of Trustees held its first meeting November 15, 1790. In 1792 a site was selected and on the 12th of October, 1793, the cornerstone of the

Old East Building was laid. When the doors of the University formally opened on January 15, 1795, it became the first state university in the United States. One hundred and fifty years ago today Hinton James became the first student in the first state university—February 12, 1795. At the end of its first term, the University found itself with only two professors and forty-one students, and for fifty years public funds made available to it did not exceed an average of $6,000 per annum.

We may not easily remember all of the dates and amounts incident to the establishment of the University. But with ever increasing pride we can and should remember that from the very inception of this Republic our far-sighted and liberal-minded forefathers well understood that education was necessary to the development of free institutions. It is timely that we should be mindful of the courage and determination with which they met and overcame the stubborn difficulties of their day as we struggle through the present and face new problems and responsibilities sure to come in the years that lie immediately ahead.

During the one hundred fifty years since Hinton James became the first student at the first state university in the United States, almost 45,000 regular students have matriculated. These thousands have come to the University from all walks of life, and mostly from North Carolina. They have come from good stock, from homes of the rich and of the poor, the high and the low, the learned and the unlearned, seeking the tools and the spiritual inspiration with which to forge a better way of life for themselves and for their state and nation. They have passed through the halls of this institution, have lived in its rooms, walked its walks, learned and loved its life, and have been gripped by its natural beauty. They have learned here the meaning of self-government and free institutions. On this campus student government in one form or another has existed through the years and has been woven into the warp and woof of the life of students who have learned through experience that freedom is not license, and that to abuse freedom is to destroy it. They have absorbed while here something of the depth and meaning of the university life, and its indescribable spirit has become part and parcel of the spiritual and mental equipment of those who have passed through its portals.

Teachers dedicated to the art and science of teaching have given freely of themselves to their students, and from its beginning the loyalty of the teaching staff of this institution has been, and is, an outstanding example of unselfish dedication to the training of youth, the building of character, and the development of this state. Somehow these teachers, and this place, have been able to impart visions and concepts of service to those who have passed this way as students, and have sent them back into the life of the state and nation, qualified to furnish direction and leadership in every phase of our life. Their able and unselfish services have enabled those who have plowed deep into the soil and who have searched deep into the soul of this place to say, amidst life's fiercest struggles,

> In every high and stormy gale
> My anchor holds within the veil.

Created almost fifty years before the establishment of a public school system in North Carolina, this University furnished many of the men who led the movement for a public school system, and many of them have devoted their lives to the cause of universal education. From the spiritual, cultural, and scientific resources which have been placed in its keeping by the people of the state, it sent forth men equipped with the best it could give, and fired with a burning desire to pour back into the flow of human life something of the majesty and leadership of their alma mater. Many of them came here during periods of stress and strain, and at times when there was much opposition to the expenditure of public funds for the support of a state university. These witnessed at first hand the struggles of this institution, not only to exist, but constantly to improve its status, and they have had the satisfaction and the added assurance of knowing that from its small beginnings it has grown as the state has grown, has improved as the state has improved, until today it is one of the great institutions of learning of the Republic.

Neither time nor the proprieties of this occasion permit me to undertake to name the leaders whom this institution has furnished the state and nation in every field of human endeavor. Suffice it to say, that most of them, as they have passed on to their respective places in life, have carried with them something of the stamp or brand of this University, something of its tremendous spiritual power, something of the breath of freedom which has not left this campus in these one hundred and fifty years. As they have become alumni, they have become workmen and toilers in the business of living and in the affairs of this state.

There is no adequate means of determining or measuring the influence of this University upon the progress and development of our Commonwealth and our Republic. Suffice it to say that in all matters affecting the sound progress of our people, its alumni are always to be found in the forefront, striving always for a higher level of intellectual, economic, and spiritual attainment. It has been, and increasingly continues to be, a symbol of intellectual freedom, placing its prime emphasis upon spiritual values, and the dignity of the human soul.

On its one hundred and fiftieth birthday, the University has high rank, not only in this state, but throughout the nation. The physical plant here at Chapel Hill is valued at approximately fifteen million dollars. The student enrollment the last full year before the impact of war reached about 4,500 students. Its faculty has been for many years, and is now, outstanding in ability and unselfish dedication to the cause of education, and unsurpassed in loyalty.

In the laboratories, in the schoolrooms, on the farms, in the factories, on the railroads and ships, in the halls of Congress, in the courts of the land, as governors of states, as presidents of educational institutions, in the churches, and wherever men are found doing things, leaders whose lamps were lit at this University are showing the way along the trails of human achievement. This ancient institution, the property and pride of the people of the State of North Carolina, has achieved an enviable position in the hearts of the citizens of the Commonwealth.

This could not have been accomplished without the splendid contributions which have been made to the development of higher education and learning by the other colleges and universities in this state. The friendly rivalry of leaders of thought; the competition in the development of science; the race for intellectual supremacy; the contest in literature and art; the thrill of rendering the greatest public service—these have constituted a constant challenge to all the institutions of higher learning in the state, and the University, along with the rest of them, has found from experience that the development of one contributes to the development of all. Gone are the days when serious consideration was given to the plea that the state should not appropriate funds for institutions of higher learning.

Conceived in a period of revolution, born within thirty days of the adoption of the Constitution of the United States by North Carolina, this institution has struggled to create here on this continent a free republic and free institutions, where men are free to think, to worship, and to govern themselves, subject only to the standards of good morals and the supremacy of the law. This explains why the University, through the years, has not seen fit to follow, but rather always has been struggling to lead, in the advancement of free institutions, the maintenance of individual liberty, and the recognition of the dignity of the human soul.

Along with other Americans, almost 8,000 University alumni are today fighting the battle of freedom on, over, and under all the seas, on and over all the continents, and on and over many of the world's islands, in every branch of the service of the United States. Its facilities and personnel have been tendered to and measurably used by the Government in connection with the war, while its President and many members of its Faculty and staff have rendered service to the Government during the emergency.

On the University's one hundred and fiftieth birthday, its past accomplishments and present status impel us briefly to consider its future. All that the University is and has belongs to the people of the state. Many times it has been called "The University of the People." It has not asked, and should not ask, anything for itself, except those things necessary to meet the needs of our state and republic. The Trustees, officers and Faculty are temporary custodians of the University for the benefit and use of all the people of North Carolina. They must, during their tenure of service, maintain here on this campus freedom in the search for truth. Its officers and Faculty and those charged with its management should stand solidly on all questions affecting this basic principle, but in doing so should, so far as possible, avoid unnecessary irritants which hamper its possibilities and usefulness.

Through its outstanding two-year Medical School, its regional School of Public Health, and in other ways, the University is making a great and continuing contribution to the public health and well-being of our Commonwealth. The establishment of a state-wide medical program, including a central hospital and a four-year medical school here in Chapel Hill, is now pending before the General Assembly of North Carolina. This program was recommended by a commission of fifty outstanding citizens of the state after thorough and careful investigation. It is my belief that the essential elements of the well-balanced proposed plan should be adopted now.

It is no credit to North Carolina that among the forty-eight states of the Union it now ranks forty-second in the number of hospital beds per one thousand population; forty-fifth in the number of physicians; forty-first in the percentage of mothers dying in child-birth; thirty-ninth in percentage of infant deaths; and forty-eighth in percentage of service rejections for physical defects.

The medical training and hospital and medical care envisioned by this far-reaching state-wide program should and does, I believe, have the unqualified support of the educational institutions of the state and of a great majority of the citizens of this Commonwealth. It will reach and serve our people in every county of the state. North Carolina is not rich enough to afford the terrific loss now suffered for lack of medical treatment and hospital facilities. The simple teachings of the Great Physician demand that the humane people of this progressive state do no less than make every possible effort to train doctors and provide medical treatment and hospital facilities which will result in the building of sound bodies, capable of performing life's work. If we are to claim a place in the march of progress and believe in the application of the simple teachings of the Christian religion, we can do no less than get this great program under way. To fail to do this would, in my judgment, leave unanswered the call of suffering humanity in North Carolina. The University is ready to assume whatever responsibility in connection with this program that the state may place upon it.

Another thing is the perfection of the organization of the Consolidated University. Those who have studied the matter most feel that it would be beneficial to the institutions involved and to the state as a whole. The full co-operation of the alumni of each of the three institutions involved will be necessary if the Consolidated University is to attain its greatest usefulness.

The alumni are interested in and love the University, but sometimes have a poor way of showing it. Certainly most alumni could and should join the Alumni Association. This organization, with its limited means, has done a splendid job. Its operating funds and staff are insufficient for the job. It needs the active support of all the alumni. By building up the Alumni Association to the point where it can participate more actively and effectively in the affairs of the University, as it should do, the alumni can make a powerful contribution to its future and to the welfare of the state.

The alumni could and should make a greater effort to translate to the people of the state the service the University is rendering and the real meaning of its leadership. They should, I think, investigate before criticizing what happens at the University, and if mistakes are found to exist, do more about correcting them in a proper way. Certainly they could and should be more anxious to encourage in every possible way all of the institutions of higher education in the state. They could and should, in my opinion, co-operate more effectively with the officials of this institution and with those of the Consolidated University. This is essential to its welfare; and its welfare, so definitely linked with the destiny of the state, should be a matter of prime importance to all of us.

In brief consideration of the future in broader outline, we quickly agree that winning the global war in which we are engaged comes first. What the cost of victory may be we cannot know. We do know that it will be great. I do not mean the cost as measured by the staggering financial obligations we are assuming, but rather by the hardships and sacrifices and suffering along far-flung battle lines in the skies, in the seas, and on the land the world over, plus the fear, anxiety, strain, and heartaches from end to end of our beloved country, and the lifeblood of American youth whose courage and gallantry command the respect of the world. War was not of our choosing, but the die has been cast, our involvement is complete, and no matter what the cost, there is no way for us short of victory. God hasten the day.

Winning the war lies across the threshold of every consideration of the future. But victory, devoutly as we hope and pray for it, will not solve the world's problems. It would be childish to conclude that when hostilities cease we will revert automatically to the state existing before the war. We will not. Civilization the world over is receiving a body blow. Only when victory comes will we be able to know the cost and fully appraise the damage. But we know now that foreign and domestic problems fundamental to the well-being of mankind exist and will multiply as we approach and pass the climax. No enumeration will be attempted in this well-informed presence. We know that a broken world is, and will be ours, and that the extent of its wounds must be commensurate with the most extensive and intense, the most wasteful and destructive, and the cruelest conflict in which the human race has been involved. Upon those who survive the conflict must rest the terrible responsibility not only of meeting the instant problems and healing as best we may the broken places, but of daring to lift the world itself to that higher ground where repetition will be impossible.

What part shall the University of North Carolina play in the rehabilitation and future security of the world? Through a century and a half it has had opportunity to grow strong and great to an extent that excites universal admiration. We rejoice in this, but we must also realize that thereby the degree of our responsibility is enhanced. We have confidence that as it has not failed in the long and honorable past, it will not fail now fully to measure up to the highest degree of its responsibility.

But in doing this it will need, as seldom before, the loyal and steadfast support of every officer, every trustee, every teacher, every student, every alumnus, and every friend. Reference already has been made to the extent to which this group, particularly the alumni, are participating in the war. In every part of the globe tonight there are those who hold in their hearts precious memories of pleasant and profitable days spent at this grand old institution which they love as they do their country. In a large way it represents the quintessence of what they are fighting to preserve. In sorrow we realize that many of them will never see this campus again, but thoughts of it must strengthen their arms and stimulate their courage in meeting daily the grim hardships of relentless war. Their example should be an inspiration to us.

At the end of a hundred and fifty years we find the talents and tools placed in our hands. The hour of great responsibility has struck. Some of the old problems and some of the present problems will be ours. The immediate future holds new and unpredictable problems. Let us not be afraid. Let us not delay. Let this ancient temple of learning, with its unparalleled heritage and great record of achievement, and all present and future students and alumni, with eyes fixed upon the stars and roots deep in the soil and tradition of North Carolina, march steadily forward upon the highroad of progress in the search for greater freedom and greater truth. Let us be confident in the faith that the omnipotent power of the Supreme Judge of the World has not changed, and that it still guides the destinies of men; that there is no substitute for religious faith and spiritual values in the affairs of men and nations; that there is no substitute for rugged honesty and honest toil; and finally, let us have faith that peace, so difficult to attain, can and will, in the fullness of time, become a reality.

A Student Comes to Chapel Hill

"The Program of Exercises" for Hinton James Day was so attractively printed that it was preserved as a souvenir by many of those taking part in the Celebration. The first page of the handsome four-page quarto folder carries a fine black and white sketch of the north end of Old East Building. It is drawn by Jack Manly Rosé, illustrator of *Northeast from Boston* and *Williamsburg—Today and Yesterday*. The fourth page of the program gives the following information concerning this first state university student:

Near Wilmington, N. C., was born in 1776 Hinton James. In the same year at Halifax, N. C., the Colony of North Carolina became the State of North Carolina with the adoption of the Halifax Constitution of 1776. That Constitution called for the establishment of a university. During Hinton James's early years the American Revolution was fought and independence for the colonies was won. Hinton James was thirteen years old when the University was chartered at Fayetteville by the Legislature of the State. He and his parents probably heard the news in 1792 that a site for the new University had been chosen at a cross-roads hilltop on which there had been a Chapel of the Church of England. When Hinton James was seventeen the news perhaps reached him that the cornerstone had been laid for the first building at Chapel Hill—on October 12, 1793.

At the age of nineteen James arrived in Chapel Hill—the story being that he walked all the way from his home near Wilmington—to become on February 12, 1795, the first student of the new institution. For two weeks he was the sole student.

Dr. Battle in his *History of the University of North Carolina*, writes: "The faculty records show that he [James] performed his duties faithfully and with ability." It was an early custom that students should give an original composition which they were required to read on each Saturday. The better compositions were posted in a record book. Hinton James's name is recorded numerous times. Subjects on which he wrote are recorded, too, and the titles of his compositions indicate that he was particularly interested in scientific subjects. Also, he must have enjoyed his college experience, for one topic on which he wrote was "The Pleasures of College Life."

By the end of the first University term, forty-one students had enrolled at the new University. The first public examination (and in those days the students were examined in the presence of the Trustees, including the Governor of the state) was held on July 13, 1795. A newspaper editorial of the time reports the event with enthusiasm: "The spirit of improvement, order and harmony, which reigns in this little community, emulously engaged in the noble work of cultivating the human mind, is most commendable."

Hinton James was graduated, receiving the A.B. degree in July, 1798. He became an engineer and was in charge of channel improvements on the Cape Fear River, among the first improvements of inland waterways to be undertaken in the state. In

1807, James was elected to the North Carolina legislature and served for three terms. He was also at one time Mayor of Wilmington. . . .

To those humble beginnings, the University of North Carolina today looks back across a hundred and fifty years. In the time intervening, 44,802 matriculates have enrolled at Chapel Hill. To this total might be added hundreds of normal-school students in summer sessions, thousands of students who have come to Chapel Hill for short courses and institutes, and many others in the state and elsewhere who have been served by extension classes and correspondence instruction. To the total also may be added other groups, for example, the 15,000 cadets of the Navy's Pre-Flight School who have studied and trained at Chapel Hill in preparation for their roles in the present global war.

In 1945 the University looks forward even more eagerly than it looks back upon its historic past. Pausing today in observing its one hundred and fifty years of service, the University also is planning for the years ahead, as President Graham has said: "On this day of commemoration and dedication we pledge anew the people's university in the people's war for the people's freedom and the people's peace."

VI

THE CONFERENCE ON RESEARCH AND REGIONAL WELFARE

O N MAY 9-11, 1945, the University held a conference on Research and Regional Welfare as a part of the Sesquicentennial Celebration. In doing so, it was moved by several major considerations.

In the first place, the University has long recognized that while it is the function of all educational institutions to disseminate knowledge, it is the particular function of a *university* to discover and extend knowledge. As a state university, by virtue of its public support, the obligation unmistakably rests upon the University of North Carolina to employ its libraries, its laboratories, and its personnel in the prosecution of research not only for the discovery of new knowledge, but also for the advancement of the material, intellectual, and spiritual welfare of the public which it serves through the application of knowledge thus discovered. In evidence of its understanding of this responsibility, the University can point to the long record of sustained investigation and publication which appears in *The Graduate School: Research and Publications*, and *The Graduate School: Dissertations and Theses* issued by the University in its Sesquicentennial Publications.

The second consideration has grown out of the recognition of distinct limitations which the University has experienced in the development and support of its research program. These limitations have been made evident in many ways. They have been most notable, however, in deficiency of funds, of laboratory and library facilities, and of personnel to carry on an extensive program at a high level. World War II clearly revealed this situation in that the assistance, though extensive and highly important, which the University could render the armed services of the United States was largely limited to the provision of physical facilities, of instruction, and of research at lower levels in a few fields rather than at higher levels and in many fields. The University could not participate in the more highly specialized types of investigation with the major universities of the Northeast and the Middle West, governmental research agencies, private research foundations, and industry.

The third consideration stemmed from the obvious lag in the development of industrial research in North Carolina and the South generally. Industry, in this region of abundance of raw materials, has depended to a far greater extent than it should on research carried on elsewhere. Consequently, the region has not enjoyed the advantages which flow from the application of the findings of laboratories to the processes of manufacturing, commerce, and agriculture. Obviously, this lag must be eliminated, and the best in science and technology must be put to work on a large scale for the advancement of the public good.

The final reason for holding the Conference was the very compelling one that the hour of the South's greatest opportunity has struck. The tremendous advances made during the war through research and the applications of research must be released and extended to the people in the post-war period. Pure and applied research, made possible through universities, governmental agencies, foundations, and industrial organizations, must be put to work on a scale commensurate with the needs and resources of North Carolina and the region. By greatly extending its own program of research, and by joining other institutions and organizations in the South in promoting fundamental and applied research—and by these means only—can the University of North Carolina, in all of its branches, play the part of a modern state university and make its full contribution to the civilization of tomorrow.

Sessions of the Conference were held at the Carolina Inn, Hill Music Hall, and Gerrard Hall and papers were presented as follows:

Introduction: The Need for Research, Robert E. Coker, Kenan Professor of Zoology, University of North Carolina.

I. The Key to the Future: Research for the Commonwealth, the Honorable R. Gregg Cherry, Governor of North Carolina; The Opportunity and Responsibility of Research, Frank Porter

Graham, President of the University of North Carolina; The Usefulness of Useful Knowledge, Wilson Compton, President of Washington State College.

II. Research in the South: Research for Prosperity in the Industrial South, Wilbur A. Lazier, Director of Southern Research Institute; The Development of Southern Research, Raymond R. Paty, President of the University of Alabama.

III. Nutrition and Public Health: Research in Nutrition: Importance to the Public Health, Russell M. Wilder, Division of Medicine, Mayo Clinic, Head, Department of Medicine, The Mayo Foundation for Medical Education and Research; Medical Research: The Foundation for Future Progress and Health and Public Welfare in the South, James Stevens Simmons, Brigadier General, U.S.A., Chief, Preventive Medicine Service, Office of the Surgeon General, U.S. Army.

IV. The Humanities and Social Science: Literary Research in Modern Life, D. C. Allen, Associate Professor of English, School of Higher Studies, Johns Hopkins University; History and Social Reconstruction, Avery Craven, Professor of History, the University of Chicago.

V. The Physical Sciences and Industry: Research and Industry as a Factor in Southern Development, Milton H. Fies, Consulting Engineer, Birmingham, Alabama, Trustee and Treasurer, Southern Research Institute; Needs and Opportunities for Research in Industry, Reuben B. Robertson, Executive Vice President, Champion Paper and Fibre Company.

VI. The Biological Sciences: Research in the Fisheries for the Betterment of the South, Harden F. Taylor, Former President, Atlantic Coast Fisheries Company; Research and the Southern Farmer, George J. Wilds, President, Coker's Pedigreed Seed Company.

VII. Research, The Foundation of the Future: The Moral Responsibility of Research, David E. Lilienthal, Chairman, Tennessee Valley Authority; Wartime Science Builds for Peace, Georges F. Doriot, Brigadier General, U.S.A., Director Military Planning, Office of the Quartermaster General, U.S. Army, For the Under Secretary of War, Robert P. Patterson.

The following persons served as presiding officers at the various sessions: Robert B. House, Chancellor and Vice-President, University of North Carolina, Chapel Hill; Howard W. Odum, Head, Sociology Department, University of North Carolina; Milton J. Rosenau, Dean, School of Public Health, University of North Carolina; Newman I. White, Professor of English, Duke University; J. E. Mills, Chief Chemist, Sonoco Products Company, Hartsville, S. C.; L. D. Baver, Director, Agricultural Experiment Station, North Carolina State College of Agriculture and Engineering of the University of North Carolina; J. M. Broughton, Ex-Governor of North Carolina, Raleigh, N. C. Representing Under Secretary of War Robert P. Patterson, who was unavoidably absent, Brigadier General Georges F. Doriot, Director, Military Planning, Office of the Quartermaster General, U.S. Army, delivered an address, "Wartime Science Builds for Peace." The paper was accompanied by an exhibit concerning the application of research in the solution of problems met with by the Office of the Quartermaster General in providing food and equipment for the Army.

The papers have been published under the title *Research and Regional Welfare*. Unfortunately the comments of the presiding officers and of others participating in the discussions were not available for publication.

The Conference was made possible through the contribution of funds by a number of alumni friends of the University and through the planning of a special committee representing the Divisions of the Humanities, the Social Sciences, and the Physical Sciences, and other units of the University, as follows: Dr. R. E. Coker, Chairman, F. K. Cameron, H. R. Huse, C. S. Jones, A. R. Newsome, H. W. Odum, Sherman Smith, and Louis R. Wilson.

The attendance at the various sessions was excellent and the reporting and editorial comment of the state and national press was extensive and highly commendatory.

VII

THE FIRST COMMENCEMENT

THE COMMENCEMENT of 1945 was, according to the early plans of the Sesquicentennial Committee, to have been the culminating and climactic event of the Sesquicentennial ceremonies. But World War II decreed otherwise. Even some of the plans being carried out as late as June 1, 1945, had to be modified or cancelled on account of rulings of the Office of Defense Transportation restricting travel. Alumni reunions were frowned upon, special events were taboo, and it was even urged that honorary degrees be granted *in absentia* and that parents be advised not to attend the graduation of their sons and daughters! Even food was so seriously limited, that it elicited the facetious comment from Chancellor House that only three kinds of sea food were available: haddock for the Senior luncheon; shrimp for the Alumni luncheon; and perch for any one staying over for another day!

Under these conditions, only three events of the Commencement were featured as parts of the Sesquicentennial—the Baccalaureate Sermon, the Commencement Cantata, and the Baccalaureate Address. These parts of the program, however, were carried out with the first Commencement of 1795 constantly in mind.

THE FIRST COMMENCEMENT, 1795

The first Commencement in 1795 was quite different from what the American public has become accustomed to in the intervening hundred and fifty years. It was held on July 13, 1795. Notice concerning it was given in the newspapers of the time over the signature of Richard Dobbs Spaight, then Governor of North Carolina. No students were ready to receive degrees. No classes were holding reunions. No dances were scheduled, and, according to the meager records of the event, the only woman present was Mrs. Spaight, wife of the Governor. Mrs. Ker, wife of the "Presiding Professor," may also have been in attendance!

The exercises, according to statements at the time by General William Richardson Davie and letters written by Hinton James when he was sixty years old, consisted of examinations of the students in the presence of the Governor, the Trustees, and the public; declamations; and the reading of compositions in one of the rooms of Old East Building.

In an enthusiastic editorial in the contemporary *North Carolina Journal*, it was stated that the "young gentlemen had submitted with a degree of cheerfulness and promptitude to the regulations of the University, which does them the greatest honor . . . The spirit of improvement, order and harmony, which reigns in the little community, emulously engaged in the notable work of cultivating the mind, is most commendable."

The Baccalaureate Sermon for 1945 was delivered in Memorial Hall at 11 o'clock on Sunday, June 24, by Bishop Robert E. Gribbin, of the Diocese of Western North Carolina. Bishop Gribbin spoke impressively to the graduating class and to a large audience.

BISHOP GRIBBIN

The Bible is a book of religion, and as such it deals with relationships—the relationship of God with man, man with God, and the resulting relationship of man with his fellow man. It also presents the record of God's dealing with nations and their responsibility to Him and to one another.

There are in the Bible terse expressions of these relationships such as, "God is Love," "Fear God and Keep his Commandments," "For the nation and the kingdom that will not serve Thee shall perish; yea, those nations shall be utterly wasted."

However, most of the message of the Bible is presented in history, laws, prophecy, poetry, even drama—such as that of Job, and short stories like that of Ruth. Just as a gem should be seen in its proper setting to be appreciated, so many Bible passages need to be interpreted in their literary form if one would receive their full meaning.

Such a passage is the dramatic prophecy contained in the first eight verses of the sixth chapter of the Book of the Prophet Micah. The persons of this simple drama are God, his people Israel, and the Mountains personified. Balaam is cited as a witness but he is not heard. The scene opens with God arraigning his people Israel and calling upon the Mountains to hear his controversy. God recites what he has done for his people—bringing them out of Egypt, redeeming them from servitude, and giving them Moses, Aaron, and Miriam as leaders. The people, conscious of their failure to use properly the opportunity which God has given them and realizing their guilt, cry out, "Wherewith shall I come before the Lord, and bow myself before the high God? Shall I come before him with burnt offerings, with calves of a year old? Will the Lord be pleased with thousands of rams, or with ten thousands of rivers of oil?" And then as the enormity of their offense deepens in their minds, the agony of their souls is shown as they conclude, "Shall I give my first-born for my transgression, the fruit of my body for the sin of my soul?"

At this juncture, the Mountains exclaim as the voice of nature and experience, "He hath shown thee, O man, what is good; and what doth the Lord require of thee, but to do justly, to love mercy, and to walk humbly with thy God?" The question is rhetorical and shows that the hearers already have that answer.

It is worthy of note that this statement of what God requires has not only the approval of the Jewish and Christian tradition but it also has a peculiar place in our nation. In the central reading room of the Library of Congress there are large stucco figures, one of which represents religion. When the figure, Religion, was erected, a nation-wide poll was made to determine what statement would best express our citizens' idea of religion. The majority replying to the poll did so in these words, "He hath showed thee, O man, what is good, and what doth the Lord require of thee but to do justly, to love mercy, and to walk humbly with thy God?" Thus we may say that it is the common denominator of our idea of religion.

Today we as individuals, as citizens of this country, and as members of the human race are arraigned before the Mountains. Certainly no one here, as student, member of the faculty, preacher, or in any other capacity is conceited enough to say that he has used properly the power which God has given him. We are aware that this nation of ours, with much to its credit and glory, has at the same time failed to bear its part of the burdens of the world. The voices of those we can hear in other lands are asking what can be done to right the wrongs and preserve peace. On this Sunday before the meeting of the United Nations adjourns in San Francisco and when our people through our Senate will be presented the charter for the new world organization; at this time when this University rejoices in its century and a half of service to state, nation, and world; and just as these young people fare forth on a high adventure, we ask what principle may we take which will improve on the record of the past and be a guide for the future. Such it seems is found in the words kept for us by Micah, "do justly, love mercy, and walk humbly with thy God."

To do justly one must first of all be just to himself. Realism and idealism unite in affirming that one cannot be false to others who is true to himself. Justice is more than a passive virtue. It means refraining from doing wrong, and doing what is right, cost what it may. The Goddess of Justice is pictured as blindfolded and holding scales evenly balanced. This idea is easily understood, but it seems that Justice should have both eyes and both ears open. She should not be near or farsighted, and certainly not suffering from uncorrected astigmatism. She must see that all are treated fairly and especially those not able to bring their own case into court. Nothing has proved truer in the long run than the principle, "With what measure ye mete it shall be measured to you again." How well Edwin Markham voices this truth:

> There's a destiny that makes us brothers,
> No man lives his life alone.
> All we put into the lives of others
> Comes back into our own.

If we want justice we must practice it to receive it. Justice is a debt we owe to all. Justice has been defined as truth in action.

In the Revised Version of the Bible you will observe that "love mercy" is translated "love kindness." Kindness is another way of saying "kinness," showing mercy to our kind. Religion is not alone in proclaiming that all nations of men that dwell on the earth are of one blood. A statesman-politician has popularized the thought contained in these two words, "One world." Two thousand psychologists of our country have united in a statement which contains ten basic principles which should be considered in planning peace. The third one of these principles is in part, "Racial, national, and group hatreds can, to a considerable degree, be controlled. . . . They can learn that members of one racial, national, or cultural group are basically similar to those of other groups, and have similar problems, hopes, aspirations, and needs. Prejudice is a matter of attitude, and attitudes are to a considerable extent a matter of training and information." In the liberal atmosphere of this University we can be sure that there has been also a liberating influence as a result of the study of the social sciences. Kindness is a universal language, even more so than music because the deaf can hear and the blind can see kindness. We show our estimate of ourselves in the way we treat others. Terence in the passage beginning, "*Homo sum*," says "I am a man, and nothing that is human is alien to me." Even the cold philosophy of Kant comes to the same conclusion when he counsels, "Accordingly the practical imperative will be as follows: So act as to treat humanity, whether in thine own person or in that of any other, in every case as an end withal, never as means only." We are not showing kindness or mercy when we treat others as means and not as ends in themselves.

Walk humbly with thy God. The poet has expressed something of the feeling of humility which should possess us all when he was unable to explain the flower in the crannied wall and the surge of the sea as it broke over the cold gray stones. If we view the world with a microscope or a telescope we are moved to repeat that "we stand in the presence of an energy from which all things proceed." As we think the thoughts of God after him, to use the expressive phrase of Pascal (who, in a recent essay by Charles Morgan, was described as a "dramatist of the soul"), we can exclaim with others, "What hath God wrought." Again it is not alone the professional preacher who calls upon us to honor God, and by so doing to walk humbly with Him.

With the program of the United Nations before us and the approach of July the Fourth, let us recall that our founding fathers in the Declaration of Independence said the truth was self-evident, "that all men . . . are endowed by their Creator with certain unalienable rights"—they are God-given, not man-conferred. We stand at attention when the "Star Spangled Banner" is played. In the second stanza of the anthem we find these words, "Praise the power that hath made and preserved us a nation." On the thin dimes in our pockets or purses are the words, "In God we trust." We can not be good citizens of our country without according God the first place in individual and national life.

This ancient statement, "do justly, love mercy, and walk humbly with thy God," is not a counsel of perfection to be attained by a few choice souls but something for "man," for all to have as guide. God requires its observance. There are many things in the Bible and outside of it which we do not understand; yet the fact remains that those who have given themselves to following the way of life as set forward in the Bible, using the knowledge they have, have attained to a peace which the world cannot give, and what is more, a peace which the world cannot take away. We needs must love the highest when once we have seen it.

May you young people of the graduating class as you grow in age, grow in grace, and in the knowledge and love of God. May all of us take heed, at this solemn moment in world history as we are gathered in the presence of God Himself, of his requirement—as true as He is true—do justly, love mercy, and walk humbly with thy God.

BRAHMS'S "REQUIEM"

The *Requiem* by Johannes Brahms was presented in Hill Music Hall, Sunday, June 24, at 8:30 P.M., by the Chapel Hill Choral Club, the University Glee Club, and the University Orchestra, with Paul Young, conductor, and Barbara Troxell and Robert Grooters, soloists. Approximately one hundred and thirty persons participated in the choral singing and forty in the orchestral accompaniment.

The graduating exercises, scheduled for 7:00 P.M. in the Kenan Stadium, were transferred to Memorial Hall on account of rain in the afternoon. The address to the graduating class, composed preponderantly of women on account of the absence of men in the armed services, was delivered by Kemp D. Battle, of the Class of 1909, a classmate of President Graham and grandson of Kemp Plummer Battle, President of the University, 1876-1891. It dealt significantly with the responsibilities of the graduates for the organization and preservation of peace in the postwar world.

KEMP D. BATTLE

When "the world is too much with us" and we are distraught with the anxieties and sorrows and perplexities and urgencies of a world still at war, it is helpful to deflate the importunities of the moment by backing off from our individual preoccupations and letting them fall into perspective against the background of the majestic sweep of Geologic Time.

H. G. Wells strikingly puts Man in his place by pointing out that if the period since Man's branch of the animal kingdom, Mammals, appeared on earth be expressed in terms of distance as one mile, then the period since the birth of Christ would represent one inch. James Harvey Robinson in his *Mind in the Making* carries this thought to an even more picturesque illustration. Let us suppose the whole age of Man on earth to be represented by one individual fifty years old. Then each year of the life of our symbolic Overman would represent 10,000 years of the life of the race, assuming that 500,000 years since Pithecanthropus is as good a guess as any. Pithecanthropus Erectus, as you know, was our distinguished ancestor whose fossil bones found on Java are the only known relics of that race of ape men who first walked erect. On this scale, Man was 40 years old when he stopped wandering and hunting where chance beckoned, and began to provide for his needs by planting crops. At 49½ he learned to write and then the speed of his progress really went into high gear. At 49¾ literature, art, and philosophy were well established. For the past two months he has lived under the influence of Christianity. The printing press is two weeks old, the steam engine a week. For three days he has been riding trains and steamships, since yesterday using electricity. For a few hours only he has been sailing in the air and under the water, and for the last few minutes using those discoveries in warfare terrible beyond compare. A week ago, he was burning alive those who differed from him in religious opinion and hanging old women if anyone accused them of trafficking with an imaginary devil. A year ago, he was a naked and painted savage. When we reflect on this newness of civilization and the potent force of savage intuitions and instincts, racial memories and taboos, animal reversions and all the unanalyzed projections of the past on the present, we can perhaps understand better the spectacle of Contemporary Man waging terrific warfare and can take heart from the thought that he hasn't really had time to develop dependable good habits.

A hopeful body might have thought that Man, even if he were only a short time from savagery, might have had more sense. His brilliant exploits in harnessing the forces of nature to his service showed the possession of a brain of sorts. One of his oddities has been a queer perverseness in deeming the higher law of less binding authority than the lower law. He has exalted the material at the expense of the spiritual, the practical at the expense of the ideal. Countless prophets have tried to set his feet in the narrow way that leads to the better life. Hear the words of John Donne: "No man is an Iland, intire of itselfe; every man is a peece of the Continent, a part of the maine; if a Clod bee washed away by the Sea, Europe is the lesse, as well as if a Promontorie were, as well as if a Mannor of thy friends or of thine owne were; any mans death diminishes me, because I am involved in Mankinde; And therefore never send to know for whom the bell tolls; It tolls for thee."

Let us give the devil his due. It took Hitler finally to burn into our very souls the answer to that question of Cain's which has come ringing down the corridors of time: "Am I my brother's keeper?" Man has been deaf to the moral law until the answer to Cain's question has come home to him in thundering tones on a thousand fields of battle. That answer is the theme of the greatest tragedy ever played on the stage of life. We may appropriate Carlyle's language: "Did not Schickelgruber present his Hitler

Opera with all too stupendous setting? With music of cannon volleys and the murder shrieks of a world, his stage lights were the fires of conflagration, his rhyme and recitative the march of embattled hosts and the crash of falling cities."

Yes, young people, the world is old but Man in the annals of time is young and the future is before him. We are passing through a great historic convulsion and countless homes will be desolate and countless bodies broken. As to those of whom in the fortunes of war a great measure of sacrifice is required, we shall hold them ever tenderly in our hearts and strengthen them resolutely with our arms. But for the world itself, there is ample reason to think that we are at the dawn of a new epoch, an era in which Man's breath-taking speed in the mastery of physical law is about to be paralleled by a similar progress in his management of himself and his fellow man.

Fervently do I hope that you and all young Americans will never flag nor falter in your insistence that our country lead in the efforts so to organize the nations of the world that this ghastly tragedy shall not again lay its crushing blight on God's children. Must it take another war and another million dead and wounded American boys to teach us that whenever people in any part of the globe are living under such injustice that they are desperate, then every mother's son of us is in danger?

Let us recur to our symbolic Overman of 50, now about to reach a real milestone. At 49, he began to grow crops. At 49½ he could read and write. At 50 two of his clans have been killing innocent women and children, shooting hostages, torturing prisoners, and in every way reverting to the barbarism which, biologically speaking, is just under the skin of all of us. Can Man, at this stage of his development, achieve the great forward step of settling international disputes by reason instead of by force? Without America it cannot be done. It comes down to this—can America, you and I and millions like us, manage to bring forth for the healing of the nations the spiritual power to overcome every devisive and defeatist influence? If the answer is "Nay," Man will likely slip back an aeon or two. Civilization as we know it cannot survive recurrent wars made increasingly devastating by its own inventive genius. If the answer is an "Everlasting Yea," the progress, which has in our era been so rapid, can go on in majesty and in glory.

It will not be easy. Belief in isolationism, temporarily silenced, is still deeply bred in countless Americans. Differences of language, customs, ideals, and purposes among the United Nations will require every resource of patience, imagination, understanding, and good will which they can command. Age is set in its ways. It is tired. It endures more readily than it changes. It will accept defeat if victory be too long delayed.

You are youth and the future is yours. If that future be black, on you will the shadow fall. If that future sparkle with the light of peace, yours will be the blessing. Never cease to struggle for it. Never accept defeat. The plan of Dumbarton Oaks, implemented at San Francisco, glows with promise, but it is, after all, the first step in a long and tedious process. We must accept it and through the years strive to perfect it. Around that goal cluster the brightest hopes of mankind. For it our sons have died and our mothers have prayed. It is indeed the only good thing we can get out of the war. With it, every sacrifice will be justified. Without it, our whole national effort will be meaningless. What a tragedy if we allow it to be frustrated by distrust of our allies, by the poison of suspicion and national selfishness and racial antagonism! Against those who sow such dragon's seed you must resolutely set your face. Let no cautious statesman represent you if he appeals to your lower self. Hold high the torch of generosity and tolerance and understanding among men. Are you your brother's keeper? Yea, verily, and only by keeping him shall you abide in safety.

What does this University have to say to you on this theme? It celebrates this year one hundred and fifty years of service to this state and nation. In the life of our symbolic Overman that is a very short time, less than a week according to the scale which I have described. But in the idiom of Churchill, "Some week!" It has been sufficient to build here a noble and distinguished tradition. In that time Alma Mater has gone through trials which tested the courage of her sons but always her message has been "Let my children serve their fellows."

Shall we whose souls have been nourished under these majestic oaks and along these quiet paths lose heart at the difficulties of building a fairer world on the ruins of the old? If our faith begins to falter, let us refresh it by reflecting upon the courage of those who have furthered this particular institution in other days of stress. Consider two epochs in its past, and first of all its very birth. The University was born as a mere disembodied statement of policy and declaration of purpose in the constitution adopted for the new free State of North Carolina, in that little 20x20 building at Halifax in December, 1776. Picture the situation of those dauntless patriots, in the language of the University's historian: "Without an army or navy, they had entered on a war for existence with a nation powerful, populous, and wealthy, having the tradition of invincibility; which had, under Marlborough, within the century broken the power of the great Louis of France; had with heavy hand crushed the fortunes of the Pretender at Culloden; had sent Wolfe to storm the Heights of Quebec; had swept the seas with her fleets. The Revolution, if it failed, was rebellion. The penalty of defeat was the doom of traitors. The state had barely 200,000 inhabitants, widely scattered, badly armed, divided in sentiment. But notwithstanding these odds, this Congress, with wisdom unparalleled and faith approaching sublimity, provided for the interest of unborn children. They made the requirement of the University a part of the fundamental law."

The second epoch occurred within the memory of men still living. In the utter demoralization which followed the collapse of the Confederacy, the doom of the University was clearly discernible and swept toward its climax so that in the fall of 1868 Mrs. Spencer, sitting under the Davie Poplar, wrote: "For 75 years this old poplar has spread a benignant shade over the gay throngs that wandered through the campus, or pressed into the Chapel in the glorious old days. The old tree still stands guard, but over grounds that are now empty and forlorn. The dry grass rustles to my solitary foot-steps, and a rabbit starts from yonder tangled and dying rosebush. . . . The sun shines down on the Old East and Old West, the Library walls, and recitation rooms; but the doors are all closed, the place is haunted. Strong and ineffaceable memories rush unbidden and my eyes are dimmed as I gaze on this Niobe sitting thus discrowned and childless."

Saddled with a carpet-bag administration, lacking both money and credit, the University finally closed as of February 1, 1871. Within five years we find a small committee of the old trustees undertaking the incredible task of canvassing the state for private contributions to restore the buildings and resuscitate their prostrate Alma Mater. The dauntless courage and exalted faith of that venture rank among the choice exploits of the human spirit. The state, ravished by war, was bankrupt; its bonds repudiated; the State Bank in liquidation. The currency of the Confederacy was worthless and its bonds dishonored. The wealth of the upper classes had been destroyed, partly by emancipation of slaves, partly by destruction of physical property, partly by the failure of business enterprise. The panic of 1873 had completely demoralized such beginning as had been made toward a revival of business. And yet that forlorn hope of a soliciting committee within six weeks reported contributions of $18,800, a fabulous sum in those days. From that time to this, the history of our University has been one of constant growth in stature and in favor with God and man. Successive generations of the sons of Carolina have builded here an institution not made with hands, an emanation of the brains and hearts of those who have loved it and sacrificed for it.

The illustrious dead who conceived the University in the throes of a desperate war for freedom, and those who revived it from the ashes of defeat, cry "courage" to you, her sons and daughters, who face a world in which even the survival of civilization may depend upon the ability of our Overman to make a step forward more momentous than any in his 50 years, each an aeon in itself. What answer will you make to your forefathers who struggled here that you might know the truth and that it might make you free? Perhaps our own Paul Green has phrased it:

> Now down the trackless, hollow years
> Which swallowed them but not their song
> We send response. . . .
> The dream still lives!
> It lives! It lives!
> And shall not die.

VIII

THE CONTRIBUTION OF THE UNIVERSITY TO PUBLIC EDUCATION

THE University of North Carolina, the first university to be established and supported by a state for the education of the people of a state, has not only served as an example of publicly supported education, but throughout its entire history has consistently and signally contributed to the advancement of public education generally. Its role in this particular has been one of great importance, and is second to that of no other state university in the nation.

This aspect of the University's life was set forth in a stimulating address entitled "The Contribution of the University to Public Education" on the evening of July 27, 1945, at the Carolina Inn, by Dr. E. W. Knight, Kenan Professor of the History of Education, at a dinner meeting at which a hundred and fifty members of the University and the educational interests of the state were present.

Introduced by Chancellor House, Dr. Knight spoke as follows:

DR. KNIGHT

Over the front of the William L. Clements Memorial Library of the University of Michigan, which contains the invaluable collection of maps, manuscripts and books relating to the discovery and settlement of America, early colonial history, and the Revolutionary period, appear two statements of historical and educational significance and also of prophetic warning for the people of any country or state: "In darkness dwells the people which knows its annals not." "Tradition fades but the written record remains ever fresh."

On the campus of the University of North Carolina are many reminders of the contributions of members of its family to the cause of education in this state,—contributions of its students, alumni, trustees, faculty, and other devoted friends. In considering these contributions to that cause it is appropriate to ask: Why do we call that building Davie? that one Caldwell? that one Murphey? that one Person? that one Swain? that one Battle? that one Alderman? that one Venable? that one Carr? that one Pettigrew? that one Graham? that one Spencer? that one Vance? that one Wilson? that one Bingham? that one Saunders? that one Hill? that one Woollen? Who were these people? What did they do for North Carolina and for education in this state? And we may ask similar questions as we study those tablets in Memorial Hall.

The answers to these questions are clear in the annals and written record of the University of North Carolina. Each of the names commemorated on this campus (and some also distinguished if yet uncommemorated) represents an effective and useful member of the University's family, who loved and labored for it and for the educational interests of the state that gave it birth and of which it is at once the product and the ornament, and who helped to keep alive in this campus and state the University's long and noble tradition of obligation to public service.

The contributions of the University family to the educational life of the state properly extend throughout its long history and are matters of proud record. While it is significant that public education in North Carolina began as a program supported and controlled by the state, alumni early became leaders in movements to establish schools, academies, and colleges. William Hooper, of the class of 1809, was chairman of the Baptist State Convention's Committee on Education in 1832 (when he was professor of ancient languages in the University) that led the way to the establishment of Wake Forest College; William H. Battle, of the class of 1820, introduced and championed in the House of Commons in 1833 the bill to charter that institution; and when vigorous and bitter opposition developed against the proposed charter, another alumnus, William D. Mosely, of the class of 1818, Speaker of the Senate, broke the tie in that body and gave the institution the right to live. It was a member of the class of 1818, Robert Hall Morrison, who was the moving spirit in the Concord Presbytery that resolved to establish Davidson

College, which, he said, "we begged into existence." Morrison became president of the institution March 1, 1837. Alumni were leaders in the movements to establish State College, the Women's College, Appalachian State Teachers College, and East Carolina Teachers College in North Carolina.

The influence of the University on public education in North Carolina reaches back to its early days. Alumni early became leaders in movements to promote public education. Archibald D. Murphey, class of 1799, properly gained the title of "The Father of the Public Schools" of the state; William Miller, class of 1806, first alumnus to become governor of the state (1814), made a recommendation that schools and education receive legislative support that led to the appointment of the first legislative committees on education in North Carolina. Bartlett Yancey, class of 1808, wrote the bill establishing the ante-bellum permanent educational school fund which became the basis of public educational support in the state prior to 1860. Calvin H. Wiley, class of 1840, led in the legislature a movement for state supervision and was himself initially appointed as the chief state school officer in 1852, taking office the following year. He and Governor Zebulon Vance, class of 1855, saved the public school fund during the Civil War. Kemp P. Battle, class of 1849, after Reconstruction organized and directed the first summer school for public school teachers ever to be established under the auspices of a college or university in this country. Alumni were leaders in the movement to secure the first legislative appropriation for public schools in 1899. Charles B. Aycock, class of 1880, while still a student in the University, made speeches in behalf of public education and became in the early part of the twentieth century the great educational governor of the state by throwing his personality and the prestige of his office into the movement that gave North Carolina its educational Renaissance. James Y. Joyner, class of 1881, laid the foundations during seventeen years (1902-1919) of devoted service as state superintendent for a system of public education that attracted the attention of the nation. Nathan W. Walker, class of 1903, working in close co-operation under the leadership of Dr. Joyner, helped to establish and develop in the first quarter of this century the public high school system and the farm life schools of the state. Hundreds of alumni participated actively in the movement early in the century which gave North Carolina its greatest educational awakening; and since that time they have led in movements for compulsory school attendance legislation, local taxes, and better financial support for education, have extended school terms, a system of twelve grades for the public schools, have extended facilities for the education and tenure of teachers, state-aid for public libraries, the protection of public education from bigotry and intolerance, the movement for better support of the state institutions, and many other extensions of public educational effort. These achievements may be fairly well known, especially those of Joseph Caldwell, Archibald D. Murphey, Bartlett Yancey, Calvin H. Wiley, Kemp P. Battle, Edwin A. Alderman, Charles D. McIver, James Y. Joyner, and Edward K. Graham, but in the following pages attention will be called to some of them and to the achievements of others who helped to relate the University of North Carolina to the schools about it.

There is no known way to measure accurately and fully the influence of a teacher, although some observer of this worker in the realm of mind and morals has said that immortality for a teacher is gained only when he blossoms and develops in the lives and works of others. There is no known way accurately and fully to measure the influence of an educational institution. Not only is it difficult to measure its influence upon students while they are in the institution, but it is more difficult to measure its influence upon its immediate environment, its constituency, the state in which it lives and moves and has its being, or in the nation; and it is more difficult still to measure those unseen and intangible, sometimes undreamed of, influences that do, however, radiate from a center of learning, teaching, inquiry, and publication.

But by the same test that the influence of a teacher is measured is the influence of a university also measured. Does it blossom and develop in the manifold interests and activities of the state? Does the university influence and promote the best interests of the economic and industrial, political, social and educational, religious and moral, aesthetic and artistic needs of the people it is set up and designed to serve?

While it is not possible to measure accurately and fully the influence of a teacher or university, it is possible to point out the major areas in which both have worked and to describe the nature and extent of the activities in which they have engaged. In the case of the University of North Carolina, established following the American Revolution and the adoption of the Federal Constitution in response to the demand of the people that public education be provided through a state-supported institution, it is possible to indicate the nature of its work in the field of public education and to describe, at least, the major contributions made by it within that field. If it is asked what have been the relations of this first American state university to the public schools of North Carolina and its influence upon them, the answer appears in a record of high achievement in public educational relations, even though the record may not always seem entirely flawless or always to reveal complete sensitiveness and alertness by the University to all the needs of the schools and education in the state. Specifically the record shows that the University, throughout the one hundred and fifty years of its service as a state-supported institution, established as the first unit in the state's system of public education, has promoted public education in five major ways: (1) The University has insisted upon the inseparability of itself and the public schools; (2) it has assumed large responsibility for the education of teachers and for the improvement of teaching; (3) it has championed the cause of public education when that cause has been threatened in several crises; (4) it has furnished, through members of the University family, the chief architects and builders of the public educational structure of North Carolina; (5) it has promoted the establishment of public, school, and college libraries, and the provision of extension service, both of which are fundamentally essential to the support of an enriched educational program.

I. THE INSEPARABILITY OF THE UNIVERSITY AND THE SCHOOLS

The truth that the educational and social history of a state or nation speaks with many tongues finds abundant illustration in the educational and social history of North Carolina. It finds illustration in the history of the University, now one hundred and fifty years old; in the history of its public elementary-school system, now one hundred and six years old; in the history of its public secondary-school system, now only thirty-eight years old; in the history of technological education, the higher education of women, the history of the education and training of teachers for the schools of the state,—a story almost as long as the life of the institution itself; and it finds illustration also even in the history of its influence upon the establishment of non-public academic and collegiate educational institutions.

The educational and social history of North Carolina has spoken through constitutional and statutory provisions for education, first and most persuasively through Article Forty-one, the initial constitutional provision for a university and schools, made at Halifax one hundred and sixty-nine years ago:

"That a school or schools shall be established by the Legislature for the convenient instruction of youth, with such salaries to the masters paid by the public, as may enable them to instruct at low prices; and all useful learning shall be duly encouraged and promoted in one or more universities."

After that historic date in the life of North Carolina, the educational and social history of the state spoke through the charter of this institution, provided for December 11, 1789, three weeks after North Carolina at Fayetteville had ratified the Federal Constitution. The preamble to that charter made the University by obligation the head of the public school system of North Carolina. And now for more than a century the fortunes of the University and those of the public schools of the state have been so closely identified as to make each dependent upon the other. Early it became known and long has it been recognized in this state that the public schools and the University of North Carolina must stand or fall together. The preamble to the charter of the University of North Carolina is highly competent evidence of remarkable prescience and prophecy of the relation between this institution and the public schools, later to be established:

"In all well regulated governments it is the indispensable duty of every legislature to consult the happiness of a rising generation, and endeavor to fit them for an honorable discharge of the social duties of life by paying the strictest attention to their education, and, that, a University, supported by permanent funds and well endowed, would have the most direct tendency to answer the above purpose."

The relation of the University to the public schools of the state and its responsibility and opportunity for their promotion were early recognized by the University leaders. Concerning this relation Dr. Kemp P. Battle, in his *History of the University of North Carolina*,[1] says: "That our forefathers thought that the University and the public school system were necessarily part of one organism is proved by their connection in the Constitution." And, commenting on Article Forty-one of the Constitution, he also says that it was clear to the statesmen in 1789, "and it ought not to require argument to prove it, that money spent for schools without providing teachers is mere waste and folly." All historians and other writers on the subject have pointed to this constitutional provision as the basis for a comprehensive educational plan for the State.[2]

The father of the University, William R. Davie, who moved in convention the ratification of the Federal Constitution, introduced in the House of Commons the bill to charter the University. Samuel E. McCorkle, an original trustee and foremost teacher, said in his address at the laying of the cornerstone of Old East October 12, 1793, that the "happiness of mankind is increased by the advancement of learning and science," that "liberty and law call for general knowledge in the people and extensive knowledge in matters of the State, and these in turn demand public places of education." "Education is the business of the public and should not be delegated," declared Joseph Caldwell, the first president of the University, in reply to bitter attacks on the institution in its infancy. And every president from Caldwell's day to this, whatever his political, denominational or educational background and training, has acknowledged the obligation of the University to the needs of the public schools:

1. Raleigh, Edwards and Broughton Printing Company, 1912, I, 2.
2. See R. D. W. Connor, *North Carolina: Rebuilding An Ancient Commonwealth* (Chicago, The American Historical Society, Inc., 1909), I, 386.

Caldwell, classicist, theologian, and Presbyterian minister; David L. Swain, statesman, political leader, and constitutional reformer; Solomon Pool, Methodist minister; Kemp P. Battle, historian; George T. Winston, classicist; Edward A. Alderman, educator and finished orator; Francis P. Venable, chemist; Edward K. Graham, humanist; Harry W. Chase, psychologist; Frank P. Graham, historian—each of these men worked for the improvement of education in the state, often against heavy odds and on unpopular issues.

In expressing the University's obligation for leadership in public education, it was only natural that Joseph Caldwell should have led the way. Pupil of John Witherspoon of Nassau Hall (Princeton), where he was graduated in 1791, Caldwell became professor of mathematics here five years later and in 1804 the first president of the University; and except for a brief period he served in that high position until his death in 1835, holding a professorship for twelve and the presidency for twenty-seven years. Sound, energetic and careful teacher; able executive; persuasive preacher of the Gospel; diligent supervisor of student discipline, Caldwell found time also to examine into and to stimulate discussion of pressing needs of the new state and the obligation of the new University to meet them. Voluminous were his able papers on the needs for improved facilities of transportation,"[3] for a state-wide public school system, for the education of teachers, and for the proper education and training of North Carolinians generally for service to the state. Joseph Caldwell is believed also to be the first man in North Carolina to urge the establishment of facilities for the education of women teachers for the schools of the state.

His significant services for education in North Carolina are numerous. Chief among these services, however, was a courageous address before a conference in Raleigh in 1829, on the subject of internal improvements, in which he declared North Carolina to be three centuries behind in education and internal improvements chiefly because of the radical and fatal delusion that "taxation is contrary to the genius of a republican govern-

3. His *Numbers of Carlton*, on transportation, was published in 1828 (New York, G. Long).

ment." No one, he declared, could be a real friend of education, or other public services who opposed the moderate taxes necessary to provide them; and he also made it clear that every citizen in the state had the right not only but was in conscience bound to help mold public opinion to promote all the best interests of the state. These were bold words for the president of a university more than a century ago.

But even bolder were President Caldwell's "Letters on Popular Education, Addressed to the People of North Carolina," in which was embodied his proposal for a state system of public education and his highly cherished plan for a school for the proper education of teachers.[4] In these eleven letters the backward condition of education and of the primary teachers of the state were clearly and unsparingly described. And, while a resolution was introduced into the legislature looking to the establishment of a central school "for the purpose of educating and preparing instructors of elementary schools," the proposal was unfortunately unsuccessful because funds were not then available for the purpose. But in a few years his work and the work of Archibald D. Murphey, and of Murphey's student, Bartlett Yancey, of the class of 1809, and of others of the University family bore fruit in the enactment of legislation in 1839 on which North Carolina established its first state-wide public school system now recognized to have been the best established in the South and among the best in the United States prior to 1860.

David L. Swain saw, as had his able predecessor, the obligation and the strategic value of relating the University and its activities as closely as possible to education and other public interests of the state. During his administration from 1835 to 1868 there was more emphasis upon preparation of men "for public service," to which Swain was himself devoted, and during those thirty-three years the institution grew in popularity and by 1858 had reached its peak enrollment of 456.

Even the Reverend Solomon Pool, in those disastrous days of

4. These letters, published at Hillsboro, in 1832, "Printed by Dennis Heartt," may be found in full in Charles L. Coon's *The Beginnings of Public Education in North Carolina—A Documentary History, 1790-1840* (Publications of the North Carolina Historical Commission, Raleigh, Edwards and Broughton Printing Company, 1908), II, 545-613.

the political rascality of Reconstruction, saw the University and the public schools as parts of the same educational system. Fortunately his administration as president of the University was brief. Battle describes him as "narrow in his views" but says he was "a man of decided ability and a good writer" and that his reports and some articles on "The University and the Public Schools" showed "thoughtfulness and literary power, but at the time of his election he had no State reputation."[5]

In those articles, however, which appeared in the *Raleigh Sentinel* in 1869 and were signed "A North Carolinian," Pool said that the Constitution of North Carolina gave the University and the public schools inseparable connection, with the University as head. Noting also that the Constitution called for a department of Normal instruction at the University, he emphasized the importance of teacher-education. He said that the public schools must prepare and send students to the University which should send them back as teachers in the schools "until the name of the University is written upon every schoolhouse, and across every heart in North Carolina. The University, as the constitutional head and center of the public school system, must shed its light all over the State, while the public and primary schools reflect its splendid glory. . . . Streams rise and flow down from their fountain head to invigorate and enliven the plains. Light radiates from its central luminary."

The distinctive contributions of President Kemp P. Battle in promoting public relations of good will with the state and the University's constituency are also matters of record. Often called the "father of the new University," Battle's energetic efforts to restore the usefulness and prestige of the institution following the ravages of war and the disasters of Reconstruction were to promote the best interests of the state through the services of the University, and his many activities practically expressed his faith in the close connection between it and those interests. High tribute to this faith of President Battle has often been paid, but never better perhaps than at commencement in 1900 by Dr. George T. Winston, who had been a member of the faculty from 1875 to 1891 and its president from 1891 to 1896. Winston's

5. *Op. cit.*, II, 10.

address had to do with the work and the opportunity of the first faculty after the reopening of the University in 1875. It and the addresses by President Edwin A. Alderman and by Dr. Battle are tonic for any who may nowadays tend to despair. Those addresses, read now after forty-five years, seem to leap out of cold type, make the reader exult with pride at the institution's past achievements on meager financial resources and other discouraging obstacles, and in doing so tend to subdue him also to a sense of humility. Those addresses seem to hurl challenges to those now here to face up to present and future opportunities and responsibilities of the University, with enlarged resources and facilities for promoting the best interests of the state. It is said that when Santa Anna was captured at San Jacinto he asked Sam Houston how he was able with such a small force to win such a complete and signal victory. Drawing from his pocket an ear of corn Houston is said to have replied: "When patriots fight on such rations, they are unconquerable."

In his address, Dr. Winston said, speaking of the hard days of the University after 1875:

"But a new era had come, the era of popular education both in lower schools and in higher. It was well for this era to be heralded by the opening of the new University, a people's University, and to be marked by a new right, the right of the people acting through their own representatives to tax themselves for the higher education of their sons in their own institutions." And he also said: "The people learned that a new University, the State's University, meant neither aristocracy nor theocracy, but eternal democracy. But the lesson was slow to learn, and its teaching was attended with amazing difficulties. Those early years were full of struggle, glorious and heroic, but difficult to bear and doubtful in issue. Surely no institution ever survived a more precarious childhood."[6]

As successor to President Battle, Dr. Winston was also energetic in relating the University closely to the public schools. In 1893 he said the immediate task of the University "and possibly its greatest, is to build up a system of education whereby each child in the State may achieve the largest possible development of

6. Battle, *op. cit.*, II, 578.

all its faculties. It recognizes its right and its duty to be the head and the heart of a life-giving system of education which carry cheer to the humblest cabin, strength to the weakest child, faith and hope to all that love humanity."[7]

Winston's successor, President Edwin A. Alderman, said in 1899: "Fifteen years ago the State's duty toward its children was a debatable proposition, but today it is an axiom and measures the growth of the public conscience and the sweep of the public vision during that period. . . ." He noted that the unity of the educational process in North Carolina, with which the people had been struggling for sixty years, was not yet fully recognized, and that "intelligent study of the whole subject has not been made since Archibald Murphey submitted his celebrated report of 1816. A good public school system is our supremest need and I may say with Jefferson that as my first plea in life was for public schools, my latest plea here shall be for them also, but the University is as much a part of this system as the log school house. . . . The University is the dynamo, the public schools, the incandescent light."[8]

The view that the University and the public schools of the state were of the same body educational and in close partnership runs through the official annual reports of President Venable and many of his addresses on educational subjects. His emphasis was that there could be "no efficient public school system without a strong University at its head. The stand taken by the University and the excellence of its work determine in large measure the conditions of all the schools from secondary to the humblest primary. If the University sends out good teachers and demands high attainments, there will be strong secondary schools; and if these are strong, there will be good teachers for the primary schools."[9]

In his report for 1906 President Venable said that greater aid should be extended to the schools of the state "and a closer connection maintained with them." And in his report for 1907,

7. "The University of Today," *University of North Carolina Magazine*, XIII (1893-94), p. 327.
8. "The University of Today: Its Work and Needs," *University of North Carolina Magazine*, XVII (1899-1900), pp. 291-92.
9. *The University Record*, VI, No. 4 (January, 1901), 23.

when the state established its first system of public secondary schools, President Venable was quick to see the significance of this forward educational step and the responsibility and opportunity which it meant for the University. He pointed to the need for teachers for these public high schools and the obligation of the University to help in supplying them. And all through these years he was proudly reporting those graduates and former students in the University who were going into teaching.

Edward K. Graham kept steadfastly to the same view, which he held before he became president and which he consistently expressed throughout his brief administration. Nowhere did he better set forth his idea of this partnership in the service of the state than in his report in 1916 where he said: "The welfare of the common schools, the high schools, the farm-life schools, the normal schools, and of all the educational institutions of the State, and the University's own welfare are one." But sound teachers and sound teaching were to Edward K. Graham the heart and soul of any educational system.

President H. W. Chase, who became head of the University in 1919, viewed state universities as institutions "with a peculiar obligation to the life of their commonwealths. Growing as they did out of the public concern in higher education, their traditions have inevitably been those of democracy and liberalism. This has, on the whole, been manifest in the point of view from which they have regarded their public duties. . . . They have regarded seriously their obligation as a part of the public school systems of their states, by the nature of their admission requirements and processes, by their work for the training of teachers through schools of education, summer schools, educational conferences, and so on. . . .

"Again, in the tradition of the modern state university is the conception of its direct responsibility to the state through extension work, service of its faculty on boards and commissions, the loan of its services for fact-finding; in other words the conception of itself as not only a bulwark for the future, but a servant of the present.

". . . .the state university of today still holds by those impulses of a democratic civilization that gave it birth. Here is both a satisfaction and a warning for the future. For, I do not believe that, in the long run, there is anything that can replace in a state university that sense of obligation to its commonwealth as a whole on which it was founded. If the state university should lose that sense, then we may expect to see once more repeated that struggle of a people to express its ideas in institutional form and the creation of other types of institutions adapted to the spirit of the age. The origin and development of state universities show, if they show anything at all, how any generation tends to create in some fashion the forms that it feels express its own necessities."

The personal and official view of President Frank P. Graham on the relation of the University of North Carolina and the schools is well known to all of us. All along, both before and since he became the University's president, he has viewed both as integral parts of the state's public educational system. He has seen both as rising or falling together, as he has many times said, especially in his address before the Citizens' Mass Meeting in Raleigh, January 31, 1933, when he closed as follows:

"It is only natural that the spokesman for higher education and the University of North Carolina should take his stand on, with, and for the public schools. The public schools of North Carolina were born at Chapel Hill. Caldwell, Murphey, Yancey, Wiley, Alderman, McIver, and Aycock are dead, but the public schools which they dreamed, founded, and builded still live and will live as long as North Carolinians carry on their precious tradition and develop the resources of their strength. In taking a stand for the University and higher education we are standing for the public schools. The public schools, the colleges, the universities, the farm, the factories, stores, banks, libraries, churches, and the people and their children, rich and poor, black and white, are all tied inextricably together in this commonwealth. The schools and the University of the people go up or down together."

II. TEACHERS AND TEACHING

The inseparable connection of the University and the schools early led to the institution's interest in the preparation of teachers and managers of schools, academies, and other educational institutions in North Carolina and the improvement of teachers in them. One of the original trustees of the University, Reverend Samuel E. McCorkle, was a pioneer in teacher-education, and had established near Salisbury in 1785 an academy with "a department for preparing school teachers," the first attempt at teacher-training in North Carolina and believed to be the first in the United States. The high order of scholarship and the influence of the school and its eminent leader appear in the fact that six of the seven members of the first graduating class of the University of North Carolina received their collegiate preparation under Dr. McCorkle. What appears to be the first definite proposal in the United States for a school designed exclusively for the training of teachers was made by Denison Olmsted in an address at Yale College in 1816, when he recommended a school in which prospective teachers could "study and recite whatever they themselves were afterwards to teach," in order to gain a better knowledge of the subjects and of the "principles and the art of teaching." Olmsted, appointed to the faculty of the University of North Carolina in that year and given a year's leave to study, later became eminent as professor of chemistry here and continued his interest not only in the subject which he discussed in 1816 but also in other means for identifying the University with the interests of the state. In 1817 he began the first geological survey of North Carolina and perhaps the first in the United States.

Joseph Caldwell occupies high place in the movement for the education of teachers. In the letters addressed to the people of the state in 1832, which were intended to arouse public interest in the establishment of a common school system, he emphasized the need for well qualified teachers. And he proposed that the state establish and maintain a central school for their preparation for the elementary schools "upon the most improved methods of instruction." He went into great detail in outlining his plan and how it could be made practicable, and insisted that the proper education of teachers was of far greater importance to the permanent well-being of the state than that of any other workers in the commonwealth. Although many years were to pass before the proposals of Caldwell were to be realized, his letters in

1832 were not without their influence in stimulating public discussion and leading to legislative action for a public school system in 1839.

A definite step toward teacher-education was taken by North Carolina nearly a century ago through the work of Braxton Craven, principal of Union Institute Academy in Randolph County, which grew into Trinity College and later into Duke University. In this work Calvin H. Wiley, an alumnus of the University, class of 1840, who in 1853 became the state's first superintendent of common schools, closely co-operated. Craven wrote Wiley (December 24, 1850), who represented Guilford County in the Senate, and urged support for a bill prepared by Craven to charter "the normal college" and make it an appropriation of $1,000 from the Literary Fund. The result was an act of the General Assembly that year by which Union Institute Academy became Normal College and was given authority to issue certificates to its graduates as "sufficient evidence of ability to teach in any of the common schools in this State, without re-examination of the county committees." In 1852 the charter of Normal College was altered and the Governor of the State became *ex officio* president and the State Superintendent of Common Schools *ex officio* secretary of the trustees. From that date until 1859,[10] when the name of the institution was changed to Trinity College and all relations with the state were severed, Normal College continued its work of preparing teachers for the public schools of North Carolina in co-operation with Superintendent Wiley and his office in Raleigh. This arrangement between the state and an educational institution established under denominational auspices (which had received a loan of $10,000 from the Literary Fund) is an illustration of co-operation in the education of teachers which fortunately has continued in North Carolina until the present.

The spirit of public service to the state through teaching also

10. An account of this early cooperative effort in teacher-education in North Carolina appears in E. M. Highsmith's *American State Normal School Curricula* (unpublished doctoral dissertation at the University of North Carolina, 1924). See also, by the same author, "The State Normal School Idea in North Carolina," *Meredith College Quarterly Bulletin*, Series 17, No. 1 (November, 1923).

early characterized the leading graduates of the University. Before the public school system was established in 1839 the people of North Carolina depended for their educational facilities largely upon voluntary local arrangements of wide variety— "old field" schools, "hedge" schools, "forest" schools, "community" schools, some of which were also known as academies, which were generally chartered by the state, privately controlled and managed by an incorporated board of trustees. Denominational groups also established their own schools, some of which attained high distinction, as for example, David Caldwell's "log college" near Greensboro; James Hall's Clio's Nursery and Science Hall, in Iredell County; Samuel E. McCorkle's Zion Parnassus, near Salisbury; James Tate's Academy, at Wilmington; Crowfield Academy, near Charlotte; and Queen's Museum or Liberty Hall Academy, near Charlotte, to list a few of those established before the Revolution. And after 1790 these schools became very numerous.

The interest and activities of the graduates of the University in such schools as these and in educational work generally in the state from its early days form a significant part of the record of the close relation of the institution to and its concern for education in North Carolina. The story of that interest and these activities has been told by Charles L. Coon,[11] but its significance may here be briefly indicated. From 1801, when Andrew Flinn, of Mecklenburg County, a graduate of the class of 1799, and classmate of Archibald D. Murphey, became principal of the Hillsboro Academy, the sponsors of which included trustees and other friends of the University, graduates or former students of this institution very properly continued to go into the academies and schools and colleges of this state to advance learning and the cause of education. The names of these graduates of the University who engaged in educational work are numerous even for the early days, and many of them are distinguished in the history of education in this state. Besides Flinn, who also served as head of the Fayetteville Academy, and who seems to have been

11. *North Carolina Schools and Academies—1790-1840* (Publications of North Carolina Historical Commission, Raleigh, Edwards and Broughton Printing Company, 1915), pp. v-ix.

the first of these University alumni to go into teaching, there were Chesley Daniel and William Hall, both of Halifax County, of the class of 1803; Bartlett Yancey, of Caswell County, class of 1809 and one of the most eminent men of his time, who was assistant principal of Caswell Academy where he taught "the English language gramatically"—a practice some people should welcome in the schools nowadays; William C. Love, of Orange County, class of 1806, in Springfield Academy, in Caswell County; Richard Henderson, in Hillsboro Academy; John B. Bobbitt, principal of Westrayville Academy, in Nash County; William Crawford, principal of Warrenton Academy; Murdock McLean, Laurel Hill Academy, in Robeson County; Robert Hall, Tarboro Academy; Andrew Rhea, Williamsboro Academy, and many others.

These young men who went out from Chapel Hill seem to have been highly regarded as teachers everywhere they went. The influence of the University upon the schools in the state, through its graduates, and the high respect in which its graduates were held as teachers may be seen by the advertisements of these schools and academies and the editorials on them in the press of the period. Frequently the trustees and sponsors of these schools proudly announced that their teacher or principal was a University man, or said: "A graduate of the University of North Carolina"; "students will be prepared for any grade of the University"; "a graduate of our own University"; "the different branches of education as established by the Faculty of the University of this State will be adopted in this institution"; "this school is strictly preparatory to the University"; "students may here be prepared for the Freshman or Sophomore class in the University"; "the plan of education is calculated to prepare young men for the University"; "the sessions and vacations of the school will be regulated for the present, by those of the University of North Carolina"; and numerous similar expressions of confidence which the schools of the state had in the University.

President Joseph Caldwell seems to have kept in close touch with these schools, and his visit to the Raleigh Academy in 1810 to see "some of the most material parts of the Examinations" was reported in the *Raleigh Register*. And the Hillsboro Academy was such "an uncommonly good classical school" that President Caldwell induced it to become "preparatory" to the University and to permit the faculty of the University to participate in the academy's periodic examinations. In 1823 it was announced that by this means "fifteen young gentlemen were approved on the studies preparatory to the Freshman class, and six for the Sophomore." In 1834 the trustees of Warrenton Academy announced that they had engaged Solomon Lea, of the class of 1833, of Caswell County, as principal, and said: "In his talents and all the qualifications required in a good teacher they have entire confidence. To those unacquainted, it will be sufficient to know that he graduated from Chapel Hill, and is recommended by the Faculty of that celebrated school." More than two decades earlier an editorial in the *Raleigh Star*,[12] referring to Westrayville Academy in Nash County, had said: "Of the merits of the Institution we know nothing. No small recommendation of its Teacher is that he is a graduate of the University of North Carolina. We cannot therefore doubt his fitness for his vocation."

The First Summer School

The important place of the teacher in the state and the obligation of the University to prepare teachers were early recognized by the institution. Interest in this activity had been expressed by Murphey and Caldwell, and was later emphasized by the presidents and other members of the faculty down to the present. But the first systematic effort at teacher-education by the University was made in 1877.

Largely through the interests and the influence of President Battle and the faculty and of Governor Zeb Vance and other alumni of the University, and on their recommendation, the legislature of that year authorized the State Board of Education to establish at Chapel Hill a summer school for the training of young white men for teaching in the schools of the state, and made an appropriation of $2,000 a year for two years for its support. A like sum was appropriated by the same legislature for the training of Negro teachers at other places in the state. Dr. Barnas

12. January 3, 1811.

Sears, of the Peabody Fund, made a grant of $500 to provide for those teachers who were unable to pay their own expenses. Of the significance of the plans for this first summer school to be established in a college or university in the United States, Governor Vance said: "With such a project we can electrify the state from Cherokee to Currituck." President Battle said in his report to the trustees that the results of the summer school would be "of lasting benefit to the cause of education in the state."

This novel but significant effort of the University to lead the way in the education of teachers in those dismal and discouraging days that followed the reopening of the institution, attracted considerable attention and made quite an impression on leading educational workers in the state, some of whom visited the school and participated in its exercises. Many things and many men seem to have contributed "to its splendid success," wrote Dr. Sears, in congratulation to President Battle August 18, 1877, "but I know enough of such matters to know that he who has had the marshalling of all the forces has been the chief agent. I feel obliged to you for the wisdom, energy and great labor on your part, which has made the whole movement so auspicious."

The organization and direction of this pioneer summer session were in charge of President Battle and State Superintendent of Public Instruction John C. Scarborough, a graduate of Wake Forest College, "who always worked in entire harmony." Competent people, "whether residents of North Carolina or elsewhere" were engaged to conduct the work and give the lectures; and Battle records that: "Prominent inhabitants of Chapel Hill, not connected with the schools, attended regularly these lectures."[13]

Although the act establishing the school provided that the benefits of the appropriation should be extended only to men, the University and the State Board of Education took the position that women should be allowed to attend the sessions, and some of the money appropriated by the Peabody Fund was used for that purpose. The restriction against women was fortunately later removed when the legislative appropriation was renewed, an action which President Battle considered very happy: "Of course

13. *Op. cit.,* II, 143.

among so many young people gathered together in the beautiful campus, there was some love making, but never a scandal or harsh criticism. Some happy marriages owe their beginning to the social attraction of the University of North Carolina Summer School."[14] And Dr. Battle added that among those happy unions "the eminent Father of higher female education by the state, Dr. Charles D. McIver, gained his life partner here." Who is to say, then, that but for the first university summer school in America our sister at Greensboro might not have been born in 1893?

Wide interest and even enthusiasm were created by this significant effort of President Battle and the Faculty of the University sixty-eight years ago, in co-operation with the State Board of Education and other educational leaders in the state, to improve the teachers and teaching in the public schools. It appears also that the undertaking stimulated imitation by the University of Virginia, the University of South Carolina, and the University of Mississippi, and perhaps other institutions, and Dr. Battle said that it was the fountain and source of many graded schools. Dr. Barnas Sears wrote President Battle a second letter, September 10, 1877, in which he said: "The University men are to throw their light on all the lower schools, and these in turn are to be feeders of the higher. . . . You are now doing a great thing for the State."

Major Robert Bingham, an honor graduate of the class of 1857, whose reputation as a teacher has probably never been excelled by a graduate of this institution, said in a public address that "The establishment of the Normal School was the greatest event in the history of North Carolina of the past one hundred years. Its successes are more direct and effect the future of the state more than any event that has occurred or is likely to occur.

"Again, this state is the first to connect the Normal School with her University, and put it under the control of the same. In this the state has done wisely. President Battle has done more for North Carolina in his efforts for education than any other man in the state. This is the first time in the annals of the state that females have enjoyed the benefits of the public money. . . . It will be a sad day in the state when the sun of the Normal School shines for the last time on the University Campus."

14. *Ibid.*, p. 148.

During the life of this first summer school established on the campus of an American university or college, the total enrollments were 2,480, almost equally divided between men and women, from most of the counties of the state. This novel effort of the University became the inspiration of that movement in the latter part of the past and the early part of the present century which awakened North Carolina to a consciousness of the need for better teachers and teaching in the schools—those energetic educational campaigns under Alderman, McIver, Noble, Alexander Graham, and others in the 1880's and 1890's which led in the early part of this century to the educational awakening under Governor Aycock and Superintendent Joyner.

The summer school was discontinued in 1884, but was revived in 1894 and continued for eleven years, when it was again suspended. During this period it enrolled 1,541. It was revived again in 1907 and has had a continuous existence to the present. Closely connected with the work of the summer school and the School and Department of Education have been the numerous activities of the University Extension Division organized in 1912-13, under the direction of Dr. L. R. Wilson. Many of the activities of this Division of the University have been in the field of teacher-education in which the School and Department of Education have co-operated.

Following the suspension of the school in 1884 announcement was made that the courses of study would be rearranged and strengthened and that "a thoroughly equipped course of Normal Instruction for the training of teachers will offer all the advantages of a permanent Normal School." The instruction, "both theoretical and practice in teaching," was to begin in September of that year. In 1885 Nelson B. Henry, of Missouri, became professor of the Science and Art of Teaching, among the first chairs established in this subject in American universities, and apparently the first in the South.[15] As early as the academic year 1885-1886 this work was called "The School of Normal Instruction." It appears that it was discontinued in 1887-1888

15. Other chairs or professorships in this field included those at Brown University, the State University of Iowa, the University of Michigan, the University of Wisconsin, the University of Missouri, and New York University.

when the legislative appropriation was withdrawn. The catalogue of the next year noted: "Special courses, adapted to teachers, are offered in each department of study, beginning each
year about February 15 and continuing three months. No entrance or other examination will be required. There are no
charges for tuition."

This arrangement seems to have continued until 1893 when
Edwin A. Alderman, of the class of 1882, became professor of the
history and philosophy of education, a post in which he served
with distinction until 1896 when he became president of the
University. In 1898, Marcus Cicero Stephens Noble, of the class
of 1879, who had taught in the famous Bingham School and had
served as the first superintendent of the public schools of Wilmington from 1882 to 1898, became professor of pedagogy in
the University; and when the School of Education was organized
in 1912, Professor Noble became its dean, a post which he held
until 1934 when he retired from active administrative duties.
Professor N. W. Walker, of the class of 1903, who came to the
University in 1907 as professor of secondary education and the
first state inspector of high schools, served as acting-dean of the
School of Education from 1921 to 1935. Professor Walker
served also as Director of the Summer Session from 1909 to
1934, when ill health forced him to give up the work. Under
consolidation of the University, State College, and the Woman's
College in 1934, the School of Education at Chapel Hill became
a Department in the College of Arts and Sciences.

Leaders of the University have applauded the function of
good teaching in the life of the state and have held that immortality for a teacher is gained only when he blossoms in the lives
and works of others. This view of the teacher and of teaching
has often been expressed by its presidents and other leaders in
the University's household. Caldwell, Swain, and Battle expressed their pride in the quality of the teachers who went out
from Chapel Hill into the academies and other educational institutions, and so also have their successors. President Winston
believed that the leadership and success of the University in the
educational life of the state, and not the least of its glory, were
due primarily to its standards of thoroughness and excellence,

the "high requirements of scholarship," which the University maintained and demanded in its work, which he said elevated "the teaching standard throughout the State." This he said was accomplished mainly "by the election of well qualified and competent professors for all the chairs of instruction." The great work of the new University in the education of teachers in those days placed emphasis upon general education, Dr. Winston said, "to fit men for technical and professional education by broad and generous education; to hammer iron into steel before fashioning it into tools."

President Alderman, with an eloquence unmatched in the educational history of this state, glorified the office of the teacher, and never ceased to acknowledge his own debt to Edward P. Moses and to pay tribute to the influence of that effective educational leader who did blossom in the life and work of Alderman and of many other leaders in education in this state, who in turn touched the lives and works of others. Alderman described Moses as "a flaming mass of enthusiasm, unselfishness, intelligence, and progress. I personally would never have become a teacher, but for his example," Alderman wrote near the end of a long life of usefulness. "The spectacle of that man on fire with interest, skillful and devoted, captured my youthful imagination." President Kemp P. Battle's faith in the teacher's place in the life of the state was known by his works generally but was especially revealed in his presentation of Alderman to be inducted as president of the University in 1897. His address then was more than a tribute to an educational leader who saw in teaching one of the highest human activities; it exhibited also Dr. Battle's own faith in the power of sound teaching in this or any other American commonwealth and the continuing need for teachers and managers in our schools of high intellectual qualities, and cultivated minds and manners.

President Venable also highly magnified the place of good teaching in the life of this state, and in an address before the Summer Session here June 21, 1911,[16] on "The Mission of the Teacher," this chemist of international eminence brought encouragement to those who then were going about the villages and rural places of the state teaching.

16. *North Carolina High School Bulletin*, II (1911), 101-9.

Few if any leaders in the University have had higher esteem for good teaching than Edward K. Graham, who exhibited in his own teaching admiration for good workmanship, and inspired among his students the desire for thoroughness and for personal excellence, an ideal of teaching to which we may need nowadays to return. Nowhere is his philosophy of teaching better set out than in an address made at the Summer School here in 1917 on "The War-Time Duty of Teachers,"[17] in which he tried to make clear that the function of teaching does not change with the wind or with every wind of pedagogical doctrine, and that in emergencies, whether military or economic, teachers should keep their eyes on their main business and do better what they are expected to do anyway. Then, as they were to be in the Great Depression and again in the Second World War, teachers in this state and elsewhere in this country were confused by the extraordinary demands upon them. Then, as too often in times of peace and comparative quietude, teachers were inclined to feel "negligible and of no account" to themselves or others, as being amiable old gentlemen or ladies engaged in conducting prayer-meetings "while lynching parties were in full swing" just around the corner. This great teacher reached out a steadying hand to the teachers and raised and answered a question which every institution that assumes responsibility for the education of teachers, every teacher of teachers, and every State Department of Education that certificates teachers, must face up to in manly manner or eventually admit delinquency and defeat:

". . . Whatever the social demands of service by the teacher to the community in times of peace or war, and the confusions that these obligations make, one fundamental fact stands out white and clear as the source of all our real and permanent worth as a profession: the teacher is not a gardener, nor a canner, nor a Red Cross nurse, nor a sanitary officer. The teacher, as a guide of life and a productive force in wholesome growth, is a student, and a man or woman of thought. His leadership comes from a belief in life based upon a passion for the intelligent way of doing things. His faith is in the controlling power of the mind to find the best path in the confusions that beset men, and its superiority

17. *Ibid.*, VIII (1917), 115-21.

in contrast to every other power. Under this standard as a teacher he renders his great service, and under it he is the priest and prophet of his world, whether it is bounded by the limits of a little school district or the confines of the nation." The teacher, he said, should be "the community's student and representative man of thought. . . ." Teaching was his principal primary occupation, "under any and all circumstances," and no extraneous conditions could minimize in civilized society the primary importance of the teacher's teaching, "the bread of life and the water of life to men." As spokesman of and for the University of North Carolina, President Graham emphasized the fact that "the source of any authority a teacher has is in his mastery of the content of the knowledge he professes" and ability to communicate it to others; that the teacher's "real and fruitful source of a sound content and sound method is a quick and eager interest in ideas, a clean, tireless curiosity that amounts to enthusiasm for understanding not only the structure of the world about him, but for its sources and ends and aims and for the development of human excellence in all its forms. . . . The trumpet that calls across the world for men to rise to higher and completer and more heroic service calls to none with such a depth of need as to the teacher in whose care is the very ark of the covenant of life." Successful response to the summons for leadership to the teachers of North Carolina and to the institutions that sent them into the schools of the state, "will not be through any divine right of our profession to lead, but through the mastery of the content of the knowledge we profess; through our insight and vision in applying it to the life around us, and through the authority of the personality we develop through which we speak louder than everything we can say."

And this brilliant teacher had a perspective for the teachers of this state as an organized and united body for educational leadership which we today could well examine and with immense benefit to our profession try to gain. "The Teachers' Assembly," he had said in an address before that body in 1909, "should be the most intellectual gathering that presents itself to the consideration of the State; it should be the one most practically patriotic; it should be most keenly stirred by educational problems, and although divided into whatever pedagogical factions you please, it should be profoundly united and inspired by a sense of service to the immediate needs of the State. But you will share with me perhaps the doubt that we are as keenly stirred by professional problems as the State Medical Association is; that we are as confidently intellectual as the State Bar Association; that we have the 'class consciousness', the professional self-confidence and self-respect of either of these. . . ."

President Chase and President Frank P. Graham both saw the obligation of the University to emphasize and to set examples in excellence of teaching. In his inaugural President Chase declared that those whom the University sends out into the schools must not only know their subjects and how to teach them, "but they must go out quick in the faith that the future of democracy is in their hands; that day by day they are laying the very foundation-stones of the new Southern civilization." President Frank P. Graham sees in research also a powerfully sustaining resource of the teacher in the classroom, and gave emphasis to this resource in his report for 1932-33, when he wrote of the "sense of reverent humility in him who has to dig in the sources of his own facts and ideas" and of the "contagious enthusiasm" that is gained by students from the "teacher who comes fresh from the mine bringing the ore in the hands that dug it out. . . ."

Few if any alumni or members of the faculty have ever been more deeply interested in good teaching in the schools or worked more diligently to advance their cause than the late Professors M. C. S. Noble, of the class of 1879, and N. W. Walker, of the class of 1903. Good teachers themselves, they exalted the office of the teacher and saw in teaching one of the most satisfying and rewarding of all human activities. Their annual reports constantly emphasized the importance of good teaching in the life of this state and the obligation of the University of North Carolina to prepare good teachers for the schools.

As State Inspector of High Schools from 1907 to 1919, Professor Walker blazed new trails in a commonwealth that had to be taught that secondary education was a legitimate function of the state. As professor of secondary education here from 1907 until his death in 1936, as acting-dean of the School of

Education for many years, and as leader in the North Carolina College Conference, Mr. Walker was always intelligently energetic in efforts to raise the level of the educational life of his native state. No son of the University ever rendered public secondary education in this state a greater and more lasting service.

The place which Professor Noble made in the educational life of the state was best expressed by a memorial sketch prepared by a committee of the faculty and adopted by that body following Dr. Noble's death in 1942, at the age of eighty-seven:

"If North Carolina is today in the vanguard of progressive states, and if the University of North Carolina is regarded as a leader among the State supported institutions of the nation, Marcus Cicero Stephens Noble was in some measure responsible. . . . For 63 years he was a teacher. He believed that to teach, to inspire, to be a companion with, the young led a man to the full enjoyment of one of the most rewarding professions in the world. . . ."

In his report for 1909, Professor Noble called attention, as he had done for a decade, to the steadily growing need for better teachers in the public schools, and said that it was the obligation of the University, as head of the public school system of North Carolina to meet that need more effectively; that many young men of ability were eager to go into public educational service and they should have ample opportunity for broadening their scholarship and their general preparation for this work; and he proudly pointed to the fact that the University was then sending "practically half of her graduates to service in the field of educational endeavor, as many as it sends into all the other professions combined." Impressive also was the report of Professor Walker for that year in which he showed the continued close co-operation between the University and the State Department of Education, under the enlightened leadership of State Superintendent J. Y. Joyner, in the interest of better schools and their teachers.

III. THE UNIVERSITY'S MANLY STANDS FOR THE SCHOOLS

That the University of North Carolina has taken manly stands in crises that threatened the cause of public education is also a matter of a record which shows how members and friends of the University family united under its leadership for the protection of the schools and itself. Some of these crises are clear in the record, while others can be judiciously reported perhaps only after the passing of many years.

The period of the 1890's was marked in North Carolina by intense feelings and even bitterness over the "crisis of conflicts in higher education." The fight on the University by the major denominational colleges, whose leaders appeared to be advocating fuller legislative aid for the public schools and a decrease of appropriations to the University, reached its highest intensity in those years. That fight, which had long been developing, is one of the most extraordinary chapters in the history of education in this or any other state, but North Carolina did not have a monopoly on such conflicts, which appeared in other states as well if not always so violent as here. And in it members of the family of the University stood up for the public schools while defending also the rights of the University, and taking the position that both were integral parts of the public educational system of the state. The story of this conflict has been well told by Dr. Luther L. Gobbel,[18] President of Greensboro College, and attempts to repeat it in detail here are unnecessary.

One of the crises that serve to show how closely the interests and fortunes of public education in this state have all along been joined with those of the University, was met during the administration of President Winston. An unholy alliance sought in the early 1890's actually to cripple the University by preventing legislative appropriations for its support, but under the guise of trying to help the public schools. Among the charges against the institution was its alleged competition with the private or denominational colleges of the state, particularly Davidson, Trinity, and Wake Forest, which united in the attack under the leadership of President John B. Shearer, of Davidson. The success of the attack would have retarded the public schools as well as the University. A bill, introduced into the legislature to "unify

18. *Church-State Relations in Education in North Carolina Since 1776,* Durham, N. C., Duke University Press, 1938.

the higher education in the State and to elevate the University to the Apex of all education in the State," was in reality designed to reduce the institution at Chapel Hill. The main issue was whether higher education should be included in the state's public educational system. If it had passed the effect would have been the weakening of the University and of the public school system of which the University was the recognized head.

In that bitter contest, President Winston led the counterattack. His work in the Summer School for teachers, his presidency of the State Teachers' Association, and his long and close relations with the educational workers of North Carolina had given him an understanding of and sympathy for the public schools that made him an energetic advocate of their cause and of education generally in the state. His arguments against the bitter attacks on the University, prepared for the information of the General Assembly of 1893, should have left no doubt as to the close relation of the University and the public schools. "In obedience to the mandate of the Constitution," he wrote, "the University was established one hundred years ago. It is not a separate isolated institution, but belongs to the State system of public institutions. . . ." He also said: "All the forces and influences of the University have been constantly exerted and are now at work to increase the public school system." And he asked whether the idea of public education in the state could be promoted "by striking down the head of the system of education?" He pointed out that the University was annually supplying the state "with a large number of teachers for both public and private schools, and is now maintaining a special department for the training of teachers and a summer school for the better training of those who are already teaching and are unable to attend the regular sessions." The annual appropriation to the University at the time was $20,000 regular and $10,000 special, a total of $30,000. This entire aid to the University by the state cost the average taxpayer less than four cents, Dr. Winston noted. At that time more than twenty per cent of the students in the University were teachers or preparing to teach, President Winston also reported.

In addition to these sobered arguments of fact, President Winston resorted to the old and effective weapon of ridicule and satire. The bill to make the University the apex of all education in the state seems to have led some people to misunderstand the meaning of "apex" and to conclude that it was a scheme to move the institution to the village of Apex, a near neighbor of the village of Cary, in Wake County. Winston wrote and had published in *The News and Observer* a letter pretending to be from a citizen of Cary, which represented the advantages of that community as the proper seat of the University. The letter, dated February 13, 1893, and signed "Cary," bore the caption "Shall the University go to Apex?" and was as follows:

If you are in favor of moving the University to Apex, you will lose friends in Cary. If the University is coming to Wake County, the place for it is Cary. Raleigh has too many institutions now. The State ought to stop building up Raleigh at the expense of other towns. The only fair and equitable plan is for the University to move around the State, not staying in one place longer than three or four years. This would help all towns alike. Mr. Editor, I have been a staunch friend of yours for many years, but if you try to draw on the treasury to push Apex ahead of Cary, I am done with you. I understand that a bill in the legislature provides fifty thousand dollars to move it to Apex. We will move it to Cary for half that much.

The president of a prominent denominational college and the president of the University of North Carolina[19] exchanged letters in *The News and Observer* March 2 and 3, 1917. Dr. Vann asked in a lengthy letter some specific questions on the attitude of the authorities of the higher educational institutions of the state toward "the Christian colleges," and whether the state institutions were antagonizing the denominational schools; whether there was prejudice or discrimination against the denominational schools on the part of the agents and friends of the state institutions; and, by implication at least, whether the state was not expending extravagant sums on its higher educational institutions in comparison with its expenditures on the public schools. Dr. Vann also charged that the superintendents of schools educated at Chapel Hill were using "their utmost endeavors to turn every

19. President R. T. Vann, of Meredith College, Raleigh, and President Edward K. Graham.

student away from the denominational colleges to those of the State," and he also said that "a number of our high school men say they are actually afraid to have a certain one of the University officials visit their institutions at all because they fear he would seek to turn their pupils to State institutions."

President Graham who, on account of bad weather and worse roads, was unable to get to Raleigh on the afternoon of March 2 to appear before the legislative committee, dictated over the telephone a reply to Dr. Vann which was transcribed in the office of an alumnus and trustee of the University in Raleigh. It was an open letter to Dr. Vann who, failing to impress the legislative committee by his speech that afternoon, very fairly and appropriately asked that President Graham's letter be published in *The News and Observer* and it was published March 3. In his brief reply to this attack on the University and the attempt to play it up against the public schools, President Graham said: "For myself I make answer that no act, attitude or feeling of mine has been other than genuine and deeply sympathetic toward the denominational schools and colleges. My whole creed and practice is that we are all at work on the same problem, and that no success in the field of education in North Carolina genuinely won can work anything other than good for every other worker in that field. I can say to you without reservation that every forward step made by any institution, from the elementary school to the college—private, denominational or public— gives me as deep a pleasure as if it were made by the one with which I chance to be associated."

More spectacular and dramatic than the attack on the University and the proposal to "move it to Apex" during the administration of President Winston or the conflict in 1917 was the crisis that threatened public education in this state in the 1920's, particularly during the legislative sessions of 1925 and 1927. In those days war clouds gathered and shock troops of the fundamentalists sought the committee rooms and the floors of the legislature to force that body to decide whether man descended from monkey or was made from mud. This frantic effort to restrict freedom of teaching in the schools of North Carolina was stopped dead in its tracks, however, by the University family, alumni, trustees, and other friends of freedom of teaching and thought in this state. All of the inside story of this fight is not a matter of authentic record, and some evidence that may be competent, if unwritten, even the most judicious historian could not well and wisely report, perhaps. Not all the University family was solidly on the same side. But it is known that an alumnus broke a tied vote in the House Committee on Education that retarded the menacing movement; that the President of the University joined forces with the President of Wake Forest College, a distinguished scientist and honorary alumnus of the class of 1906, and both stood up in Raleigh in behalf of the schools; and meantime another alumnus, later to be President of the University, while studying in England had prepared and sent to the press of North Carolina, a careful statement on "Evolution, the University, and the People," that had much to do with the outcome of that fight. In that statement he appealed to the people of North Carolina to resist "the false fear of truth and the foes of freedom" and to fight against bigotry and ancient tyranny in its latest form. "Freedom to think, freedom to speak, and freedom to print are the texture of our University standards," he asserted. Legislative appropriations may temporarily come down, he said, but never the motto of the University of North Carolina.

The impressive "Committee of One Hundred" was formed in the state, later to change its name to "The North Carolina Bible League." The Anti-Evolution League and Bible Crusaders of America rushed to the state to outlaw the theory of evolution and to place on the statute books of North Carolina legislation which would cripple and suffocate the public school system, from the first grade through the University. But discord appeared in one of the early meetings of the Committee of One Hundred, when ordained ministers lost their tempers in a fiery session which exhibited willingness and readiness to shed blood in opposition to teaching in tax-supported schools any theories which clashed with the Mosaic explanation of creation.

When this warfare was raging in the state, North Carolina was doing less than any of its forty-seven sisters for public libraries. Many of its teachers did not have a standard high school education; hundreds of them had never heard of Darwin; more than

300,000 of the children of North Carolina had only six months' schooling a year; half of the farm workers of the state still toiled in tenancy; and almost a hundred thousand native white men and women were cursed by sheer illiteracy and its suffocating loneliness, unable to read a single word of *Origin of Species* or of the Book which the Carolina Crusaders would protect from Darwinian attacks. Between 1921 and 1929 thirty-seven bills similar to the bill introduced into the legislature of North Carolina in 1925 were introduced into a score of American state legislatures. Most of these anti-evolution bills failed as in this state and in Minnesota, but many teachers were dismissed for holding certain scientific views, and loud were the rumblings of the conflict "in the corridors of American public schools." It was in this fateful hour that the University of North Carolina, through its faculty, alumni, and friends, stepped in to protect the public schools.

IV. BUILDING THE PUBLIC EDUCATIONAL STRUCTURE

It is clear that, all along, the University has considered itself and its fortunes inseparably connected with the schools about it, has recognized its obligation to prepare teachers and has emphasized the importance of good teaching, and has stood by the schools in manly manner when these were faced with crises that threatened their progress and usefulness. It is a matter of proud record also that members of the University family have been the chief architects and builders of the public educational structure of the state.

The period from 1825 to 1860 in North Carolina was marked by increased interest in the economic, political, social, and educational development of the state by a small group of men among whose leaders were many alumni and other members of the University family. Two sons of the University stand out conspicuously as distinguished leaders in building the structure for public education in the ante-bellum period,—Archibald D. Murphey, of the class of 1799, and Calvin H. Wiley, of the class of 1840. Efforts for educational reform had been stimulated by the able papers and plans of Archibald D. Murphey in 1816 and 1817; and in 1825 one part of Murphey's elaborate educational plan of

1817 was provided by act of legislation. This was for a permanent public school endowment, known as the Literary Fund. The author of the law was Bartlett Yancey, of the class of 1809 and a former student of law under Murphey. The fund became the basis of state aid for public schools prior to 1860 and greatly stimulated local educational taxation in the counties of the state. Immediately preceding Commencement at the University six years later, alumni, trustees, members of the faculty and other friends of education organized in Chapel Hill the North Carolina Institute of Education, the purpose of which was "to diffuse knowledge on the subject of public education, and by every proper means to improve the condition of common schools and other literary institutions in our State."[20] Although the organization had a short life, apparently holding meetings only in 1832 and 1833, it nevertheless stimulated wide interest in the movement for public schools that led in 1839 to the enactment of the state's initial public school law. And in 1832 Joseph Caldwell, first president of the University, published his well-known letters on public education, referred to above, which had wide influence on public discussion that culminated in the legislation which became the basis of the state's public educational system prior to the Civil War.

Murphey had been prepared for college in David Caldwell's famous school in Guilford County, and was graduated from the University of North Carolina in 1799 "with the highest distinction." William A. Graham, of the class of 1824, in an article in the *North Carolina University Magazine*,[21] wrote of Murphey's ability to write "like Goldsmith, and with an ease and rapidity that Goldsmith could not have equalled. . . ." Murphey served as professor of languages in the University, being appointed immediately upon his graduation, and was admitted to the bar in 1802. It is the testimony of all Murphey's students and of his contemporaries and historians, that he was one of the most distinguished characters in North Carolina, with extraordinary attributes of the statesman and philosopher, a man who excelled "all his contemporaries in the State," and in the application of his mind to problems of North Carolina "he had few equals or sec-

20. *Raleigh Register*, July 7, 1831.
21. X (1860-61), 1-12.

onds." He was distinguished as an advocate at the bar, a jurist on the bench, a farseeing "legislator of comprehensive intelligence, enterprise and patriotism, a literary man of classic taste, attainments and style in composition." His fame has been "a source of just pride to his friends and his country."

Murphey represented Orange County in the state Senate from 1812 to 1818, and to him perhaps more than to any other was due the effort to inaugurate a new and advanced period in the public policy of the state. His influence in the counsels of North Carolina was probably wider than that of any other citizen. He brought to legislative consideration an "energetic spirit of patriotism," had the most comprehensive view of the needs of North Carolina, and proposed bolder and more intelligent measures for the improvement and advancement of the state than any other man of his generation. Graham said that whether the failure promptly to realize some of his proposed measures was due to "error in their conception or timidity in his contemporaries to meet and boldly sustain them, the historian must pronounce that his reports and other writings in regard to them are the noblest monuments of philosophic statesmanship to be found in our public archives since the days of our Revolution."

His vision and labors for internal improvements, which would have done credit to DeWitt Clinton of New York to whom he has been compared, his interest in improving the means of transportation, in the development of cities with a view to making North Carolina commercially independent of other states, and his vision for a system of education from the primary schools through secondary schools and the University, are unexcelled in the social history of the United States. Other enterprises in which he was greatly interested included an institution for the deaf and dumb, and the writing and publication of a comprehensive history of his state. Of the proposed history Murphey wrote in 1821: "We want such a work. We neither know ourselves nor are we known to others. Such a work, well executed, would add very much to our standing in the Union, and make our State respectable in our own eyes."[22]

22. William Henry Hoyt (ed.), *The Papers of Archibald D. Murphey* (Raleigh, E. M. Uzzell and Company, 1914. Publications of the North Carolina Historical Commission), I, 211.

Of the University in 1817, "in a state of extreme depression," he said: "When the pride of the State is awakening and an honorable ambition is cherished for her glory, an appeal is made to the patriotism and generous feelings of the Legislature in favor of an institution, which in all civilized nations has been regarded as the nursery of moral greatness and the palladium of civil liberty." He said that a people who cultivate science and the arts with greatest success excel other people. "It is due to North Carolina, it is due to the great men who first proposed the foundation of the University, to foster it with parental fondness, and to give to it an importance commensurate with the high destinies of the State." Murphey conceived of the University as the proper place of leadership in North Carolina. His services to his state properly give him the name of the "father of public schools," "father of internal improvements" of North Carolina, "the first native historian" of the state, and "the projector of the first geological work done under government auspices in America."[23] His plan for a public school system ranks very high among the best proposals ever made for a state system of education in this country. The report, in which Murphey thoroughly elaborated his theory of education by and for the state, appears in full in Charles L. Coon's *The Beginnings of Public Education in North Carolina: A Documentary History, 1790-1840*[24] and has been treated in many places by historians and other writers on education in North Carolina.[25] Murphey's work was the subject of lengthy discussion in *The North American Review*, January, 1821,[26] when that magazine was under the editorship of Edward Everett. The writer of the article said that the documents of Murphey "prove that the legislature of North Carolina has engaged in the noble undertaking of internal improvement with an enlargement of plan, and a firmness of purpose not surpassed by any other state. Nor has everything evaporated in deliberations and

23. *Ibid.*, I, ii.
24. I, 123-45.
25. See Edgar W. Knight, *Public School Education in North Carolina.* Boston, Houghton Mifflin Company, 1916; M. C. S. Noble, *A History of the Public Schools of North Carolina.* Chapel Hill, The University of North Carolina Press, 1930.
26. III, No. II, New Series.

schemes. In the proceedings thus far, we discover much wisdom in projecting, and much energy in acting."[27] The article also said: "While on the subject of North Carolina, we cannot resist the inclination which we feel to bring forward one or two other particulars which exhibit the present condition and future prospects of this state in a most favorable light. In an ardent and increasing zeal for the establishment of schools and academies for several years past, we do not believe it has been outdone by a single state."

Another son of the University who took high place in educational leadership of the state before 1860 was Calvin H. Wiley, who became the first state superintendent of schools in North Carolina. Born in Guilford County in 1819, prepared for college at Dr. David Caldwell's "log college" near Greensboro, Wiley was graduated from the University in 1840, later studied law, was admitted to the bar, and located at Oxford for the practice of his profession. He was interested also in journalism and for a time edited the *Oxford Mercury* and later the *Southern Weekly Post*, a paper published at Raleigh and devoted to civic, educational, and industrial improvement. He became a member of the legislature in 1850, and there devoted his energies to educational interests. Chief among these was legislation which provided for the establishment of the state superintendency of the public schools which had been established in 1839. The bill creating this office was enacted into law December 4, 1852, chiefly through his leadership, and he was appointed to the position by the Legislature. He took office January 1, 1853.

This alumnus of the University of North Carolina, who had many qualities in common and compared favorably with the most eminent American educational leaders of his generation, continued in that office until 1866. One of the interesting facts in connection with his long and distinguished service in behalf of public education and the proper education of teachers for the state is that although a Whig, Wiley was appointed or elected to the office by a Democratic legislature and continued to be so

27. *Ibid.*, p. 21. As matters turned out, this report of Everett or the writer of the article was too optimistic, of course. Murphey's plans for his state were too advanced for his time.

appointed until the office was abolished in 1866. In addition to his co-operation with Dr. Craven at Normal College for the improvement of teaching in the state, Wiley urged the formation of library associations for improving the professional qualifications of teachers; formed an educational association of North Carolina; established *The North Carolina Journal of Education;* labored consistently for a complete reorganization and improvement of the educational forces of the state; lectured in every county to arouse interest in the cause of popular education, and advised neighboring states concerning the educational work of North Carolina which, at the close of the ante-bellum period, was "attracting the favorable attention of the States south, west and north of us. . . ." This spiritual and educational successor to Caldwell and Murphey served his state as chief state school officer longer than it has ever been served by another superintendent of North Carolina except Dr. James Y. Joyner, of the class of 1881.

The contributions of Wiley to the educational development of the state are matters of record. His reports of educational conditions in the state during his superintendency are among the best of the official accounts made by chief state school officers in this country prior to 1860. He used those reports not only to provide information about the schools and their progress, but to point out their weaknesses and to suggest reforms, and also to create and direct public opinion on educational matters, especially on the subject of universal and free public schools. His philosophy of education was simple: that public education is the only sure and safe foundation in a democratic society and that "a system of common schools for a great and growing state is a vast and sublime moral organization." Wiley believed that education should be universal and free and open to all, rich and poor alike, and at the close of the war he was very decided in his advocacy of the education of the freedmen.

The last quarter of the past century was a difficult period for public education in North Carolina and the other Southern States. Economic, political, and racial conditions, whose roots reached back to the war and Congressional Reconstruction, retarded educational progress. Until these conditions were improved around the turn of the century, opportunities for substantial public educational leadership were heavily restricted. Dr. J. Y. Joyner was the first state superintendent of public instruction in North Carolina after the war who had a fair chance for such leadership, although two other superintendents before Joyner's administration had served the cause of education as well as conditions would permit. These were John C. Scarborough, a graduate of Wake Forest, who served from 1877 to 1885 and again from 1893 to 1897, and Charles H. Mebane, who served from 1897 to 1901. Notwithstanding the difficult conditions under which these two men served, their real contributions to public education have not been properly acknowledged by writers on education in North Carolina.

The member of the University family who, since the Civil War, has made the most distinguished contribution to the structure of the public educational system of the state is James Y. Joyner, class of 1881, who served as state superintendent of public instruction from 1902 to 1919. Under his leadership the principle of equality of educational opportunity came to be recognized and accepted as did also the duty of the state to protect children through compulsory-attendance legislation. During his administration, public support for schools increased four-fold and their term nearly fifty per cent; there was a ten-fold increase in library facilities; local-taxation districts increased from about 200 to more than 2,000; nearly three hundred state high schools and a score or more of farm-life schools were established; a schoolhouse a day was built every day in the year during a large part of his administration; and the state gained a new perspective of teaching and of professional educational administration.

Dr. Joyner, who was the third Southerner ever to be elevated to the presidency of the National Education Association, saw in his position as state superintendent an opportunity for energetic and wise educational leadership and for strengthening the structure of the public school system and through it to serve the state he loved and to promote its best interests through the advancement of the welfare of children always and everywhere. An indefatigable worker and wise leader, marked by that precious quality of patience, he could fight when he had to do so, but he never entered into warfare merely for the joy of the struggle. For thirty-seven years he served the public educational interests of this state, as county superintendent before he could vote, as chairman of a county board of education, as teacher in and superintendent of public schools, as professor and dean in the Woman's College, and for seventeen years as state superintendent of public instruction, and through that high office was the recognized public educational leader of his state. In the face of discouragement and opposition, Dr. Joyner laid strong and deep the foundations for a better public educational structure of his state.

V. LIBRARIES AND EXTENSION SERVICE

University leaders have been aware, however, that more is needed than the structure and organization of an educational system if it is to function in the lives of those it is set up to serve. Hence, the long and energetic interest of the University in helping to prepare good teachers for the schools of the state, as already noted, and to assist teachers in service through its Extension Division. Energetic has been the interest of members of the University family in enriching the work of the schools through the encouragement of school, public, and college libraries and the stimulation of habits of reading among the people of North Carolina; and distinctive has been the University's leadership in strengthening the library as the great ally and support of the public educational program of the state. Members of the University family were foremost leaders in the organization of the North Carolina Library Association, in the Citizens' Library Movement, and in the campaigns that led the legislature in 1941 to make its first appropriation for state-aid to libraries. This aid in the sum of $100,000 (exactly the amount first appropriated by the legislature in 1899 for public schools) was increased in 1943 to $125,000. Through the libraries thus provided the public educational structure of the state has been strengthened and enabled to do its work more effectively; and through its Extension Division the University now for more than three decades has also sought to strengthen that structure and thus to increase the effectiveness of the schools.

VI. FUTURE RESPONSIBILITIES AND OPPORTUNITIES

It is difficult enough for one to try to reconstruct the history of the educational past in North Carolina, with fairly adequate annals and records. It is more difficult for one to try to appraise the present or recent educational scene here; and it is even perilous for him to assume the role of the prophet and attempt to predict the future of public education in this state. But the relation of the University of North Carolina to public education in the past is a matter of record, in which any state or its university could well have pride. What of conditions during the present and recent period? What of responsibilities and opportunities of the University for public educational leadership in the future? What will the future historian report?

Among other things the future historian will naturally discover that the latter part of the past and the early part of the present century were the days of the public educational pioneers in this state and the South. He will point out that the spirit of pioneers is marked by energy, faith, and spirited resourcefulness. No university ever sent out in such a brief period so many able, inspiring, and effective educational leaders as went out from Chapel Hill in the last decades of the past and the early years of the present century. By their records here and out there they held their own with the leading citizens in the communities whose schools they served as teachers and managers. They were energetic and often apostolic in their zeal for the promotion of public education and for the advancement of learning. Here they had acquired a liberal education rather than mechanical training in pedagogy and as a result exhibited a steadying philosophy that comes only from broad and generous education.

The future historian will look in vain for these qualities in public educational leadership and also among the teachers of teachers in this and the recent period. He will find that public education is not nowadays attracting a healthy quota of the best and most promising young men and women from the colleges and universities. It may seem a hard saying, but the future historian will look in vain in the present and recent period for those lively, courageous, and well educated leaders who in other periods aroused this commonwealth from educational and intellectual lethargy to energetic activity and set this state ablaze in behalf of better schools and better teachers.

What will his explanation be? Of course, he will find that occupational opportunities are more numerous now than then. But he will also find that teacher-educational institutions, including the University of North Carolina, have been somewhat casual in permitting professional education to be divorced in isolation from those other subjects and disciplines which in the past doubtless accounted largely for the quality of teachers and managers of the schools. He will find that the rapid inflation of pedagogical courses has caused the collegiate and university study of education to fall under a heavy cloud of suspicion of other departments and discouraged able and promising young men and women from going into educational work. He will find heavy emphasis upon pedagogical techniques and methods and "tricks of the trade" and perhaps an opportunism and a myopic concern with transient and transitory educational objectives to the neglect of substantial content.

The future historian will have to report also that institutions engaged in mass production in graduate work in education should have seen the danger of creating for themselves an artificial prestige and the lowering of educational standards. He will observe the comparatively little intellectual inconvenience by which graduate degrees were acquired in this comparatively new discipline, and will find that professional education was extending itself in many different and vague directions and weakening itself under the weight of assumed tasks and the promise of offering solutions for all social ills. He will find that teachers of teachers of the present period were trying to make teachers jacks-of-all pedagogical trades, by assuming to increase their functions and to make them at the same time physicians, nurses, oculists, dentists, policemen, experts on taxation, economics, flood control, international and racial relations, politics, soil conservation, and numerous other problems. The future historian will point out that this view of the function of teachers assumes that the schools can work miracles in places where miracles need to be worked indeed, but which teachers should not be required to undertake. And the future historian will point to the danger, which educational leaders of the present should have seen, in the tendency to dump a little of everything in the curricula of teacher-educational institutions, sometimes in superficial manner, through coercion by or courtesy to every wind of passion or prejudice or every pressure group, in the implied promise that teachers can cure all the social distempers of a confused world and remove all the painful conditions of a muddled social and economic environment. The future historian will have to note the many attempts in the present and recent period to erect a showy superstructure upon an insufficient foundation and the ambition of professional teachers of teachers to have the schools undertake everything.

The future historian may also discover in the present and recent period a strong tendency toward a pedagogical priestcraft, through the "super-analysis and hyper-dissection of the teaching process" and the creation of a pedagogical jargon peculiar to and understood only by the craft. And he may find evidence of danger that lurked in making the art of teaching complex rather than keeping it the simple process that in reality it is.

In these conditions appear the responsibilities and opportunities of the University of North Carolina. By constitutional authority this institution has been recognized officially and by the people themselves now for one hundred and fifty years as the head of public education in the state. This leader in the state's educational system is itself crowned by its graduate and professional work, whose influence should be preeminent in determining purposes and policies in the educational system of the state. No other institution or agency in North Carolina has larger potential opportunities for giving direction to the elementary and secondary schools and even to teacher-educational institutions; and impressive is the educational responsibility which thus rests fully and finally upon its University which has accepted educational leadership in North Carolina. At the inauguration of President Chase here twenty-five years ago, Dr. E. C. Brooks, State Superintendent of Public Instruction, said that an educational system is as comprehensive as its manifold resources, and that "Such a system unified becomes a great spiritual temple, having for its base the infant school, and its crown the University."

Properly considered the state university is an institution of leadership in all aspects of the life of the commonwealth in which it lives and serves. Nowadays, more than ever before, it has come to be looked upon not only as an institution where distinguished teaching is done, where independence of thinking is encouraged and fostered along with its "ardent love for truth and righteousness," but where no phase of civic, social, educational, political, and industrial life is beyond its obligation to study for the sole purpose of promoting the highest interests of all the people of the state. Not only must the state university be a leader in the intellectual life of the society in which it exists; but more and more is it expected also to be "the mother of reforms." Sometimes it may have to defy and vigorously oppose what someone has called "the momentum of inertia" on new questions and issues; but always must it bravely fight against prejudice and selfish vested interests and bid ignorance defiance always and everywhere. Otherwise, it is not a university in the real sense, nor can it be true to its own conscience and the commonwealth. It must also stand vigorously against any tendencies to a one-sided development of the society in which it lives. It must resist and curb any hasty and feverish educational spirit of the times that would ignore or neglect the past, and constantly keep before the people the warning that "in darkness dwells the people which knows its annals not." The state university must have the clear eyes of the prophet to foresee dangers and the moral courage and intellectual honesty to forewarn against them. It must be a robust and sturdy influence that never truckles nor yields obsequiously to the fancies and fads of the passing moment or generation, while being at the same time, however, sensitive and responsible to the real needs of the present.

Education is fundamentally richer and more extensive than the study of methods and techniques of instruction with which it has unfortunately come to be confused in recent times. Professional education is a derivative discipline and draws its contributions from many other disciplines and subjects. For this reason attempts to establish it as an isolated intellectual discipline or

science are bound to be disappointing. Attempts in the past by
energetic enthusiasts in the field of psychology, statistics, and
administration have had short and disappointing lives. The technician or mechanic in education can assert with high confidence
that he has the figures, but he does not always know what the
figures mean, because for the meaning and values of education
it is necessary to draw on other sources and resources than technical pedagogy. When Plato set out to answer the question,
"What is Justice?" and to discover the foundations of the just
state, he came out with *The Republic,* the first treatise on education and still one of the most vital of all discussions on the
subject. Here and in his other writings Plato made the head of
education in his ideal society the most important of all state
officials because, he wrote, "If young men have been or are well
brought up, all things go swimmingly" in the state. And his distinguished disciple, Aristotle, maintained that there is nothing
which the science of government should "take so much pains
with as producing a certain character in the citizens, that is,
making them good and able to do fine actions."

The history of education in this state during the life of this
institution demonstrates nothing more clearly than that the
professional education of teachers is more than the study of
educational theories and techniques. The late Sir Michael Sadler
long ago pointed out that a state system of education is a living
thing and has in it the secret workings of the life of the state.
"It reflects, while seeking to remedy, the failings of the State.
. . ." And he made it clear that professional education should
deal primarily with those forces that give education meaning
and life, those forces which reveal the hopes, the aspirations,
and the culture of the state in which it exists.

The influence of the University in providing leadership for
public education has been very definite and far-reaching. The
structure of a great system of public education has been cred-
itably erected. Much has been done. But the undone work still
is vast. The most persistent and pressing part of the undone
work is that on which Dr. Joyner wrote so eloquently more
than forty years ago in his first report as state superintendent
of public instruction, to his college-mate, Governor Charles B.

Aycock. Dr. Joyner said: "The first essential of a teacher is the knowledge of the subject to be taught. As is the teacher, so will be the school."

The origin and growth of the University of North Carolina and the public schools form one of the most significant chapters in the history of this state, one of the most fascinating of our entire democratic epic. The University was designed to serve the manifold interests of the state which created it. More than any other type of educational arrangement ever devised in North Carolina, its University is a public-service institution. Its life and success have depended upon and will continue to depend upon the public, the public will, and sympathetic public appreciation. Its resources should always be at the intelligent service of the people wherever good purposes are to be served. As a social institution and a public servant, the University of North Carolina is in partnership with the commonwealth. It must faithfully meet not only its primary obligation to teach and to keep aloft the lamp of learning but it must also extend the boundaries of knowledge; and its zeal for sound teaching and productive scholarship must be kept robust, unflagging, and unsullied. And we are confident that to this high trust and opportunity this mother of state universities will be faithful.

IX

UNIVERSITY DAY, 1945

U NIVERSITY DAY, October 12, 1945, one of the most notable in the history of the University, was celebrated in
conjunction with the forty-sixth annual meeting of the
Association of American Universities, with Duke University and
the University of North Carolina as hosts to the Association.
The day was October at its best with brilliant sunshine and flame
in the maples along the Avenue vying with the colors of the academic procession augmented by the delegates attending the meeting of the Association.

The program of the day included four events: a Sesquicentennial Convocation at 10:45 devoted to the celebration of University Day and to an address delivered by Dr. James Bryant
Conant, President of Harvard University; a luncheon tendered
the Association by the University, at which President Graham
was the speaker; an afternoon session at which the Association
considered the problems of accrediting higher institutions; and
a dinner meeting at which the University was host to the Association, with short addresses on aspects of research in the South
by Dr. Paul Gross, of Duke University, Dr. Howard W. Odum,
of the University of North Carolina, and Dr. James Southall
Wilson, of the University of Virginia.

The program for the convocation, over which Chancellor
House presided, included: The Invocation, by Dr. Howard E.
Rondthaler, President of Salem College; "The Star Spangled
Banner," by the combined Men's and Women's Glee Clubs;
Responsive Reading in "Praise of Famous Men," led by Chan-
cellor House; "Integer Vitae," by the Men's Glee Club; Intro-
duction of the Delegates, by Dean W. W. Pierson, Jr.; "How
Lovely Is Thy Dwelling-place," by the Glee Clubs; Introduction
of the Speaker, President James B. Conant, of Harvard Uni-
versity, and the Awarding of an Honorary Degree, by President
Frank P. Graham; "The Future of the American University,"

by President Conant; The University Hymn, by the audience; the Benediction, by Dr. Rondthaler.

The invocation was offered by Dr. Rondthaler.

DR. RONDTHALER

Our Heavenly Father: As we are counselled in Thy Holy Word, we do pray that we may seek to: "Remember the Rock whence we are hewn," and likewise, to: "Ask our Elders and they will tell us, and inquire from our fathers and they will show us."

Increase we pray Thee our sense of obligation to the mighty past of this our beloved University.

May we indeed believe that Thou hast carried it through these long years "in the hollow of Thy hand," and that Thy protection has been about these walls lo these many generations.

In Thy light may we see light, and in Thy strength may we address ourselves, with added assurance to the challenge of this new day of peace.

Thou must indeed have great purposes in Thy divine care so long bestowed upon this institution, and may none of us be found lacking in this time of our renewed opportunity.

This we ask in the name of Jesus our Saviour. Amen.

TRIBUTE TO GENERAL JULIAN S. CARR

Before the audience was asked to stand in silence in honor of the members of the faculty and of the alumni who had died since last University Day, a list which included the names of 226 individuals, of whom 117 died in the armed services, Chancellor House read the following tribute to the late General Julian S. Carr, whose one hundredth anniversary was being celebrated in Durham:

Our memorial service is, as always, in honor of all University men and women who have died since last University Day. But it is fitting to remember with special affection General Julian S. Carr. Today is the one-hundredth anniversary of his birth. It is being observed as a public holiday in his home city of Durham and by special tributes in all of North Carolina. The University has sent Dr. Archibald Henderson as its special delegate to the exercises in Durham. General Carr, student-soldier of 1862-1864, A.B. in 1911 with other Civil War veterans as of 1866, trustee, friend and benefactor of the University, Trinity College, and Duke University, lives in his works in industry, education, religion, and philanthropy. On this day, celebrating education in the international scene, we remember that his benefactions to the father of the Soong sisters of China links him through them with liberty and education in China and the world today.

Introduced by President Graham in a ceremony in which he was the recipient of the honorary degree of Doctor of Laws, President Conant spoke upon the subject, "The Future of the American University."

President Conant

We are gathered here today to celebrate the one hundredth and fiftieth anniversary of the opening of the first state university in America. The University of North Carolina was the first of the educational institutions chartered *de novo* by one of the thirteen states to open its doors. It started as a state university; it has remained such to this day. On the other hand, the history of the colleges or universities which were already in existence at the time of the American Revolution took another course. Even those incorporated into the framework of the new sovereign states harked back to the independence of a chartered seventeenth century corporation and became less and less formal agencies of the state. For example, the college in Cambridge was ambitiously designated as The University in Chapter V of the Massachusetts Constitution of 1780; and a century and a half ago I doubt if the President of Harvard would have thought of his institution as being of a different type from the university just opening in the state of North Carolina. In those days Harvard was as much a state university as any that were planned. Only toward the middle of the nineteenth century did the distinction now current between state universities and privately controlled or privately endowed universities come to have significance in educational thinking. Perhaps a century hence this distinction will again have disappeared; universities are among the most persistent of human organizations—they outlive many political and social changes.

I mention this bit of history, President Graham, not in order to enter my own horse in competition for the priority prize, but to emphasize my belief that in interpreting the past record of American universities and forecasting their future, the less said about the differences between state universities and others the better. Therefore, you will forgive me, I feel sure, if after offering my heartiest congratulations to North Carolina on her one hundred and fiftieth birthday I suggest that we are also celebrating today the evolution of a new type of educational institution—the American University.

To be sure, a hundred and fifty years ago, or even one hundred years ago, no one could have foreseen that the university tradition as imported to this continent in colonial times was to undergo a significant mutation. No one then could have predicted that exposure to the social and political climate of the United States, to alternate blasts of Jeffersonian and Jacksonian democracy in particular, was to bring about an academic revolution and that the state universities were to play a leading role in the transformation; but such was in fact the case.

Indeed, only in the last fifty years has the reality of the change in species become apparent to all observers, and only in the last twenty-five years has the true significance of the change been widely understood. Even today there are those who regard the alteration as a mere temporary and extremely regrettable aberration to be attacked by drastic surgery; pruned or cut back, as it were, to conform to the older European model of a perfect university.

But what is this university tradition which, according to my thesis this morning, has undergone a revolution in American hands—a revolution equivalent to a biological mutation? Indeed, what is a university? How shall we define the *genus?* For well on a thousand years there have been universities in the western world; to understand the present institutions, we must therefore comprehend something of their history. For while there have been several clear and distinct changes in the pattern, the essence of the university tradition has through all these years remained constant. We can describe a university, it seems to me, as a community of scholars with a considerable degree of independence and self-government which is concerned with professional education, the advancement of knowledge, and the general education of the leading citizens. To accomplish these three ends, it has been found desirable often—but not always—to incorporate into the community of scholars a community of students. Thus arose what has been termed the "collegiate way of living." Thus came about the emphasis on what we now call the "extracurricular" educational values.

As the university tradition came to America, it was thus based on four ultimate sources of strength: the cultivation of learning for its own sake, the educational stream that makes possible the professions, the general educational stream of the liberal arts, and lastly, the never-failing river of student life carrying all the power that comes from the gregarious impulses of human beings. According to my view, universities have flourished when these four elements have been properly in balance; and, conversely, when one or more of these same elements has diminished or dried up the academies of advanced instruction have failed signally in performing a relevant social function.

The cultivation of learning alone produces not a university but a research institute; sole concern with student life produces in these days either an academic country club or a football team manoeuvring under a collegiate banner; professional education by itself results in nothing but a trade school; an institution concerned with general education, even in the best liberal arts tradition, divorced from research and education for the professions is admittedly not a university but a college. Therefore, to my mind, the future of the American university depends primarily on keeping a proper balance between these four traditional elements of strength. These four elements were the basis of the properly balanced plan in a time when universities were flourishing; they must continue to be in balance if institutions of advanced instruction are to fulfill their proper functions in the times that are to come.

But what about this American mutation, you may ask? What is there new about the American university, and how does the novelty (if any) affect the prospects for its future? The mutation, I believe, occurred in two of the four historic elements of which I speak, namely, professional education, and general education of the leading citizens. The first was a change in content, an enormous growth; the second, a change in type of student. Both represent a vast broadening of the educational goals, both present us with problems still unsolved. The changes have been to a large degree unconscious responses to social forces, and often the rationalization of the transformations have been in other terms than I shall use. Indeed, many of you here today may well disagree completely with my analysis both of the history of education and of the current scene. If so, perhaps we shall be to a large degree quarrelling about metaphors for with my conclusions, which will be quite conventional, I feel sure most of you must agree.

As public secondary education expanded in the last decades of the nineteenth and the first half of the twentieth century, the colleges and universities likewise expanded. Not only were the applicants more numerous, they were much more heterogeneous as to backgrounds and ambitions. Furthermore, the political, social and economic development of the United States vastly altered the way in which the public regarded education. As the years went by it became more and more evident that in our complex industrialized society mere ability to read and write added to native wit was not enough. With the passing of the frontier, the pioneer spirit was turned away from new lands toward new industries. And to manage modern industry requires more than a high school education—at least for all but the very exceptional man. With increasing industrialization went increasing urbanization, a higher standard of living and a vast number of services available for city and town dwellers, more and more new mechanical and electrical devices distributed widely among the population—automobiles, electric refrigerators and radios, to mention the most obvious examples. All this industrial expansion required more and more men and women with a larger and different educational experience than would have been necessary fifty years earlier to run a farm, a store, or even a local bank.

The pressure on the universities, therefore, to educate men and women for specific vocations both increased and diversified. Beginning with the Morrill Acts the public had recognized the need for education in agriculture and the mechanical and industrial arts. Many a state in the Union made the significant step of combining the new agricultural and industrial arts colleges with an older state college of arts and letters. Perhaps one could say that from this union came the new American university. But, if so, the transformation rapidly spread elsewhere. Even before the great influx in numbers, the pattern had been set in publicly controlled and privately controlled universities alike; the mechanical and industrial arts (later to be known as engineering) and agriculture were recognized as being on a par (at least in theory) with divinity, medicine and law.

It thus came about that as the twentieth century grew older both the enrollments in our universities and the diversity of the training increased with each decade. The word "profession," in danger of being stretched beyond the elastic limit, was supplemented by the phrase "semi-profession." But soon the voice of harsh critics was heard throughout the land. Able and distinguished citizens became alarmed at this transformation of the idea of a university in American hands. When you once abandon the concept of a university as a home of learning, a place where the life of the mind is to be cultivated at all costs, you have destroyed our centers of higher educations, they declared. But in spite of these outcries and lamentations, the development proceeded on its way. One of our oldest universities strengthened its school of business administration, another continued to give degrees in forestry and nursing, while privately controlled universities in urban areas were as catholic in their offerings as any financed by the state. One element of the ancient four—professional education—had received nourishment from the combination of democracy and industrialization. It was forced to proliferate in a way to shock the admirers of the ancient stem. All manner of new vocations were assimilated within the sacred walls of a university, and graduates armed with special training in a variety of skills stood on the commencement platform as proudly as the future members of the church or bar.

In short, in the course of seventy-five years or so the forces of democracy had taken the European idea of a university and transformed it. The American university today is as different from the nineteenth century British or Continental universities as the Renaissance universities of Italy and the Netherlands were different from those of the Middle Ages. Personally, I think the basic philosophy which almost unconsciously has shaped the growth of the modern American university is sound, for it is none other than a philosophy hostile to the supremacy of a few vocations; it is a philosophy moving toward the social equality of all useful labor. But the implications of this philosophy are revolutionary and those who react against it have, if anything, understated the extent and radical nature of the change.

Now, as an offset to this increased emphasis on professional training (for I regard all university vocational education as a derivative of the ancient professions), there came about a strong movement to make American universities centers of scholarly work and scientific investigation. This movement was not only to some degree a counterbalance to the educational forces associated with the agricultural and mechanical colleges, but also a response to a challenge to make of some of the older institutions something more than advanced boarding schools for a special group. In the middle of the last century the head of one of the Oxford colleges, an eminent scholar and educational reformer, saw no evidence that the university tradition had ever taken root in the United States. "America has no universities, as we understand the term," he wrote, "the institutions so-called being merely places for granting titular degrees." Taken literally this harsh judgment is undoubtedly false, yet it probably is not a gross exaggeration of the situation which then existed. The new spirit moving within the educational institutions of the country had not become evident to those outside the academic walls. It was not until the Johns Hopkins University was opened at Baltimore that the idea of a university as a center of advanced learning came to have a prominent place in the public mind. It was not until Gilman had boldly proclaimed that "all departments of learning should be promoted" and that "the glory of the university should rest upon the character of the teachers and scholars . . . and not upon their number nor upon the buildings constructed for their use,"—it was not until then that scholarship came into its own again as part of the University tradition of this land.

From this development, as we all know, came the growth of the graduate schools of arts and sciences, the introduction of new standards of excellence in regard to original work by scientists and scholars, and the growth of what is now sometimes referred to as the Ph.D. octopus. All this was slow at first, but like the other changes in the universities of America gained speed during the period just before and just after the First World War. As a consequence, the American university has been in recent years something of a mental patient suffering from a schizophrenic disorder:—on one day, or during one administration, the disciplines grouped under the banner of the arts, letters and sciences represent the dominant personality; another day, or during another administration, it is the vocational procession led by law and medicine and sweeps all before it. As a reminder of this split personality we have the Association of American Universities (which is meeting here this week) which has been for years in reality an association of graduate schools of arts and sciences; even the most distinguished and ancient professions are scarcely mentioned. As another example, we see a wealthy foundation supporting a history of American universities which is in fact a history of the departments which award a Ph.D. degree.

But, as so often happens in the delightful chaos of American democracy, the various pressure groups to a large degree cancelled out. Looking back over the history of this century we can see the American universities drew strength from many different sources. The fact that the forces making for the new developments were often not only totally unrelated but at times seemed to be working one against another made little difference; the expansion and strengthening of the entire institution continued almost without interruption. The nature of the typical American university had emerged; whether any given institution was state controlled or privately supported made little difference in the pattern. In some states there was a comprehensive system comprised of several constituent members as in North Carolina; in others all work was included in one academic institution. As to the variety of the vocational training, one university or one university system might show considerable divergence from another; as to the strength of their faculties, there were, of course, wide differences; but as to their ideas of undergraduate education and their devotion to the welfare of the students there was remarkable uniformity among them all. But the significant fact was that no one university which gave degrees in the ancient professions of medicine or law remained aloof from also giving degrees in such modern subjects as business administration, engineering, journalism, forestry, architecture, nursing or education. And many were awarding bachelor's degrees for courses of study in vocational fields very distant, indeed, from the traditional disciplines of the arts and sciences.

To complete this brief and inadequate account of the Americanization of the university idea, it remains only to discuss general education as apart from vocational education. I have earlier referred to the "general education of the leading citizens" as one of the traditional elements in the university pattern which has remained constant through the centuries. A volume would be required to do justice to this aspect of the work of universities in different countries and in different periods of history. In a sense, this phase of university education is a by-product of the two main pre-occupations of the scholars—the advancement of learning, and education for the professions which includes, of course, the training of new scholars. In a sense, it is a by-product; yet a by-product which in the public eye (including the eye of future students) has often loomed as large as all the other functions of the university put together. And the larger it loomed the more emphasis we find put on student life which has manifested itself in ways as different as the Oxford colleges, the German duelling clubs, and the American zest for intercollegiate athletics.

If we examine the role of the universities in the English speaking countries in the seventeenth and eighteenth centuries, we find a fair proportion of the students preparing not for the church or bar, but for public service or a career in letters. In England only slowly, in the Colonies more rapidly, the merchant families came to send their boys to a college or university in order to obtain the sort of general education required by the business positions they would later occupy. In terms of the total population, the number of young men who pursued this road, however, was very, very small indeed. For the most part only a special set of relatively wealthy families patronized the colleges and universities for this purpose; the poor boy entered only if he desired to become a scholar or a member of a learned profession.

The numbers were small in the eighteenth and first part of the nineteenth centuries because the education thus acquired was of but little significance in later life. The fact that Harvard College was not available in the eighteenth century for boys of Benjamin Franklin's social and financial status made little or no difference to either this genius or many of his much less gifted contemporaries who grew up in equal poverty. The same may be said of the situation throughout America as late as the middle of the last century. But then matters began to change. As part of the educational expansion of which I have already spoken, more and more boys began to enter colleges and universities not to study for the professions, but for a general education as a preparation for later life in the business world.

An acute observer reared in another culture might have seen at the turn of the century that American educational policy was steering American educational philosophy toward an ugly dilemma—a dilemma only now apparent and still often dodged. As long as education beyond the high school was a matter for a very small fraction of the population and, except for learned and literary men, of no great moment in terms of subsequent success, it mattered little who went to college. But as more and more doors of opportunity in an increasingly industrialized society became closed to the non-college man, the question of who went to college raised new social and political problems. Today, we see out of the corner of our eyes, at least, such awkward queries as: Have we real equality of educational opportunity at the college level? If not, what is the proper remedy? Is everyone to go to college? If so, what kind of college? If not, on what basis are some to be denied "the privileges of a higher education?"

Here we run into some of the thorniest problems in modern education. If we are to continue the expansion of public education so that the opportunity of formal instruction beyond high school is given to still greater numbers irrespective of financial status, what sorts of colleges and universities must we provide? To my mind, such phrases as "the privileges of a higher education" confuse the issue greatly. If we could eliminate the words "higher education" we could at least make a start toward thinking more clearly about the relation of our colleges to the structure of American society. For the adjective "higher" implies at once that those who do not go to a four-year college are forever on a lower plane. And any discerning teacher in our secondary schools will testify that the social implications of "going to college" weigh quite as heavily with parents and children as does proven aptitude for college work. Furthermore, any placement officer of a college knows full well that it is a rare holder of a bachelor's degree who is anxious to take up as his life work a trade or vocation for which he might have been trained in a technical high school.

If we substitute the word "advanced" for "higher" we get squared away for a discussion of high school and college in terms of the basic premise of American society, equality of educational opportunity. Instead of raising the question, "Who should be educated?" we would then pose the problem, "How long should be the education of the members of each vocation?" Instead of asking who should go to college, we inquire, "What types of education beyond the high school are needed of the members of each vocation?" Considered in these terms, the answers can be given within fairly narrow limits. It is beyond argument that certain callings require longer periods of formal education than do others. Public health now tops the list; medicine and the academic careers requiring a Ph.D. in arts or letters next—research in science is not far behind; then come law and engineering, to name only a few of the well-recognized professions.

Since the major cost of advanced education, if the student is away from home, is board and lodging, one can argue that as far as possible the expansion of public education beyond high school should be provided locally. Otherwise we would have to envisage using public funds to provide two to four years of free board and room for a considerable fraction of our high school graduates.

But there are various types of professional and vocational education which can be given at only a few centers in even a very populous state. To tap the reservoir of national talent for these professions we need a vastly expanded scholarship policy, for these students must for the most part live away from home. It is literally impossible, for example, to give adequate instruction in clinical medicine except in cities of sufficient size to support large hospitals, or except in a state university teaching hospital, which is the one focus of a state-wide hospital program. How are boys with little financial backing who come from other cities and towns to be financed if they are to study medicine? Similarly, advanced work in the arts, sciences and letters can be done only where adequate libraries and laboratories are at hand. Is it not in the national interest to get all the latent talent available for the lengthy training that research careers demand? To establish research centers at every point in the United States where general education beyond the high schools is desired would be not merely uneconomical, but literally impossible. The alternative, to strengthen our present universities and establish a national system of scholarships, seems the only answer.

The logic of events in this country and this century, therefore, leads to the conclusion that the undergraduate college in a typical American university must be closely integrated in its work with the other functions of the institution, advancing knowledge and professional or vocational education. The pattern of the education offered in such colleges may be of little relevance, therefore, for the two-year colleges which can provide locally in many instances for those who need no advanced training for the vocations they will enter. Not that I would suggest the university divorce itself from the two-year colleges any more than from the high schools; quite the contrary. The university, because of its interest in professional education, in the advancement of learning in all fields in the training of teachers, and because of its concern with basic educational problems is in a position in every state to exert leadership in the whole field. But the methods by which a university provides general and professional education to its students may in detail be very different from what is desired in other institutions with shorter courses and different educational goals.

At the risk of being redundant, I return to my original proposition: the health of our universities depends on keeping a balance between the advancement of knowledge, professional education, general education, and the demands of student life. From time to time, every institution will be threatened by the overgrowth of one of these four elements or the atrophy of one or more. But by and large it seems clear that in the next few years it is the advancement of knowledge which will be in need of the greatest encouragement and support. I say this in spite of the present public concern with supporting research in the physical and biological sciences. I say it in part because of this concern. I am afraid that there will be so many research institutes founded by industry and philanthropy for very specific purposes that the university faculties will be drained dry of their productive men. What few laymen seem to realize is the simple fact that it is men that count, and that first-rate investigators and original scholars are relatively rare phenomena, and require long and careful training. That is why, to me, the spending of state and federal money on a scholarship policy is equally as important as the establishment of a suitable federal agency to support basic research in our universities.

I say equally important as I yield to no one in my hearty support of all the provisions of the Magnuson bill which is now before Congress. And I may remark parenthetically that if this bill is passed and it becomes demonstrated that a federal agency can allocate research funds wisely and fairly and support a scholarship program in the natural sciences, the scope of the federal government's concern with professional education should be broadened. I hope that a careful report will be prepared, showing what are the national needs for research funds and scholarships in such fields as social psychology, cultural anthropology, educational psychology, sociology and economics. A very strong case can be made for the necessity for strengthening our universities in these areas quite as much as in the so-called natural sciences. An even stronger case can be made, in my opinion, for the need of attracting a large number of men of ability, originality and wide imagination into academic careers in what I may call the philosophic aspects of the social studies—in particular, into philosophy itself.

Let any university president assume that he could call any professor to his institution whom he chose, and then compare the situation he is confronted with in philosophy or jurisprudence with that in physics or mechanical engineering. The dearth of outstanding men in the first two areas is as striking as the abundance of professors of eminence in the others. How to right the balance between the philosophic and the more practical aspects of each field of human learning seems to me the great question mark of the day. I have no answer; but where the weight should be thrown by administrators and trustees is certainly evident to all who believe in a balanced plan as a prerequisite for academic health.

Thus far I have spoken of the future of American universities largely in terms of their importance as measured by the subsequent performance of their graduates. Let me, in conclusion, emphasize another role of great significance for the nation which has been played with such conspicuous success by the institution whose 150th anniversary we are celebrating here today. I refer to intellectual, educational and moral leadership,—leadership not only of a state but of an entire section. This leadership of a community of scholars, like the leadership of an individual, requires: first, capacity based on expert knowledge; second, broad vision; third, courage. And of these the last is by no means the least significant. More and more I believe the nation and different groups within the nation (geographic, social, or economic groups) must look to the university scholars for guidance in handling basic social and economic problems. To this end the professors of these subjects must explore vigorously not only the fundamental aspects of man's behaviour but the applications of our present knowledge.

But for this, one condition is essential. This is absolute freedom of discussion, absolutely unmolested inquiry. We must have a spirit of tolerance which allows the expression of all opinions, however heretical they may appear. On this point there can be no compromise. We are either afraid of heresy within our universities, or we are not. If we are afraid, there will be no adequate discussion of the great questions of the day, no fearless exploration of the basic problems forced on us by the age in which we live. The door will be shut to the development of a culture which will satisfy our needs.

But we have no reason to be unduly apprehensive. The public has come to understand both the function of the universities and the necessary conditions for their health. Therefore, I view the future of our institutions with the greatest confidence. I see the American scholar defined in the days ahead as he was a century ago,—defined as "that man who must take up into himself all the ability of the time, all the contributions of the past, all the hopes of the future." I see the American universities as leading the way in the development of a unified, coherent culture, the expression of a true democracy in a scientific age.

The convocation was concluded with the singing of the University Hymn by the Glee Club and the audience and by the pronouncing of the Benediction by Dr. Rondthaler. The University was then host to the Association of American Universities at a luncheon at the Carolina Inn.

At the conclusion of the luncheon, over which Chancellor House presided, President Graham spoke on "Some Observations, Occasioned by the Atomic Bomb, on the Influence of Universities and Mechanisms in the Great Transitions of History."

President Graham

The Association of American Universities, as the guest of Duke University and the University of North Carolina, in the generous fellowship of universities, joins the University of North Carolina in the commemoration of the one hundred and fiftieth anniversary of the opening, in the mid-winter of 1795, of the first existing state university to open its doors in America. We express to you our deep sense of honor and gratitude.

In Chapel Hill, the historic birthplace of the University of the people, and in 1945, the historic birth year of the atomic bomb, youth is deeply aware of the fateful relations between old institutions of the people and new mechanisms of science. By consultation, correspondence, and in conferences, young men and women in many colleges and universities are petitioning for prompt amendments toward a stronger and more democratic constitution of the United Nations. The place and the hour select, from many vital factors and forces in the processes of historic transition, and make appropriate for our present consideration mainly two factors: the constant responsibility of an old institution, the university, and the high potential of a new mechanism, the atomic bomb, in the momentous transition of our times, catastrophic or regenerative for all mankind. For deeply needed values of perspective and comparison, it should be helpful to recall the origin and influence of universities and mechanisms in other great transitions of western history.

THE ORIGIN AND INFLUENCE OF UNIVERSITIES

The ancients, East and West, developed the higher learning but, as Rashdall makes clear, did not found universities. The university is a child of later medievalism, of the commercial, urban, and intellectual resurgence of the eleventh and twelfth centuries, and of the mother church. The modern university has an unbroken connection with the medieval university.

The first European university, founded in the eleventh century at a health resort, Salerno, under the influence of the revival of Graeco-Roman medicine, was devoted to the study of medicine. The second university was founded in the twelfth century at Bologna during the revival of Roman law led by the great teacher of the civil law, Irnerius, and in response also to the need for the formulation of the canon law under the leadership of the great teacher of ecclesiastical law, Gratian. Both of these universities in origin and impulses were vocational and, for that reason, gave purpose and zest to scientific and humane learning. The third university was founded at Paris in the twelfth century as an offshoot of the cathedral school under the influence of the rising scholasticism and was devoted to the study of the liberal arts, philosophy, and theology under the leadership of that master teacher of the dialectic method and that bold protagonist of intellectual curiosity, Peter Abelard. An offshoot from Paris was Oxford, in 1167; from Oxford, Cambridge, in 1209; and from Cambridge, Harvard, in 1636, whose progeny have multiplied and replenish America today. In this historic line of universities, Harvard's president, James B. Conant, standing on the high ground of her more than three hundred years of service to America and the world, summoned us all this morning to the great future of the American university for the development of "a unified and coherent culture in the service of democracy in a scientific age."

The University of Bologna, chief example of the university as a corporation of students, and the University of Paris, chief example of the university as a corporation of teachers, soon became two of the most influential institutions of the later Middle Ages. Accompanying the rise of the universities in the thirteenth century were the rise of trade and towns, the beginnings of Parliament, the building of the cathedrals, and the scholastic reconciliation of the ancient philosophy of Aristotle, the patristic faith, and medieval theology in one of the greatest works of intellectual and doctrinal synthesis ever attempted by the human mind. It was not a mere coincidence that Thomas Aquinas, who made the great medieval synthesis, Saint Francis, one of the noblest souls of all history, and Roger Bacon of Oxford University, whose ideas and experiments were prophetic of the scientific age to come four centuries later, all lived in the thirteenth century and reflected the vigor and variety of an age, some of whose original creations of the human spirit have never been surpassed. The universities, along with parliaments and cathedrals, towering from later medieval times across all the transitions of the modern age, still abide as among the noblest institutions of Western civilization. Professor Rashdall, of Oxford, in his monumental three-volume history of European universities makes it vividly clear that as surely as Rome was the center of the spiritual dominions and Germany was the theoretical seat of the medieval empire, so the University of Paris was the main center of philosophic conflict and synthesis, and intellectual energy and curiosity which stirred the minds and lifted the spirit of western and northern European peoples. The universities, stirring mightily in the minds of men, were both the flowering of the medieval mind and the seeds of the modern spirit. For all their ecclesiastical inertia, social lags, and intellectual frustrations, the medieval universities stimulated the revival of Greek medicine and philosophy, Roman law, and Arab science; promoted the study of Latin grammar, rhetoric and logic, arithmetic, geometry, astronomy, and music; mastered the scholastic synthesis; and were the source and stimulus of much spiritual energy and intellectual curiosity. In these ways the medieval universities prepared the way for the European Renaissance, which, in turn, prepared the way for the Scientific Revolution which, in its turn, prepared the way for the Industrial Revolution.

MECHANISMS OF SCIENCE IN THE GREAT HISTORIC TRANSITIONS

Along with the universities, for our timely consideration as factors in the transitions of history, have been and are the mechanisms of science. In the transition from medieval to modern times, we shall concentrate on the compass; and, in the transition from mid-modern to contemporary times, we shall concentrate on the power engine, as comparative bases for our awful concern with the atomic device for compressing and releasing the energy of the universe in the present transition to a new era whose adumbrations challenge the destiny of the human species of this planet.

THE COMPASS AND THE COMMERCIAL REVOLUTION

In the transition from medievalism, the compass, along with two other mechanisms, helped to change the status and outlook of the later medieval peoples. Gunpowder overthrew the power of the medieval castle and made the common soldier superior to the feudal knight. The printing press broke the monopoly of learning and put books and religion in the hands of laymen. The compass, a result of the ideas, gadgets, and experience of the Chinese, the Northern European, and Mediterranean peoples, made possible the new age of exploration beyond all the known horizons of the ancient and medieval world. Evolved out of the minds, hands, and necessities of many peoples, it was much perfected as a maritime device in the thirteenth century by the theoretical insights and skill of a French soldier and engineer, Peter Peregrinus, who, according to Park Benjamin, served in the army of Charles Anjou at the siege of Lucerne in southern Italy. This composite mechanism and its allied gadgets were much further improved by Italians and Portuguese in the fourteenth and fifteenth centuries and guided Columbus across fearsome seas to the discovery of America.

Ships held for thousands of years within interior seas or close to continental shorelines were released by the compass to sail all the outer oceans, to find the islands and continents of the New World and new ways to the Old World, and to change the direction of commerce and the course of great events. In the midst of the ferment of ideas and forces let loose in the world by humanism, individualism, nationalism, and commercialism, which all together wrought the disintegration of the medieval world and the reintegration of the modern world, we find the little compass connecting the ways of the earth's magnetic lines of force with the ways of the heavens and the ways of the seas thus changing the ways of men and the history of nations. Upon the compass, as one dynamic factor, with its tiny magnetic needle, pivoted and free, the medieval turned to the modern world.

The Commercial Revolution, given mighty propulsions by the little compass, in turn gave impulsions to the rise of the middle class, whose capital and capitalism helped to free the serf from the land, the land from the lord, and the lord from his own privileged power, and liberated industry and trade from medieval restrictions and boundaries. This rising middle class of business and professional people played a decisive part in the Revival of Learning, the Protestant Revolt, the new national state, the power of Parliament, the Scientific and Philosophic Revolutions, the democratic struggles for political and civil liberties, and in the coming of the Industrial Revolution which was to bring in the later modern age.

INSTRUMENTS OF PRECISION AND THE SCIENTIFIC REVOLUTION
IN THE SEVENTEENTH CENTURY

Just as the compass was a mechanism which helped to bring in the modern age, so the power engine was and is the pulsing heart of the Industrial Revolution. Between the Commercial Revolution and the Industrial Revolution came the Scientific Revolution under way in the seventeenth century with such new instruments of scientific precision as the telescope, microscope, and thermometer, and with such advanced techniques as thorough observation, experimentation through trial and error, factual data, and the inductive objectivity of free scientific inquiry, stimulating the curiosity, increasing the knowledge, testing, clarifying, and widening the insights into the nature of man and the universe, and enlarging the mastery of men over natural resources and human destiny. New societies of scientific fellows and new scientific techniques wrought a revolution in the outlook, attitude, work, and hopes of men.

The Scientific Revolution came from the summary interaction of many factors and movements. The Revival of Learning, with its idea of the roundness of the earth, made possible the Commercial Revolution. The rediscovery of the Old World led to the discovery of the New World. The Revival of Learning prepared the way for the Advancement of Learning. The mastery of the old learning caused the quest for the new learning. The quest for the new learning caused the invention of new devices of scientific precision. The resulting Scientific Revolution made possible the Industrial Revolution. The new basic scientific knowledge patiently won with the new devices in university laboratories led, in turn, to the invention of new dynamic mechanisms which caused the Industrial Revolution. The Commercial Revolution with its new attitudes and techniques of banking and trade, with its new oceans, new continents, new peoples, and vast new resources made necessary new ways for larger production, longer transportation, and quicker communication for trade in the Old World and between the Old World and the New.

THE POWER ENGINE AND THE INDUSTRIAL REVOLUTION

To meet the necessities of production and commerce in such a world came the modern steam engine. James Watt, a skilled technician and instrument mender in the basement laboratory of Professor Black in the University of Glasgow, changed the principle of an old Newcomen engine of a type which, for over sixty years, had uneconomically used atmospheric pressure over a vacuum created by condensing steam. Watt, by the device of a separate condenser, used the constant steam pressure on a piston whose reciprocating motion was converted into the rotary motion of the modern steam engine. The university professor's theory of latent heat and the expansive power of steam was mechanized by the instrument mender into a steam pump which revolutionized the modern world.

Along with the steam engine were geographic, economic, social, political, intellectual, and spiritual factors and forces, making possible and vastly enlarging the course of the Industrial Revolution. By virtue of its detached geographic position; its basic sciences in the universities; its inventions made necessary by the expanding needs of the textile, coal, and iron industries; by virtue of the alliance between the national central authority and the commercial interests; and by virtue of being the largest free trade area in Europe, Britain became the home of the Industrial Revolution. The new scientific and philosophic conception of a deistic mechanistic universe with its new basic laws of nature made for the development of the theory of the natural rights of man which supplanted the theory of the divine right of kings. This new science and philosophy of fundamental laws of nature gave sanction to corresponding economic and political theories of the inalienable rights and liberties of men inherent in nature and in the mechanically self-regulating universe. The old mercantilism with its royal monopolies, class privileges, and stifling restrictions on industry and trade, was giving way to the new theories of the natural liberty of the individual, *laissez faire*, and free enterprise in commerce and industry. This untrammeled freedom as the source of daring, initiative, and enterprise was, it was held, to be subject only to such natural laws as supply and demand in a free, competitive, self-balancing and self-regulating economic system.

It was not a mere coincidence that the *Wealth of Nations* became the declaration of the freedom of the new industrialism and that the *Declaration of Independence* became the manifesto of the liberties of the new democracy in the same year, 1776. Adam Smith, Thomas Jefferson, Ben Franklin, Quesnay, Tom Paine, and Condorcet were natural philosophers and contemporary champions of economic, political, and civil liberties, as above the lawful authority of kings and states. It was not a historical accident that the American, French, and Industrial Revolutions all came in the last quarter of the eighteenth century. The democratic victories for political, civil, and economic liberties, the liberation of trade and industry from the monopolies and restrictions of kings, guilds, and parliaments, gave a release to the daring investments and adventurous enterprises of bankers, merchants, and the new and rising manufacturers. The widening market of free trade at home and of the peoples and resources of two hemispheres gave mighty impulses to the production and transportation by steam power. The capital reserves of the Commercial Revolution now poured into the new enterprises of the Industrial Revolution. The historically significant financial and legal mechanism, the modern corporation, gathered the savings of people anywhere for the service of people everywhere. The steam engine was soon to be joined by the electric dynamo and then by the gas and oil engines which caused their own revolutions in production, illumination, communication, and transportation on land, on the seas, and in the air.

The power engines multiplied the production of goods and the population of the world. The power engines gave rise to the new industrial middle class and the mounting millions of industrial workers who are becoming powerful economic groups and the dynamic social forces of the modern world. The philosophy of the Industrial Revolution, reenforced by the Darwinian theory of the struggle for survival, seemed to give immediate sanction to the free and ruthless competitive exploitation and waste of resources and peoples. The power engines then gave impulse to social reforms; to the labor movement, as a fourth chapter of the rise of democracy in the western world; to the woman's movement when women followed machines from their homes into the new factories; and helped to give a democratic base to the stupendous public school system as workers backed up the agitation of philosophers for the universal education of children regardless of race, color, creed, or economic position. The Industrial Revolution, in making the nations more economically interdependent, gave a lift to the cause of international peace. The power engine became the driving force of an earthwide mechanical framework which holds up the structure of the modern world. Mass production in America, made possible by the power engine and the co-operation of management and labor, helped the brave people of Britain, Russia, China, and America to win the war on all the fronts of freedom.

HOPES AND DISILLUSIONMENTS

The Industrial Revolution in less than two hundred years changed the ways men work and live more than they had changed in more than two thousand years. By its mighty capacities for production, for equalizing opportunities, and for making an interdependent world, the Industrial Revolution gave men hope for abundance for all, for freedom and democracy in all nations, and for permanent peace on earth. These hopes have been crushed to earth in this generation by a world depression with wide unemployment, hunger, and human misery for hundreds of millions of forgotten people; by the rise of fascism, and the Axis Powers when lately freedom and democracy were renounced or crushed in almost half the world; and by two world wars, global, total, and destructive without parallel in any other age of history.

Confronted by such humane hopes and such terrible disillusionments, such potential capacities and such miserable frustrations, it is a clear and terrible fact that human society has not learned to master the science and technology of the modern world.

THE FRAGMENTARY VIEW OF THE UNIVERSITIES AND THE
SOCIAL LAG

In the hands of men, as animal organisms, are scientific mechanisms without corresponding political and social mechanisms of control. For the use of man with a primitive biological inheritance of untold ages is a technological power which makes necessary a social intelligence and spiritual development for its humane mastery. In a fast-changing industrial world are an almost unchanging human nature and the slow changing social mind and motive. The political and economic ideas evolved in the handicraft age reach over with controls in the age of the power engine. The shibboleths of liberty which came flaming from the soul of a Thomas Jefferson in the eighteenth century in behalf of the freedom of forgotten men were turned against the freedom of forgotten millions in the twentieth century. The universities have given youth a fragmentary view of learning, of the human being, and of human society.

As noble repositories of the great tradition of humane learning and as scientific guardians of the tested and true, the universities, reflective and creative parts of our modern society, are also parts of the social lag. The colleges and universities were mainly scholastic in renascence times, dominantly classical in scientific times, narrowly scientific in the midst of complex economic and social change, and too often they were reluctantly social minded and apologetically philosophical and spiritual minded on the eve of the greatest social, ethical, and spiritual crisis of human history.

The colleges and universities have within themselves the men and resources to help mankind onward toward the new age. The universities must help to make adjustments, not as lags in the social process, but as leaders of the people in need of the truth which can come from honest and thorough research in all fields, from informed and dedicated teaching, and from clear, responsible thinking by scholars who seek the truth and who, in their own lives, are free and unafraid to find and speak the truth as they find it. The scholars and teachers, scientists and philosophers of the universities have had a vital and creative part in every major scientific, agricultural, industrial, educational, professional, social, intellectual, and spiritual development of modern times. If society should fail now more adequately to sustain the schools, colleges, and universities, then society, in failing its own high purpose, will set in motion its own downfall. The universities cannot, without their own self-destruction, fail society in this hour.

The universities, in intensifying the specialization needed in the training of men and women for modern society, also need to equip the specialist as a better specialist with an integrated view and understanding of his specialty, himself, his society, and his world in which he is to be a responsible and fellow human being and a citizen of his local, national, and international community. The curriculum of the college, often an age behind the highest needs of the age should be highly serving, cannot afford in these times to be belated and provincial in any place on the earth or any period of history to come. The curricula should vitally represent the best of all branches of useful and humane knowledge. Human society, and therefore the curriculum of the college, needs not less science but more science, more scientific attitudes and techniques in all areas of knowledge and in all relations of human beings; not less but more social sciences as ways toward the social-scientific mastery of science and technology, our human nature, our political and economic processes. The curriculum should require more first-hand understanding of the classics of the great tradition which bring to the plastic mind and spirit of youth the fellowship of the greatest minds and noblest spirits of all nations and of all ages, whose precious experience, wisdom, and goodness provide the basis for the thoughtful perspectives and ethical valuations of our own thinking and self-expression; more fine arts for fine feeling, heightened emotion, noble imagination, the inner vision, and the beautiful creations of the human spirit. The curriculum needs more recognition of philosophy and religion as the basis of an intellectual and spiritual synthesis of the physical and moral, the vocational and liberal, personal freedom and social responsibility, stability and progress, ethics and politics, work and justice, democracy and excellence, religion and learning, and of man as belonging to the world of nature and to the world of spirit as parts of one world under the physical laws and the moral sovereignty governing man and the universe. Youth in the college needs both the scientific view and the spiritual aspirations of the whole person for the true, the beautiful, and the good in the free and responsible self-governing campus democracy, through which the students may have a vital part in their own education in preparation for their part in the great society of men and nations in the high adventure of creative cooperation toward the Kingdom of God.

THE NEED FOR INTELLIGENT POLITICAL AND SOCIAL MECHANISMS

The curriculum of the school and college is thus one of the intellectual, social, and spiritual mechanisms needed to keep the human being and human society abreast of the scientific mechanisms of an advancing technology. The scientific mechanisms carry with them the necessity for the invention of political and social mechanisms for the humane mastery of their power so that the pecuniary will be subordinated to the industrial, and the industrial subordinated to the human and spiritual. Political and social mechanisms, needed now for democratic adjustment to world depressions, world wars, and the onward sweep of the revolutions of science and technology, are: (1) the strengthened organization of the United Nations; (2) national plans for full production to stimulate private initiative and, if constructive and necessary, to supplement the creative energies of free enterprise within the reference frame of the public welfare; (3) a broader base of social security to lift the level of human liberty; (4) minimum wages for human decency both in the nation and within the states; (5) equal freedom of self organization in religion, politics, business, agriculture, labor, and the professions; (6) national and state policies for fair employment practices; (7) equal suffrage without poll tax in all America; (8) federal aid to the states for the schools under state and local control to provide equal educational opportunity for all children regardless of creed, color, race, economic status, or the place of birth; (9) federal aid to the states and localities for building hospitals and rural health centers to provide more adequate medical care for all the people in all the states; (10) the reinvigoration of the basic and historic old Bill of Rights with a new bill of rights to implement the Atlantic Charter; (11) co-operative research in all fields; and (12) not least, as we have observed, the revaluation and reintegration of the curriculum of the college as basic to the understanding and the decisions necessary for the mastery of our dynamic world. Immediately, the world, in this potentially tragic hour, needs co-operation: co-operation between nations for justice and peace; co-operation between management and labor for reconversion, full production and fair distribution; and co-operation between governments, industries, endowed institutes, agricultural and engineering experiment stations, and graduate schools of the universities for combined research, not only in science, agriculture, industry, business and medicine, with their humane and dramatic victories, but also in all fields of knowledge and human relations, whose economic and social tensions may compress psychological bombs of devastating power.

THE SECOND SCIENTIFIC REVOLUTION

The university graduate schools themselves have been the creative center of the Second Scientific Revolution which is preparing the way for another Industrial Revolution as a factor in the transition to a new era in human history. The mechanistic universe, itself a revolutionary conception of university men in the seventeenth century, with its law of gravitation, with its later theory of the conservation of matter, its theories of electromagnetic waves, its theory of the ether, and with its theory of the atom as the indivisible ultimate stuff of the universe, this universe in fifty years has been overturned by university men and women. The X-ray, radioactivity, the theory of relativity, the electron theory of matter, the quantum theory, the nuclear theory of the atom as whirling bundles of energy, and the astronomical explorations of the universe, have revolutionized our conceptions of the nature of the atom and the universe. Older men and women in university laboratories and graduate seminars have been on the quest for pure knowledge which has resulted in the capture of nothing less than the energy of the atom and the power of the universe. Younger men and women in classrooms and dormitories are demanding co-operation for the international ban on atomic bombs and international co-operation for the mutual sharing of atomic knowledge and power. A program of co-operation is imperative in such an age in which social mastery lags behind scientific knowledge and the social conscience lags behind technological power. The transitions of history impelled by the compass and later by the steam engine were processes of slow centuries and gradual adjustments. Social drift and slow adjustments did not then, on such a scale as now, mean swift, wide, and terrible social tragedy and involve mayhap the survival of the human species on this earth. The possession of the earth might revert to a species which has not learned to make mechanisms which it cannot control. Centuries are not available for mankind to wait around for social drift and slow adaptation. Human society with an atomic bomb in its bosom cannot lag in adjustment to its explosive power. Mankind, with his swift scientific inventions and his slow social adjustments, has, with much economic progress and much human misery, muddled through to this fateful hour. Confronted with the atomic bomb, men and nations through co-operation now are to master this modern mechanical civilization or be destroyed in its unregulated self-destruction.

ATOMIC POWER AND THE NEED FOR A SPIRITUAL REVOLUTION

One little atomic bomb shook the world. Thousands of planes carrying loads of bombs could destroy thousands of years of accumulated civilization. The industrial structure which sustains the modern world but which catches up a war or a depression anywhere and involves human beings everywhere can soon with the press of many buttons release the power of the universe to destroy people anywhere. The bomb which fell on Hiroshima with the explosive, inner physical power of the universe, fell also on the consciousness of mankind with the explosive, inner moral power of man and the universe, loaded with the doom or the hopes of mankind. Youth, who fight the wars, lift their voices now for the brave hopes of a new world. Responsible freedom and human decency, international justice and peace, in the view of youth in the colleges, will come not by privileged advantage, but by equal opportunity for all; not by secrecy, but by open dealing; not by monopoly, but by wise and mutual sharing; not by isolation, but by co-operation; not by autocratic force, but by democratic faith. The way of hope is not by national power without the co-operative faith and will to make peace prevail. The way of hope is the way of faith with the international power and co-operative will to stop the aggressor and bring international justice and peace under the rule of law all over the world.

The atomic revolution demands a spiritual revolution. As the home of the atomic bomb, by virtue of her geographic and economic position, international co-operation, presidential daring, congressional appropriations, business and military genius for organization and production, university research and leadership, the devotion of preeminent scientists of many lands and the loyalty of workers from many states, America has a great moral responsibility. America, for the sake of her own soul, must take the lead in putting the atomic bomb under the ban and control of a strengthened international government. America must, with wise and mutual safeguards, share the knowledge and use of atomic power with all the peoples of the United Nations for full production and fair distribution within the nations, and for justice and peace among the nations, to include in God's good time all the peoples of the earth. Standing where cross the high road and the low road of human destiny, America, with her mechanisms, her universities, and her youth, let us pray, will not, in her choice, fail mankind in this tragic hour, but will rise to the responsibility of her power and the opportunity of her greatness to give fresh hope to the stricken and fearful peoples of the earth as brothers of men and sons of God for one co-operative world in our time.

RESEARCH IN THE SOUTH

Three addresses were delivered at the dinner meeting in the Carolina Inn Ball Room at 6: 30 P.M. which dealt with the general subject of research in the South in the fields of science, social science, and the humanities. The specific topics and speakers were: "Southern Research in the Sciences," by Paul Gross; "Research in the Social Sciences in the South," by Howard W.

Odum; and "Research in the Humanities," by James Southall Wilson. The speakers were introduced by President Graham, Toastmaster for the evening.

DR. PAUL GROSS

It is not my purpose this evening to attempt any detailed survey or appraisal, even supposing I were competent to do so, of research in the physical and natural sciences in the South. Such a recital would reveal many high spots of interest and would focus attention on notable examples of individual scientific achievement here in the South. It would call to mind such names as Venable and Baskerville and their work on the chemistry of the rarer elements; that of Herty and the utilization of our southern pine forests; all three distinguished past members of the faculty of this University, to cite examples from a single field. In other fields one would immediately recall the amazing pioneering research of Goldberger in nutrition. From this, as a beginning, we would follow a whole chain of discoveries in nutrition, many from southern institutions including my own, which ultimately led to the control of what was once one of the South's worst scourges—pellagra. Looking at the current scientific research we would note the work of Beams and his group at Virginia on the effect of high centrifugal accelerations on the properties of matter; important work in genetics in Texas; the coordination of scientific research and regional planning by the Tennessee Valley Authority and the University of Tennessee; the agronomic work on grazing lands in Florida; the significant contributions of the Coker enterprises in South Carolina in developing better strains of cotton—to list but a few examples. Proceeding thus, it would be readily possible to paint a eulogistic picture of the state of southern science.

Instead, I would like to look behind this picture and attempt an analysis of the status of some of these sciences in the South in comparison with that in the nation as a whole, and also of the factors which are responsible for the discrepancies that quickly become apparent.

Evidences of these discrepancies appear in a number of directions. Thus, when one looks at the representation on national scientific organizations, such, for example, as the National Research Council, it is evident that due consideration has not been given to a reasonably proportionate representation from southern institutions. The National Research Council covers all fields of science of any significance in this country and includes in its membership much of the scientific leadership of the country. The lack of adequate southern representation is immediately brought out by an examination of the membership list for any of the years immediately preceding the war. It will be found that of the two-hundred-and-twenty-odd members of the Council, there was at no time more than a small handful of five or six scientists representing the institutional and industrial research of the thirteen southern states. In terms of population, these states represent roughly a fifth of the nation's population. They have from a sixth to a fifth of the industries of the nation. Obviously, it can be argued that we have not scientists of the proper caliber for membership in such a body, but I am sure that this is not true in fact and, even if it were, it would not constitute a sound basis for such a disproportionate representation. In saying this, no criticism of the work of the National Research Council is implied nor of its attitude toward southern research. I am merely making a plea for a broader representation for the South in national scientific affairs. This would undoubtedly be of benefit in terms of its stimulation to southern research and would provide much needed guidance in charting its future course.

This disproportionate representation in a national scientific body of this broad type has, however, some real justification in another sense. A scrutiny of the broad fields of scientific activity in the South reveals that, in a number of important and significant branches of scientific work, there is little or no research in the South. Thus, with a few notable exceptions, it would have been found before the war that work in nuclear physics was almost nonexistent in our southern institutions. As an illustration, an examination of the list of contributed papers and addresses before such a conference as that on "Applied Nuclear Physics," which was held at Massachusetts Institute of Technology in the fall of 1940, shows that of the hundred-odd contributors to the conference, only one was from the South, and he was from an industrial research laboratory. There is thus missing from the southern scientific scene significant work on one of the most active frontiers of modern science.

Looking in entirely different directions one also finds no strong development of research in plant biochemistry, plant physiology, and plant pathology in the South. The absence of these disciplines is serious in terms of the South's needs. One of the greatest of these needs is the better development of a scientific agriculture, and it is obvious that the three fields mentioned are most important in implementing a sound and effective development of this sort.

Two other fields that are conspicuously absent, again with one or two exceptions, from southern scientific activity, are those of theoretical physics and applied mathematics.

My plea that such gaps be filled is not based merely on a wish for well-rounded scientific growth in the academic sense here in the South. I feel that, in its broader implications, such development may well be essential to the future development of a sound southern economy and I would like to dwell briefly on this aspect of the matter. While industry is moving southward and industrial expansion is increasingly evident, it is still true that agriculture is the principal economic base for the South. In this situation the status of southern agricultural research becomes a matter of first importance.

Agricultural research here has been carried out by state agricultural schools and state experiment stations. We find neighboring states with much the same agricultural problems working in comparative isolation and with too little co-ordination of effort. We have carried over our strong state pride into the scientific field. More important than this, we have let the Federal Government carry a disproportionate share of the cost. With this has come federal dominance and control of research policy and direction. While this has had some obvious points in its favor, it has been, on the whole, a species of remote control, and remote control rarely solves difficult scientific problems. Of more serious consequence is the fact that this situation has failed to develop adequate local scientific leadership, especially in the agricultural field. The South has trained many able scientists and scholars. Because of lack of support for research and inadequate salaries, many of these have migrated and but few have remained. As an apt phrase current in scholarly and scientific circles puts it, "The South is a good place to come from."

Such state support as there has been has not been as effective as it should have been because of our dual system in higher education. In most of our southern states the state university and the agricultural and engineering school are separate institutions. This has too often led to competition for the limited resources that the state could provide and this in turn has not been conducive to intellectual co-operation. As a result, the applied fields of agriculture and engineering have lacked the stimulus and breadth of scientific background that comes from basic work in pure science. If one looks back over the history of the development of agriculture in our western states, it will be found, with few exceptions, that most rapid progress has been made in those states in which there has been no dual system in higher education and where agriculture and engineering have been integral parts of the state university.

Some of these situations I have outlined would be helped if we had institutes, either public or private, comparable, even on a modest scale, with the Boyce Thompson Institute for Plant Research or the Rockefeller Institute for Biological Research at Princeton. We are making some progress in this direction. One of the Regional Laboratories was located at New Orleans and recently a modest counterpart of the Mellon Institute has been established at Birmingham. This is the Southern Research Institute which is already doing good work. Until recently, in spite of the fact that many technological industries have expanded southward, they have continued to do their research in the North. The recent announcement by one of our large oil companies that it plans a large research center at Baton Rouge along with expansion of research facilities in the North is a hopeful sign.

Finally, let me turn to some of the intangibles which I feel have bearing on research development in the South. Here I must be quick to say that I am on the less sure ground of personal opinion and judgment. Some of my good northern scientific friends have seriously argued that our warm climate is not conducive to a high level of scientific activity. In the light of my own experience, I put little stock in this but am inclined to give more weight to the influence of the southern cultural climate. There is, of course, a strong and fine liberal arts tradition in education in the South. However, this, added to a species of cultural complacency in some southern thinking, has not made for ready acceptance of the consequence of the impact of new scientific advances. Dr. Charles Herty had another phrase for this—he said the South was in a condition of "static ecstasy." I must confess that at times I feel that it will require the impact of something of the order of the atomic bomb to bring about the conversion he hoped to see to what he called a condition of "dynamic ecstasy."

This same atomic bomb is, of course, the outstanding example of what can be achieved by organized and co-ordinated scientific effort directed toward the attainment of an objective. Better organization and co-ordination of southern scientific effort, better understanding of it, and better support for it is one of the surest guides by which to chart our course here in the South through these post-war years. For this to be effective our scientific thinking and planning must be on a high as well as a broad plane. Otherwise, there is but little hope that it can bring about some of the near miracles that will be required for the solution of some of the South's pressing agricultural and industrial problems.

Following Dr. Gross's address, Howard W. Odum spoke on "Research in the Social Sciences in the South."

DR. ODUM

On first thought it would seem relatively easy to say a great deal about research in the social sciences in the South. For, on every hand there is well-nigh universal agreement that unless we can do something about harnessing the knowledge and technology which we have to social ends, there will be disaster ahead. We do not need to subscribe to the extreme verdicts which predict chaos and self-destruction, man and civilization destroying themselves; or the alarm for the future of mankind, to recognize the elemental nature of society's dilemma at this the crest of technological achievement.

More specifically in the South, in addition to the universal need for the social sciences to parallel the researches of the physical sciences and for the two together to parallel the humanities, in order to achieve mastery, there are other considerations. In the first place there appears to be a widespread and substantial purpose in the South to strengthen and expand facilities for research in all fields. This is in line with a new recognition of the role of research commensurate with needs and comparable to its role in other parts of the nation.

In the second place research in the social sciences merits special attention in the South because of the great opportunity which faces the South in the next field of development and because of the South's current deficiencies in research.

Still another reason why the discussion of research in the social sciences is of special timeliness in the South is the fact that efforts now being made to secure national legislation looking toward the strengthening of research seek to incorporate co-ordinate levels of social research alongside research in the natural sciences. The supplementary funds which might accrue from this would be of special value to the South as leverage to lift its own increasing efforts in this direction.

When, however, we try to say something new or adequate for the occasion, the task is peculiarly difficult. This is true for the very reason that so much is being said and written by so many people from so many sources and angles. Then it is true again because the opportunities and the obligations of southern universities are proportionately greater. What we should like to do, therefore, is to present something of these opportunities and obligations but within the twofold framework of regional problem and the larger implications of universal need.

In order to do this we shall need to look at a number of assumptions that appear to be basic. One of the first of these is to re-emphasize the meaning of research as being of the essence of University itself. If we should select the two distinctive traits of University, one would seem to me to be that of research and the other freedom to do research and to translate and use it. On this assumption, our institutions are not universities, but colleges or professional schools until and unless they are equipped for doing research.

This means, then, that we are here making a distinction between the social sciences and the social studies; between advanced social science, the very content and methodology of which are determined by research, and the social sciences which are catalogued as subjects in a liberal education or as undergraduate courses for advanced social science. That is, economics, history, political science, sociology, cultural anthropology, human geography, social psychology, statistics, are important subjects in the curriculum, but as sciences their value and validity must depend upon research and an increasing approximation to dependable scientific method, and then to an equally important scientific premise for the application of results.

Another way of illustrating this is to say that the universities now have an increasingly large obligation to strengthen the field of philosophy and certain other aspects of the humanities and of the professions. This is true not only because these subjects are of great importance on their own account, but because they are needed more and more for larger and larger numbers of students who think they want the social sciences. Many of the best minds and the brightest students want to read and discuss, to debate and argue, and to provide action programs based upon ideological or moralistic assumptions alone. Others are minded to equip themselves for effective action duties, and others perhaps simply "love humanity" and want to do something about it. The point is that all of these are of the greatest importance and are part and parcel of democratic and professional education, but they are not social science in the sense in which we are discussing it.

In this connection, however, there are, I believe, two general assumptions that are important. One is that the social sciences are developing in increasingly closer co-operation and co-ordination with the natural sciences, both for the advantages they gain from such co-operation and from the end-results which come from genuine integration of the two great fields of science.

I scarcely need to illustrate: economic geography, ecology, biochemistry, psychology, physics with all its communication and arts phases, engineering, and the hundred and one areas of climate and weather, foods and diets, soils and vitality.

The second general observation here is that the social sciences, enriched, expanded, made increasingly more scientific, may make substantial contributions in both materials and premises to that new and dynamic humanistic education which seeks balance and harmony between man and nature, between men and machines, between culture and civilization.

Turning then to assumptions that point more specifically to the framework of our own research in the South, there are three that appear basic here.

The first is that for any successful program of research in the social sciences, including the necessity of developing and training personnel, there must be content and field adequate for concrete studies but also comprehensive enough for the integration of a social science that will focus upon human relations. We may illustrate this briefly a little later.

The second essential is that there must be laboratory and scientific method adequate for concrete studies but also comprehensive enough to develop sound theory through the synthesis of the findings of empirical research in which there is adequate range and selection of materials.

The third essential is found in the need for scientific method and practical strategy for the application of the results of research to the living society about us. This should be somewhat comparable to the effectiveness with which technology makes wide application of the results of scientific research in the natural sciences.

With reference to the content and field, there appear to be two major areas. One is the very real and measurable economic and cultural environment. The other is the area of actual human relationships. Each of these must be studied and mastered.

Within the framework of southern regional research we illustrate the field and content, first, with resources which in the modern world of science and technology become the keynote to both survival and progress. For the story of a nation or of a region or of any human society begins with the resources of the people and the influence of nature's endowment upon their culture.

As time goes on, the story continues with more emphasis upon how the people use their resources and what the people do to and with nature and the kind of spiritual culture and institutions they develop.

Resources are what the people have to live on and to do with. Sometimes they are what men live for and die for in terms of native lands they love. Always nature and resources are the physical backgrounds of the culture of people and the wealth of nations.

Nature's endowment of man consists not only in the abundance of material and natural resources, but also in the tell of time, the cycle of seasons, of days and nights, and incidence of cold and heat, sunshine and rain. It consists also in the laws of nature and of science from which flow invention and technology, and of man himself in nature.

Because Nature's endowment is translated into resources through man's capacity and will to develop, to conserve and to use wisely, the chief resources of any society are the people themselves, skilled, trained, and at work in the places where they live and in interchange with other peoples and other places.

It is often said that potential resources are not real until they are used and that the harnessing of nature is man's biggest job. It follows that the development, conservation, and wise use of resources can make a wealthy people in a lovely land, but that man's exploitation of nature or nature's exploitation of man with the resulting waste of resources can make a poor people in a barren land.

This applies more specifically to the South in a number of ways. In the first place, many years of research have shown us that the South's main deficiencies have been due to its lack of science, research, skill, organization, management, which would translate its natural resources into capital wealth which in turn could be devoted to the institutions, culture, and economy which would enrich the people and develop the region. It is to bridge the chasm between the potentialities of the South and its actual realities that the social sciences now are called upon for new reaches in research and application.

You recall that our analysis of the region showed that we excelled in natural resources and human resources but we lagged in technological wealth, capital wealth, and institutional wealth. We also have a large measure of waste. For these reasons, we have an unbalanced economy. We also have a rich heritage in southern background and culture and with it a tendency to look to the past. The challenge to the social sciences is to see that the South excels in all levels of its resources, eliminates its waste, attains a balanced culture and economy, and realizes on its heritage in such a way as to look forward in the development of new leadership.

There is another way in which this total combined research of the social sciences may focus upon the over-all problem of the development of the South in the framework of the national culture and prosperity. This is in what we may call the regional equality and balance of America which many observers feel is the most important domestic problem upon which new research and strategy must be focused. In relatively simple terms this means that research and planning must be devoted to a strategy which will guarantee that the South can produce wealth in an abundance economy and can use it wisely; that the youth of the South may have opportunity to work in the places where they live and to profit by the interregional exchange which comes from communication, technology, and education from and within other regions. It means the opportunity for the fullest development, conservation, and wise use of resources and a cultural development which integrates the South increasingly with the other regions of the nation. It means that there can be no longer isolation and separatism and that interregional and intercultural educations and relations constitute a major field for consolidated research and planning.

Perhaps more than anything else, this means that the South can never develop in any adequate way worthy of its heritage and resources except as it becomes a dynamic living part of America, in harmony and balance with all America.

All of this assumes, then, the regional social science laboratory. This laboratory, as featuring the research in the social sciences, may be envisaged on three levels. The first is reading rooms, the statistical laboratories and calculating machines, necessary to any adequate research program. Historical collections, tools for recording and collecting facts, and all the rich new facilities that are developing now become the essentials for translating our new research into reality.

The second level of the laboratory is the state or the city or the special community or industry or subregion which stems out from the immediate center of research.

The third level of the regional laboratory consists of an entire region, such as we may designate a Southeast or a Southwest. It seems clear that such a total region is the smallest unit in which all the social sciences and the physical sciences working together may find all the factors of environment, resources, time factors, and cultural and economic development adequate to give full range and fair selection of materials.

This framework of the laboratory seems to me to be even more specifically necessary when we come to examine the need and facilities for trained personnel in research. We suffer because we have not developed any reasonably well recognized methodology, because we do not have personnel adequate or matured; and because we cannot find such trained personnel. It is of the essence of this discussion or this appeal that we shall have to train and develop quickly and well hundreds of young scholars, and that the only way to do it is to put them to work in the laboratories where their learning becomes a part of the process of research and its analysis and interpretation.

We come now to the third essential of our social research program, and that has to do with making application of our results to the better ordering of a democratic society and to studying and working on the dilemma of human association. I do not believe we should blame the common man for being skeptical about what the social scientist does. I doubt if we should blame the natural scientists or the humanists for their skepticism. For, as yet, we have not developed enough laboratories, enough real scientists, and we have not been able to equip those we have adequately. It is the assumption of our discussion that it is only through some such integrated programs of co-operative research and of actual living social science laboratories that we can do the job. This is an appeal, as it were, to usher in the new period of southern development by giving this sort of regional social research in the living laboratories of the people the first priority.

But there is another reason why our work has not been more effective. It is that we have done very little in the way of making our social science understood, of translating and channeling the results of our researches into education and industrial development, into political and administrative channels, and into the heartening of the public to work together for better human relationships.

This field of application, then, is of two sorts. One is research and strategy in the fields of organization, of public administration, in all the institutional ways of our southern culture and economy. The other is then to make available these results to the people and to the people who lead.

The conclusion of this brief discussion brings us back to our perennial premise, namely that unless we can have universities equipped for scientific and technical research and leadership, and unless we can train a great many more leaders than we have and can set them to work in the South and keep them there, we shall continue to fall far short of any adequate regional development. Since research is of the essence of University, and since we have no universities of the first rank and few of a high rank, it follows that the appeal for new levels of achievement in research in the social sciences is an appeal for a university consciousness in the South.

My father, down in Georgia, now about ninety years of age, being part Irish, has a way of being positive in his expression. He likes to be positively dogmatic sometimes, as for instance when he would say: "Any man who says he loves the Lord and hates the Negro is a liar." Then he would smile beneficently and say: "At least, that's the way it seems to me."

Well, this is the way it seems to me. It is in that spirit that it seems to me that, from a partial and specialized viewpoint, the most important thing to be done in our southern universities is to strengthen this field of social research and to do it quickly. There are other things to do. But at this time, in this place, in the spirit of the Association of American Universities, and in the spirit of modern dilemma, and still more specifically on the eve of a New Southern Epoch, this seems to me to be the supreme challenge for here and now.

Dr. Odum's address was followed by that of Dr. James South-all Wilson, "Research in the Humanities."

DR. JAMES SOUTHALL WILSON

We have not yet got away from the connotation of the word "scholarship" with the erudite student of the humanities whose learning springs out of a study of the past and has historical and linguistic as well as possibly literary associations. On the other hand the word, "research," has been multiplying its affiliations with the scientists. Its methods are approved only when they can be called scientific and, among some academicians whose language is less accurate than their laboratory methods, a reference to the "research activities" of a university applies only to those of the natural sciences.

I

The War and its results have created at the same time an opportunity and a danger for research in the humanities. The danger is the more obvious and the more immediate. In a world impressed and terrified by the achievements of the atomic bomb there is not much likelihood that the importance of research in either chemistry or physics will be underestimated. The resultant emphasis upon the practical value of the natural scientists and the almost equally expanding demand for so-called "social scientists," that is, for experts in matters of economics, business, public and foreign affairs, and government, will be so great that there will be most probably a tendency to disparage the development of research in the arts, literature, language, and subjects like philosophy and the more unserviceable phases of history. It is sufficiently understood now that the most esoteric finding of pure mathematics or of science can, like the original thought of the Angel Uriel in Emerson's poem, unhinge a universe. From the theories of an Einstein to the destruction of a city of Japan was as inevitable as the steps in a mathematical formula. Not an atom's difference is made in our comfort or safety if it is proved that a William Brown and not a Sarah Wentworth Morton wrote the first American novel, *The Power of Sympathy*, or that Shakespeare wrote " 'a babbled of green fields" instead of "a table of green fields," though the difference in the words in these phrases makes all the difference between wonderful old Sir John Falstaff's dying in obloquy or into immortality. Among the ranks of the humanistic scholars themselves, even before the war began, ridicule had been turned upon the character of the research and the methods of graduate teaching in the humanities among American graduate universities. It was charged that topics and material had given out. Fantastic stories were told of the searches made for thesis subjects and ludicrous titles were quoted to indicate in what such persistent researches resulted. In unexpected quarters it was announced that the proper fruit of literary study was the ability to create literature. It was urged that the place of research in the languages and the arts should be taken by the exercise of the creative gifts. Instead of the thesis, it was proposed, let the universities accept poems, short stories, and novels, musical compositions and examples of sculpture and painting. The attack upon the validity and importance of research in the humanities before the war was largely one that sprang from special points of view and even certain temperamental predispositions. The threat now is a more far-reaching one. The danger is in an insistance upon utilitarian values that may become a nation's attitude affecting not only the providers of the means of research but the readiness to undertake it of the youth who are the potential research workers of the future in the humanities.

This is a brief statement of the danger. I said the war has created also a need and an opportunity for research in the humanities in America. If the danger is formidable, so is the need imperative. Scholars in the past have looked to England, Germany, and France as custodians of the past in the humanities. From the countries of Europe, too, have come much of the critical interpretation of our own times and their background. Partly as a result of the very successes of theoretical and practical research in the fields of natural science and their application to mechanical uses, those regions in which learning and art have been so fruitfully active have been reduced to a way of life that will force attention primarily to the stark necessities of life. It will be years before the great universities of Europe and Great Britain will restore their full facilities and recover completely the conditions and atmosphere of great centers of culture and of productive research in the humanities. On the other hand, there have developed in America great special collections like those at the Huntington and the Folger libraries. In the South resources for study are developing in special fields at the Universities of Texas, North Carolina, Duke, and Virginia. The importance of an authoritative study of America's own life, past and present, in literature, language, art, music, and all other subjects has become more and more evident. Never has the responsibility of the scholarship of the United States been so great as now for the preservation and extension of the values represented by research in the humanities. It is the one great nation in which the resources of life are so rich that it is not forced to restrict its primary activity to those necessary researches by which life is preserved and made safe. It can foster also the arts and the investigations of that culture which is a large part of what makes civilized life worth preserving.

The first prerequisite for the fulfillment of this obligation to become the vital center of humanistic studies is a full recognition by our scholars themselves of the dignity and importance of these studies and of active research in them. The second prerequisite is a more active and aggressive effort to secure financial support and endowment of research enterprises in these fields. It is only the first of these prerequisites that can be discussed here. I remember talking to a great English scholar at a dinner during the First World War. He said to me that he felt that nothing in the world was so useless as the researches of a middle-aged student of English literature. Fifteen years later I repeated to him that remark. "I have no recollection of saying that," he said. "I must have been in a bad way indeed. I cannot recall now that ever in my life I have doubted the importance of English scholarship." He had recovered from the influence of a temporary environment. The modern scholar is more a part of the general world he lives in than the scholar was in the past. He enters into its daily interests and is influenced by its common judgments. Often he accepts the value put upon his activities and their fruits by the society that surrounds him. In the United States, including the South, that society does not now put a high valuation upon the activities or the researches of the scholar in the humanities. We must first believe in ourselves and our works. We must then convince others and not be convinced of the contrary by them. It would be well if some of the leaders of organizations such as the Modern Language Association would take time out from listening to papers which are too often representative of the misdirected or trivial scholarship that justifies some of the satire of the scoffers, and consider soberly (but with a sense of humor and proportion) how the interests in their field of scholarship can be best served by the scholars in it. Perhaps habit and routine and the following of the nearest interest have blinded our eyes to higher tasks that need accomplishment. Perhaps the urgency of time and the practical desire to secure the office certificate of a degree have had too much influence in the choice of the research objectives of young university graduates.

I think that one of the potent reasons for a lack of faith in research in the humanities among scholars themselves is that their own motives for engaging in it are sometimes unworthy ones. The first initiation is through a piece of work done wholly from the practical necessity of writing a thesis as a preliminary to receiving a Ph.D. which is a prerequisite to holding a college professorship. Later publications are counted up like the credits in a college degree as tangible grounds for promotion or calls to other institutions. The South is certainly as active as the rest of the country in demanding the label rather than the spirit and zeal of scholarship, showing more interest in the label of the degree than in the character of the scholarship. If I may play on words in this sober company I would say that we judge our professors not by their works but by their titles.

There is an especial opportunity in southern universities for research in southern subjects that only a southerner can investigate understandingly. I hope that does not shock your sense of the objectivity of honest research. Not all southerners are conscious of it but there was a culture peculiar to itself in the Old South that has changed but that made its own qualifying contribution to the life in America. Interest and distance and sympathy enter into the perspectives of scholars as of other men. There was a novel called *The Prisoners of Niagara or the Errors of Education* published in Frankfort, Kentucky, in 1810 that would be discussed in every history of American fiction if it had been printed in Massachusetts. The novels of George Tucker, published in 1824 and 1827, have more real importance historically than those of several writers whose names are familiar because local interest made them so. I doubt if ten professors of English in America are familiar with the titles of these novels. The manuscripts in southern literature at Duke University and in southern history at Chapel Hill emphasize the obligations of southern research scholars. There should be funds established to underwrite the serious studies that demand publication but do not interest purchasers. But with the fullest provisions for publication, research conditions in the South will not be good until southern universities seek, find, and hold more first-rate professors and encourage their research activities. There are three especial conditions that must be altered: low salaries, heavy teaching loads, and lack of sabbatical years. Dean Taylor, of Princeton, has recently called attention to the "real dearth of scholars in their forties or early fifties" in the humanities. That dearth is at least no less noteworthy in the South than elsewhere. But were the academic groves full of productive scholars we cannot have fruitful research unless we are willing to pay for it.

II

I have been talking of the dangers to and the opportunities of research in the humanities at this time. I want to speak now of some conditions among humanistic studies, some of which increase the danger and lessen the opportunities. A reconsideration of the aims and the methods of research in every field is desirable from time to time. A clarification of the relationships in the fields of the humanities is especially needed now as we face a world with a changed outlook amid changed conditions. For one thing there should be a better understanding of the different objectives and their relationships in the several fields of the humanities. It is not wholesome for the historian who gathers the statistics and the facts and consults the documents to hold in contempt the able writer who uses his data as a basis for the dramatic presentation or the broad philosophical interpretation of the events. In the field of literature and language, there are diverse interests and aims each with its appropriate methods. The literary historical scholar has an importance no less than the student or historian of ideas, and the textual scholar no less than the analytic or the historical critic. A really scholarly piece of criticism should carry as much credit to its author if published in the *Saturday Review of Literature* as in the *Publications of the Modern Language Association*. In my own field that is one of the needs of our intellectual life: that research scholarship shall be vitalized by more application to contemporary life and that contemporary criticism shall be more informed by an intelligent awareness of the findings of scholarship.

It is not to be expected that all the findings of research shall appear, or even be, important. It is not so in the natural sciences; it will not be so ever in the humanities. Mediocre men do mediocre tasks and think commonplace thoughts. Thousands—is that an exaggeration?—of young mathematicians must be trained for the chance of training one Einstein or even one Bertrand Russell. There is always the hope of the "lucky find" for the little man, of the growth of the promising man, of the discovery of the great man. And there is always the big task for the big man. The field of literary scholarship in America is thick with important tasks waiting to be done when the right scholar finds them or perhaps even when that scholar has some confidence that he can publish the results of his labor after years of devotion. Edward Shanks has said that it is a shame to American scholarship that no authentic text of the writings of Edgar Allan Poe has ever been published. There is no such text: but who will offer the days of his youth and the sight of his eyes to the task with no assurance that any publisher will publish the next text or that any considerable number of people will be interested in the achievement? Yet we must keep our inheritance of centuries of humanistic research up-to-date. It is a mistake to suppose that the last word is ever said on anything. Shakespeare is alive today because for each generation the actors and the scholars have represented him in the interpretation of the times. The research problems in Shakespearean scholarship in the twentieth century differ as greatly from those of the early nineteenth century as do the realistic critical interpretations of his plays from the romantic rhapsodies of a century ago. Even literary biography and history changed their moods and methods with the generations. We are busier today righting the mistakes of the past in history, literary and political, than we are in finding new tasks that have never been undertaken: and the job is more important, for the worst ignorance is the possession of supposed knowledge which is demonstrably false.

I do not know what I was expected to do in a fifteen-minute paper. Whatever it was, I am sure I have not done it. But I assure you of the sincerity of my belief in the importance of keeping alive the love of learning, the curiosity to discover how men have lived and thought and written and created into words or objects or sounds of beauty or significance. I believe the fruit of this love of learning, which includes especially what we call research in the humanities, is one of the surest and highest tests of a nation's cultured civilization. It is the importance of the values that are represented by humanistic research that I have sought to stress, and that is no different in the South from what it is in all America. I maintain that in seriousness and austerity of truth it can be on a plane with that of mathematics or natural science and that its significance is no less because it relates to the dignity of the spirit of man. I have sought to stress also the desirability of a better understanding among the leaders of different phases of research in the humanities. There is the student of the text or the sources or the history. There are those who critically explain or who trace philosophically the history of ideas. There are those who give imaginative interpretation to the works of others and those who themselves are original creators. All these have importance to humanistic research. They should understand each other's aims that there may be peace in the house of the humanities.

X

THE SESQUICENTENNIAL CONVOCATION

THE FINAL events of the Sesquicentennial which had been planned for University Day in October, 1945, but had to be postponed on account of regulations of the Office of Defense Transportation governing attendance at meetings, were held April 12 and 13, 1946, after the sesquicentennial period had ended, in order to give representatives of other institutions, returning alumni, and friends of the University generally an opportunity to participate in the ceremonies and to offer their felicitations to the University. A two-day program, varied, delightful, and inspiring, was carried out for this purpose.

The program of Friday, April 12, was presented in three parts, the first of which began at 6:00 P.M. at Lenoir Hall with a dinner for the four hundred delegates from other institutions, the thirty-nine prospective recipients of honorary degrees, and other special guests of the University. Chancellor Robert Burton House presided and R. Gregg Cherry, Governor of North Carolina and President of the Board of Trustees of the University, extended the official welcome of the University.

GOVERNOR CHERRY

It has been my keen pleasure to come to the campus of the University of North Carolina on several occasions during the nearly sixteen months that I have been Governor of North Carolina. It is always a pleasure to come here.

I like Chapel Hill and the surroundings and buildings and people and institutions here, as do most North Carolinians. At this particular time of the year it is easier than at any other time to explain to a rank stranger from another state the charm and the magic of Chapel Hill. This spot is never more beautiful than in the lush of spring and it is a delight to come here from the State Capitol at Raleigh to be with you in an atmosphere that we all love.

The spring of the year is a very fine time to take an accounting. That is true with an individual, with a university, or with a state. I have been taking an informal accounting of some of North Carolina's assets and liabilities in recent weeks.

I find my attention turning again of late to the realization that the real North Carolina peacemakers are the young men and the young women of the state. The war demonstrated that this group gives us our real lift and embodies our fine hopes for the future. Talk of youthful peacemakers in North Carolina brings us quite naturally to talk of the State University.

There are reasons why the young people of our state and of America are the best in the world. First of all they are the best educated young people in the world—in spite of the fact that our educational system has yet a long way to go. Our young people are just about the most self-reliant young people on earth. Records of military service in recent years show that. Our young people think for themselves, act for themselves and handle the consequences in their own way.

There are two important things to be considered in a breakdown of our No. 1 asset—our young people.

On the liability side it is apparent that we need to take quick and sure action in the matter of health and physical fitness. We also need to eliminate the scourge of poverty that still attacks our society at its fringes and at its heart, even in these days of reasonable plenty.

To get a bumper crop of the sort of citizens that North Carolina wants and needs we must scatter over the face of this fine state a lot of healthy and intelligent people. The land is rich. Let's make the seed good. This crop of good citizens will bring in an abundant harvest of co-operative, self-supporting, happy, and productive citizens.

In this desire and in this effort ignorance is our principal enemy. We must tackle ignorance at its roots. As we eliminate ignorance and give to our young men and young women knowledge, skills, and understandings we will solve the problems of our state and the problems of the peace of the world.

Here in North Carolina the plain person—the young man or woman from a modest home and modest means—has always had a chance. That is because we are a free people and because we look for and give reward for merit.

The lives of men and women are affected by three important things over which they have some control. These things are the education or the training they receive, the man or woman they marry, and the type and kind of work they do. Here at Chapel Hill many generations of fine men and women have attended the school of their dreams. Every day North Carolinians marry the girl or boy of their dreams. In this state a vast majority of three and a half million people do the work of their dreams. I think North Carolina is a state of the heart's desire. It's a state that belongs to the people who live and work in it and who have the opportunity of going as far and as fast in it as they want to go or are willing to go.

We have some people in this state who are poor, who are dissatisfied, who have somehow missed the whole basic idea of the place or have been overlooked by fate. For the most part this minority group has either failed to see North Carolina's truly wonderful opportunities or has failed to take advantage of them in a good, earnest, hard-working way. There are those who blame conditions, who blame others, who blame their teachers, who blame their wives, but who never blame themselves.

A man who blames himself for his troubles will likely seize the next opportunity to come along. He is ready. He is ready because he is busy. The better opportunities come to those who are at work. Individuals are supposed to take care of themselves and of their work—whatever it is. No one else will do this for them.

You see I am advocating here tonight more and better things for more people. At the same time I advocate less of poverty and its penalties and less of poor health and inadequate physical fitness.

We must believe in everybody doing well in North Carolina. We must join forces and work to the end that North Carolinians live fuller lives, make more money, have more of the things of life that men and women want, get ahead, and do more and see more.

The formula for success has always been simple. It is confined to the one word "work." I challenge you to show me a truly successful man or woman who has not worked. They do the things they know they ought to do. That is how and why they are doing what they want to do, earning what they want to earn, and having what they want to have.

It is traditional here in North Carolina that we teach our young people to hold their heads up, to look any man in the eye, and to fear the wrath of no one on earth.

To that the University of North Carolina has devoted one hundred and fifty-one years of its existence. In connection with the observance of its sesquicentennial I extend compliments for the job that has been done and commend the continuation of a program built around just those ideals.

As this sesquicentennial celebration nears its end, it is fitting and timely that we again consider the courage and determination with which our ancestors met and overcame the stubborn difficulties of their day. During the one hundred and fifty-one years since the first student appeared here for instruction, nearly 50,000 regular students have matriculated here. These have come mostly from this state but also from other states. They have represented the homes of the rich and the poor, the high and the low, the learned and unlearned. They have sought after and have been provided with the tools and the inspiration to forge a better way of life here in North Carolina—for themselves and for their fellow North Carolinians. They have absorbed here at Chapel Hill something of the meaning and the depth of university life.

Here on the University campus a long line of teachers with lives dedicated to the art and the science of teaching have given freely of themselves to their students. The loyalty of the teaching staff of this institution has been, and is, an outstanding example of unselfish dedication to the training of youth, the building of character, and the development of North Carolina and the North Carolina way of life.

Created here half a century before the public school system of North Carolina, the State University has led the movement for education as it has been in a position of leadership with every other movement for good that has rolled across our state.

There is no adequate method of measuring the influence of this institution on the life of North Carolina in the century and a half that the University has been a living, throbbing, serving institution. Suffice it to say that the alumni of this University have always been on hand when any matter affected the sound progress of our people. University graduates have joined with graduates of other educational institutions in leading the way in the continuing march for a higher level of intellectual, economic, and spiritual attainment. Now in the one hundred and fifty-first year of its birth, the University of North Carolina is a symbol of intellectual freedom, ranks high among the universities of the nation, has a faculty of outstanding ability and unselfish dedication, and is at the same time the property and the pride of the three and a half million North Carolinians.

This institution holds an enviable place in the hearts of our people. In churches, in schoolrooms, on farms, in factories, in the halls of government there are leaders whose lamps were either first lit or refueled here at this University. And with the light that was kindled or reactivated here these men and women show the paths and light the trails of human achievement.

This is indeed and shall ever be "a University of the people." And that is at the same time the secret of its greatness and the assurance of the permanent security of its future. This ancient temple of learning with its unparalleled heritage and great record of achievement, still has its eyes fixed on the stars at the same time that its roots are set deep in the soil and the traditions of North Carolina. We march steadily forward upon the highroad of progress in the search for greater freedom and keener and more usable truth. There is no substitute for spiritual values in the affairs of men and of states and nations. Rugged honesty and hard work provide the key to any still unopened door.

On the eve of the series of meetings, I salute our State University now beginning the one hundred and fifty-second year of service. I commend without reservation its staff and its faculty. I congratulate the men and women who have passed through its portals to take their places in the hustle of everyday life. I bring happy greetings to those who are now daily using its walks and corridors in their search after knowledge.

The great state that we have in North Carolina has been made greater by its State University.

ORCHESTRAL CONCERT

The second part of the program was given at Hill Music Hall, with Chancellor House presiding. It consisted of a brilliantly executed orchestral concert given under the direction of Professor Earl Slocum by the University Symphony Orchestra assisted by the Chapel Hill Choral Club and Professor William S. Newman, pianist, and a comprehensive address entitled "Two Hundred Years of American Painting," by Mr. John Walker, Chief Curator of the National Gallery of Art. The three musical numbers, presented by the Orchestra, were: "Jesu, Joy of Man's Desiring," from the Cantata No. 147, by Johann Sebastian Bach; "Symphony in E Flat, Op. 2," Adagio-Allegro, Allegretto scherzando, Adagio, Allegro Maestoso, by Camille Saint-Saëns; and "The Rio Grande," for Chorus, Orchestra, and Solo Pianoforte (Poem by Sacheverell Sitwell), by Constant Lambert. In the interval between the concert and the address, Mr. Norman Cheshire Cordon, Jr., of the Metropolitan Opera Company and an alumnus of the University, delighted the audience with the rendition of "Hark the Sound of Tar Heel Voices." Introduced by Chancellor House, Mr. Walker spoke as follows:

MR. WALKER

On the twelfth day of May the United States will send to London the first important exhibition of American painting ever shown in England. The exhibition is an official gesture of good will financed by the governments of the two countries. The selection of the paintings covering two hundred years of American art has been made by two committees of museum directors, one committee for the work of artists no longer alive, the other for contemporary painting. I have been chairman of the committee selecting what we might call the "Old Masters," and this evening I want to give you a preview, so to speak, of this section of the exhibition, so that you can judge for yourselves what we have accomplished in the first two hundred years of our artistic life.

In selecting the paintings to be sent to London the committee was confronted at once with the problem: Is there an American style? When this college was founded one hundred and fifty years ago, was there anything in American art which indicated that it was more than a colonial dependency of the Old World, more than a provincial outpost of European painting? When our settlements grew into towns, when the amenities of life increased, when political independence was finally attained, did a national school of painting develop? Certainly until recent times the parenthood of Europe has remained. For example, throughout the nineteenth century every significant American artist went abroad to study. In fact, it will surprise many Englishmen to know that Copley, West, Stuart, Whistler, and Sargent are actually American painters, for these artists still appear in English catalogues under the heading, British School.

Nevertheless, I am convinced that there is a native flavor in our painting that is not derived alone from subject matter, costumes, or scenery. It is a quality which we also find in American literature. There is a parallel between the hard colloquial vividness we find in the paintings of such American realists as Bingham and the writings of Mark Twain; or the shadowy symbolic beauty apparent in the canvases of our imaginative artists like Ryder, which is very similar to the poetry of Poe or the novels of Melville and Hawthorne. Though this indigenous quality is difficult to describe except by such analogies, it is apparent that we have developed a native style distinct from Europe.

That such a style should develop is not surprising. For you must remember that the American painter, even more than the American writer, has been affected by the geographical position of the New World. He has been physically separated from the central tradition of Western Art. The center of gravity has been, until now, Europe, and our artists have been invariably drawn abroad, but these painters have arrived in Europe mature in years, yet children from the point of view of the technique of their profession. Thus, apart from the expatriated painters, the

American style compared to European painting lacks facility, is naive, brusque, even awkward, and very often curiously primitive as in the painting by Hicks of the "Peaceable Kingdom." The greatness of American painting lies neither in its dexterity nor in its virtuosity, but rather in its honesty, its sincerity, and its hard grasp of fact.

What we may consider an American School begins with the work of Copley and West, who were born in the same year, 1738. Copley's portraits are the first outstanding achievement of realism in this country, the earliest work of significance with a distinct native flavor, as can be seen in the portrait of "Nicholas Boylston."

West's allegorical and mythological subjects are the first imaginative paintings by an artist born in the New World, the earliest manifestation of a poetic strain in American painting, qualities which made him in some ways a precursor of romanticism, as can be seen in the sketch for a painting entitled "Death on a White Horse."

Of John Singleton Copley, Gilbert Stuart once said, "He knew more than all of us put together." Stuart's remark is correct, in a sense. Copley learned to transcribe exactly what he saw in front of him, to paint every detail of the shrewd Yankee countenances of his patrons. But he never learned, on the other hand, the short cuts to portraiture which had been developed in Europe, or never needed to learn them while he remained in America. For as social life in the New World offered few diversions his sitters were willing to pose for hours on end. They asked only that their portraits should be exactly like themselves. They liked the brusque, unadorned recording which Copley gave them. These Bostonians were, in fact, curiously like the patrons of the Italian Renaissance. Like the Medici and the Gonzagas and the Visconti, they were satisfied with that outmoded goal of portraiture, an honest, unflattering statement of their personalities, something no eighteenth-century patron in Europe would have permitted.

The tragedy of Copley, however, foreshadows the tragedy of many American painters who were to follow him. He had no confidence in the style he had created; he looked upon himself as a provincial cut off from the source of European tradition. He regretted having to live in a country where the art of painting was regarded as no more than any other useful trade—like that of a carpenter, tailor, or shoemaker. Yet for a long time Copley hesitated to exchange the security of Boston for a doubtful success in the London of Reynolds and his circle. In 1766 he sent to the Royal Academy the "Boy with the Squirrel." The painting arrived at the exhibition, and the hanging committee received it with immense enthusiasm; but when they looked to see who had painted the picture, they found no indication, for Copley had been too modest to sign his canvas. It was only by chance that one of the members thought of going to the wharves and asking whether any of the ships captains had brought the painting from America and thus discovered its author. In spite of the great success which the "Boy with the Squirrel" immediately had, Copley preferred to stay in New England.

As the Revolution approached, however, Copley found himself allied by marriage to one of the great Tory families in Boston. His father-in-law, who appears in the group portrait in the National Gallery of Art, was actually the consignee of the tea thrown into the harbor at the Boston Tea Party.

Having saved up enough money to travel and hating political controversy as being "neither pleasing to an artist or advantageous to the art itself," Copley sailed for Europe. In Italy he copied the Renaissance masters; and in doing so he lost the innocence of his earlier style, lost, ironically enough, the very qualities which made his earlier realism, as I have said, so like the realism of the fifteenth century.

From Italy Copley went to England, where he spent the rest of his life. His expatriation marked a turning point in his development. He was confronted with the necessity of making his way in an alien country where standards were very different from those in Boston. He suffered under great disadvantages. His competitors in England required the sitter to pose for as little as five hours of sittings for a portrait, while in America Copley had often required as many as ninety. And worst of all, his uncompromising realism, so popular in Boston and New York, would attract no patrons in London, where flattery was all-important.

CAMPUS VIEW AND BELL TOWER

A facsimile copy of the second published view of the University, engraved by W. Roberts from a drawing by William Momberger and printed in Duyckinck's *Cyclopaedia of American Literature* (II, 5), New York, 1855

CAMPUS VIEW 1860 OR AFTER

From an undated and unsigned colored print owned by the University

MEMORIAL HALL, 1885-1930

THE CENTER OF THE CAMPUS

The Well, Old East, Cameron Avenue, and South Building

OLD WEST AND CAMPUS NORTH OF
CAMERON AVENUE

SMITH HALL AT NIGHT

Formerly the Library, now the Carolina Playmakers Theatre

THE ASSOCIATION OF AMERICAN UNIVERSITIES

Representatives attending the meeting in honor of the University, October 12, 1945. President James B. Conant, of Harvard University and guest speaker, fourth from the left, bottom row

News Bureau

Wootten-Moul

THE MOREHEAD-PATTERSON BELL TOWER

News Bureau

SECRETARY OF STATE JAMES F. BYRNES AND
EX-SECRETARY OF THE NAVY, JOSEPHUS DANIELS

From the Academic Procession at the Sesquicentennial Convocation April
13, 1946

THE UNIVERSITY LIBRARY

Conscious of these handicaps, Copley decided to change his whole approach to portraiture and adopt the mannerisms of European painting.

He enjoyed a short period of success in London and was elected a member of the Royal Academy. It was during this time that his historical and allegorical subjects were received with considerable acclaim. Taste changed, however, and Copley gradually lost his popularity. During his last years he was constantly menaced by debt. He also seems to have been conscious that he had betrayed his original gifts, that he had lost his instinctive sense of realism without attaining the imaginative power required to paint in the Grand Manner. With a few rare exceptions, his work had declined from the high achievement of his American period. Today his fame rests upon the realistic probity of his colonial portraits, or those done immediately after his arrival in England, like that of "Mrs. Fort."

It was Benjamin West's admiration for Italian art that helped to draw Copley to Europe, just as it was to draw many other American artists abroad. West was born in Chester County, Pennsylvania, of Quaker parents. He was taught his colors, according to a tradition which he doubtless fostered, by the friendly Indians, and he made his first brush from the tail of the family cat. At the age of twenty-two he journeyed to Europe, where he spent the rest of his life, a prototype of the American expatriated painter.

In "The Death of Wolfe" West reveals his instinctive sense of actuality. According to a contemporary biographer, he caused a sensation by portraying the dying general and his followers in the actual costumes of 1759, when the event took place. Though the legend has been discredited that West was the first to portray a contemporary historical scene in the dress of the day and not in 'classical clothes,' his picture remains a brilliant example of the new trend toward historical realism, which was to culminate in France during the next century.

The American instinct for realism, so pronounced in the early portraits of Copley and apparent even in the historical paintings of West, ran counter to the taste of the eighteenth century. Realism therefore, flourished in centers away from the great metropolitan cities, which have always tended to standardize style. It is significant that the two outstanding realistic portrait painters of the eighteenth century, once Copley had succumbed to London, were a Scot and an American, Raeburn and Stuart. The fact that both painters worked in the provinces gave them a freedom of expression which would have been difficult, if not impossible to achieve in London.

But Stuart actually began his career as a painter in London. At first he suffered great privations. At twenty-one he wrote Benjamin West, "I find myself ignorant, without business or friends, without the necessities of life, so far that for some time I have been reduced to one miserable meal a day, and frequently not even that." West took him into his house and helped him to get established as a successful painter.

Unfortunately, Stuart's extravagances more than kept pace with his success. Painting as many as six portraits a day he could not earn enough to pay his bills, and bankruptcy finally forced him to return to America in 1792. Here he had the good fortune to persuade Washington to sit for him. The first portrait he painted from the life of the President has been identified as the Vaughn Washington in the Collection of the National Gallery of Art. Later Washington was persuaded to pose for two other portraits, the full-length Landsdowne painting and the unfinished Athenaeum head. Throughout his life Stuart earned a considerable income by making replicas of these paintings, especially the Athenaeum portrait, which he copied more than seventy times, referring to these copies as his "hundred-dollar bills."

In Philadelphia, Washington, New York, and Boston, he portrayed all the leading figures of his day. Stuart, however, was at his best with sitters of less exalted rank, and in portraits such as that of "Mrs. Richard Yates," he painted with precision and probity.

Of the many young Americans who passed through the hospitable studio of West, which is shown in the painting entitled "The American School" by the stolid Matthew Pratt, Gilbert Stuart alone achieved a supreme position as a portrait painter. There were others, however, who merit a passing remark. One of the first was Charles Willson Peale, whose many interests and accomplishments ranged from the fashioning of wooden teeth for President Washington, whose portrait he had painted years before in the regimentals of a young British colonel, to the exhuming of the first American mastodon. Incidentally, the wooden false teeth did not work very well and they were later carved in bone.

Peale, however, painted one outstanding canvas, "The Staircase Group," one of the most remarkable examples of illusionistic perspective in Anglo-American painting.

Ralph Earl was another pupil of Benjamin West who escaped the standardization which beset many minor eighteenth-century painters. Though he was made a member of the Royal Academy, he remained all his life a provincial realist. His art was devoted to the faithful portrayal of the Connecticut squires, their wives, their farms, and their homes. One has a sense, when looking at Earl's portraits, of the immense pride these New Englanders took in their possessions.

There was nothing provincial about the work of Thomas Sully, whose long life from 1783 to 1872 covered the period which saw the rise of Stuart, the passing of the men who had studied under West, and the beginning of the new realism of Winslow Homer and Thomas Eakins. Sully was one of the most accomplished artists this country has produced. His portrait of Queen Victoria, more than any English painting, has given us our conception of the future Empress at the beginning of her reign. But Sully as he grew older developed a genteel formula, a style that was symptomatic of the decline of American painting toward the middle of the last century. In his late portraits all the women are languishingly beautiful and all the men languidly well-bred. There could be no clearer evidence that the virus of sentimentality had entered the American style.

America, as the nineteenth century developed, lost the colonial character of its culture. It became an independent, turbulent nation, pushing westward and devouring a continent. Science rather than art flourished; gifted painters like Robert Fulton and Samuel F. B. Morse gave up careers as artists to become the inventors of the steamboat and the telegraph. Workshops, steel mills, and foundries produced vast and sudden wealth. The great merchant prince who was to rule American taste is triumphantly portrayed in the painting of Amos Lawrence by Chester Harding; the self-made man, who was to take the place of Sully's genteel sitters, appears in the portrait of Pat Lyon by John Neagle. Regardless of class, sitters have a look of aggressive self-confidence which was to mark the spirit of the coming age.

This self-confidence is echoed in Walt Whitman's command to the Muse to migrate to America, "For know a better, fresher, busier sphere, a wide, untried domain awaits, demands you." National pride developed a national outlook, and painters groped for a way of interpreting this vast continent so different from the Old World. John James Audubon, one of the greatest masters of design to come to this country, climbed mountains and tramped through marshes to record in oil and water color the birds and animals of North America. Painters also began to forsake the studio scenery of romantic idealists like Washington Allston. They sought to depict instead the actual appearance of this country. Members of the Hudson River School, Thomas Doughty, Asher Brown Durand, Thomas Cole, and John P. Kensett, studied the landscapes of the eastern states. They recorded the picturesque beauty of the New World with timid brush strokes, as though their thin, dry delineation of each branch, each leaf, offered security against the overwhelming vastness of the sparsely settled continent. In "Kindred Spirits," Durand portrays the poet William Cullen Bryant and the landscapist Timothy Cole on a ledge of rock over a deep gorge in the Adirondacks, obviously meditating on the heroic grandeur of mountain scenery spread out below them. The spectacular beauty of the West was later painted by Albert Bierstadt, Frederick Church, and Thomas Moran. In their effort to grapple with the immensity of their subject matter, they produced huge panoramas, which in time have sunk, as though from the weight of the mountain ranges they endlessly depict, into the cellars of our museums and public buildings. But occasionally, as in the picture by Bierstadt, "Guerrilla Warfare," they observed nature with a fidelity suggestive of the best French landscape painting of the last century.

Whitman called for "Landscapes projected masculine, full-sized and golden," but none of the artists mentioned was capable of this achievement. Inness was the first of his generation to whom Whitman's words can be applied, the first to make his landscapes at once descriptive and interpretive. Inness' early work held promise of a native style, poetic and yet firmly based on observation. "Lackawanna Valley" is typical. Inness had been commissioned by the president of the railroad to do what was virtually a portrait of the new roundhouse just built at Scranton. The artist was told how many steam engines had to appear, how many tracks, how prominent the initials of the railroad were to be shown, and all for a fee of $75.00. Yet in spite of these limitations Inness has achieved something of the ordered beauty of Poussin and Claude, whose work he must have studied on his several trips to Europe.

At his best Inness interprets and records the rich, somnolent fertility of the Connecticut Valley with poetic fervor. But during his last period he succumbed to the germ of sentimentality which entered the blood stream of taste in every country, and his belief that "a work of art is beautiful if the sentiment is beautiful, it is great if the sentiment is vital," proved a dangerous heresy, for he came to lean so heavily on beautiful and vital sentiments that he lost touch with nature and painted blurred, misty pictures, flimsily constructed.

To escape from the bad taste of the period the most significant imaginative painting done in this country was created in relative isolation. Our two most original imaginative painters, George Fuller and Albert Ryder, were both solitaries. Fuller, whose paintings have a vague, shadowy beauty suggestive of Hawthorne's stories, withdrew from the world and painted on his farm in New England. Remote from the influence of popular taste, he created a delicate, very personal style, evocative and filled with overtones of romantic revery. Though the thick pigment he loaded on his canvas has deteriorated and his colors have faded, his weak craftsmanship has not destroyed the charm of his visionary figures, with their strange, evanescent beauty, like apparitions glimpsed at twilight.

The poetic, imaginative strain in American painting, which appears in Inness and Fuller, culminates in the work of Albert

Pinkham Ryder. Like Fuller, Ryder was an intense individualist, who dwelt in the world of his own inner life and was little influenced by the work of other painters. He sought to embody in his paintings what Herman Melville, a few decades earlier, had sought to describe in words—in fact, few painters and authors have been spiritually so akin. The mystery and the elemental forces of the sea, the loneliness of sailing under windswept, moonlit skies, the terror that emanates from certain landscapes, from spellbound valleys and gaunt trees silhouetted against story clouds—scenes such as these, which also obsessed Melville's imagination, Ryder spent his life in painting. This strong resemblance between two of the most imaginative geniuses America has produced is especially apparent in such pictures as "Jonah." These have the same quality of preternatural horror, the same strange, symbolic beauty that distinguishes *Moby Dick.*

Ryder created slowly, painting and repainting a few small pictures. He worked over his forms, always simplifying them until they took on the appearance of heroic shapes, which are only vaguely related to physical reality; and with these shapes he created patterns as abstract and beautifully balanced as the designs of Eastern lacquer work, as in his extraordinary painting of the "Flying Dutchman." He loaded on his pigment, mixing and fusing it until his rich paste achieved the effect of enamel. With time the thick impasto has cracked and chipped, the colors darkened and faded, and in a few generations it will probably be difficult to appreciate the full stature of the most poetic of American painters.

The tradition of imaginative painting lost somewhat in vigor after Albert P. Ryder. Arthur B. Davies is typical of a more recent generation. His painting shows an increase in lyricism with something of the delicate, archaizing beauty, the charming and sophisticated imagery that we find in the verse of certain modern poets, especially Edna St. Vincent Millay.

The main stream of art in this country, however, has always run counter to the work of these imaginative painters. Its direction has been toward objective realism which began with the work of the colonial artists and reached an early climax in the Boston portraits of Copley. This realistic tradition was continued by the genre painters of the nineteenth century, by such artists as John Quidor, William S. Mount, George Caleb Bingham, and Eastman Johnson. With their work the American scene for the first time becomes important in painting. Quidor, illustrating American legends with a mixture of realism and romanticism; Mount, depicting scenes of rural life and occasionally creating a masterpiece of composition; Bingham, searching out characteristic examples of pioneer existence and translating them into designs reminiscent of Renaissance Art; and Eastman Johnson interpreting daily life from Massachusetts to Kentucky, anecdotal, sentimental at times, but always revealing his instinct for fine draughtsmanship—these artists have given us a native style which has recently achieved wide recognition.

The highest achievement in the nineteenth century of this American realism, which is as different from European realism as *Huckleberry Finn* from any European novel, appears in the work of two painters, Homer and Eakins.

Homer began his career as an illustrator, and it is because he remained an illustrator at heart that he did not succeed in representing optical appearance as successfully as his contemporaries among the French, the Impressionists. A sense of actuality was, of course, important to the illustrator, and this, with his superb draughtsmanship, Homer was always able to achieve; but his greatest attainment lay in his ability to evoke certain emotions, to convey the delight of sailing before a fair wind, or the terror and loneliness of storm and fog at sea, or the tense expectancy of hunting and fishing. If one has enjoyed sailing, for example, "Breezing Up" brings back with extraordinary intensity the exhilaration of swift movement before a freshening breeze, the physical joy that comes from the control of such an elemental force as wind. By contrast, a similar Impressionist picture, such as "In a Boat" (1874) by Manet, painted the same year as "Breezing Up," though it is a far better example of visual truth, of the underlying organization of the optical effect, fails to arouse these particular feelings. Though Manet was a greater master of color and composition, though he conveys more vividly a momentary impression of visual reality, he lacks Homer's power of suggestion, his sense of mood.

It is important to understand the qualities of Homer's realism to appreciate his real merit as an artist. His style was old-fashioned compared to the works of the advanced painters in France. He took no interest in the new developments here or abroad. He sought stubbornly for what he believed to be "simple and absolute truth"; and he succeeded in illustrating, probably better than any one else, certain phases of life: the pleasures, dangers, even tragedies of men who live out-of-doors, the various aspects of their contest with nature, for pleasure or for existence. He was almost unique among painters in being at home in a world of guns and traps, of fish nets and fly rods, of dories, cat boats, and canoes. He interpreted this subject matter without idealization or sentimentality, in a style lucid, simple, and virile. One cannot but regret the perfect illustrations he might have provided for mark Twain, or, if he had lived longer, for Ernest Hemingway.

Thomas Eakins had the same hard, uncompromising sense of actuality as Homer. Walt Whitman said of him, "I never knew of but one artist, and that's Tom Eakins, who could resist the temptation to see what they thought ought to be rather than what is." It was the simplicity and the sincerity of this austere realism, so American in its uncompromising grasp of fact, that made Eakins one of the great painters of the nineteenth century.

Like Homer, Eakins was indifferent to Impressionism, to Post Impressionism, to all the movements of art of his day. Like Homer, he was more concerned with illustrating the life he enjoyed, the diversions of hunting, rowing, sailing, and boxing. His response to these scenes, however, was colder, more analytical, his pictures less evocative, less suggestive of the mood of the scene.

In spite of the obvious nineteenth-century appearance of his pictures, Eakins bears a fundamental resemblance to the fifteenth-century Italian realists. He had the same burning passion for reality, and like them, he studied anatomy, worked out the mathematics of perspective, and investigated the optical effect of movement, especially in his scenes of rowers.

But it was much easier to be a realist in Florence in the fifteenth century than in Philadelphia in the nineteenth century. Incredible as it may seem, Eakins had to give up his job as a teacher at the Pennsylvania Academy because he wanted his students to draw from the female nude. The painting of William Rush, the American sculptor of an earlier generation, working from the nude model, was Eakins' reply to his critics. But the curse of prudery, which has until recent times beset American culture, triumphed, and Eakins, compelled to give up teaching, could not have supported himself if it had not been for his portraits.

As a portrait painter Thomas Eakins continued the tradition of the early works of Copley. His hard, angular characterizations are as unflattering as the most candid of photographs, and as revealing as the most analytical of psychiatric reports.

In the second half of the nineteenth century America produced six outstanding painters. The three I have mentioned, Ryder, Homer, and Eakins did almost all their work in America; but the second trio, Mary Cassatt, Whistler, and Sargent settled abroad. Recently, there has been a tendency to depreciate whatever is cosmopolitan and to over-value whatever is native; but we should bear in mind that expatriation is bad for the artist only when it affects his integrity, as it did in the case of Copley, whereas Mary Cassatt, Whistler, and Sargent suffered no more from living in Europe than had, say, Claude and Poussin from living in Rome rather than in Paris.

Mary Cassatt toward the end of her life explained why she had left America: "When I was young," she said, "it was different. Our Museums had no great paintings for the student to study." It was not easy for a man, much less a woman, to leave Pittsburgh in 1868 and go to Paris to study art. Mary Cassatt's father was brutally frank to her. He said quite simply, "I would almost rather see you dead." But Mary Cassatt knew she had to get to the European museums if she was going to be a painter. The masterpieces of the past were like wheels of emery against which she had to grind and polish her own style. She was taught to draw by the work of Holbein and Ingres, she learned subtleties of modeling from the paintings of Correggio, she studied the compositional arrangements of Oriental art, and in the case of

"The Morning Toilet" she even borrowed a pose from Michelangelo's "Bound Slave." Yet her art was never eclectic. All these different influences were fused into a style as personal as her own fiery, dominating character.

During her long residence in France, Mary Cassatt came to be closely associated with the Impressionists—particularly Degas. Like the artists of this movement she found her subject matter in the world about her. Paintings like "Woman and Child Driving," for example, evoke the elaborate refinement of the society described in the novels of her fellow expatriate, Henry James. These early pictures are marked by a fragile, feminine beauty —an impressionism of great delicacy.

Some years before Miss Cassatt's arrival in Europe James Abbott McNeill Whistler was established in Paris. He was a peculiar combination of charlatan, dandy, wit, and artist. His career was to take him as far as possible from his birthplace, Lowell, Massachusetts; yet in spite of the cosmopolitanism he subsequently attained, he always remained something of an American Puritan. A rather dry primness deprived his work of that gusto possessed by more sensuous painters.

Moreover, in spite of his reputation for eccentricity, Whistler as an artist was basically orthodox. Whereas the advanced painters he exhibited with in Paris, Monet, Pissaro, Sisley, and the other Impressionists, were doing such unexpected things as to take their canvases out-of-doors and paint exactly what their eye could take in at a quick glance, Whistler followed the established tradition of art, which he defended with brilliant phrases, such as "Nature contains the elements, in color and form, of all pictures, as the keyboard contains the notes of all music," and again "the artist is born to pick, and choose, and group with science, these elements, that the result may be beautiful." Like the old masters, he felt that "Painting after nature is something one should do at home." Any other view, he pointed out, was a heresy condemned by the great artists of the East as well as of the West.

He himself sought to combine the asymmetrical and subtly balanced designs of the Japanese print-makers with the visual realism of Velázquez. This exotic and refined eclecticism Whistler embodied so skilfully in his delicate paintings and preached so effectively in his stinging aphorisms that for a time English taste was dominated by his theories. Thus an American artist came to be the arbiter of fashion in England, and in a little more than a century America had not only ceased to be provincial, but had produced a painter whose cosmopolitanism and sophistication were envied and copied in London, and even in Paris.

Of the three great American expatriates the reputation of John Singer Sargent has declined the most. A generation ago his portraits were as sought after as were those of Sir Joshua Reynolds in the eighteenth century. For years he was the most fashionable portraitist in England and America, and he has left behind scores of distinguished portraits, most of them painted early in his career. What is the explanation then of the present eclipse of his fame? The usual answer is that he painted too fast and that he used a formula. But in fact the tragedy of Sargent is that often he did not paint fast enough and that he never found a satisfactory formula to use.

Trained in Paris by Carolus-Duran, he developed an extraordinary talent for realizing at the first glance the tone and structure of a face. No American painter could surpass his manual dexterity, nor could any artist of his generation penetrate more cruelly, on occasion, into the character of his sitter. In portraiture when he let the first statement stand, he achieved the freshness and spontaneity of an instantaneous effect. Where the sitter's character seems to be ovious—vulgar, voracious, predatory, as in the case of "Asher Wertheimer," or witty, brittle, chic, as in the case of "Madame X"—Sargent caught it without hesitation. But with personalities less obvious, less salient, he was lost. In a desperate effort to get a telling likeness he often painted and scraped out his portraits thirty and forty times, and these alterations and re-workings impaired the purity of his tone and blurred the sharpness of his vision. However, time will doubtless restore much of Sargent's fame; his early portraits painted when his eye was fresh and his confidence in his fluent brush unimpaired, will stand as a major achievement of American realism.

Mary Cassatt, Sargent, and Whistler were not the only American cosmopolitan painters. There were many others, like Duveneck and Chase, who accepted and developed the styles popular on the continent whether in Paris or in Munich, the two most influential centers of painting. A group of artists even banded together, calling themselves the Ten American Painters, to promulgate the doctrines of French Impressionism, of whose work Twachtman's "Wild Cherry Tree" is typical.

The Ten in turn were succeeded by a group which called itself the Eight. These artists were more significant from the point of view of the development of an American style. For they had in common a desire to overthrow the stereoptype and academic, which the European styles when brought to America were apt to become.

One member of the Eight was Arthur B. Davies, whose work has been touched upon as part of the imaginative tradition of American painting. Another member was Maurice B. Prendergast, a lyrical artist, who covered his canvases with a mosaic of pigment, so that his surfaces appear like pointillism under a powerful magnifying glass. A third was Ernest Lawson distinguished for the vibrant beauty of his color, for his "palette of crushed jewels," as Huneker described the tonality of his paintings.

There was, however, within the movement of the Eight a group of five painters who were united in their doctrine. These artists, Henri, Luks, Glackens, Sloan, and Shinn, who were later joined by Bellows, turned for their subject matter to the life about them. Through their work the perennial interest in the American scene was intensified. The same trend appears in the literature of the time, in the novels of Norris, Dreiser, and Anderson. The painters were in revolt against the cosmopolitanism of the expatriates and the sophisticated elegance of the Academy, the writers against the sentimental optimism typified by Howells and the genteel complexities that preoccupied Henry James.

Robert Henri was the teacher of the group. He studied abroad and brought back with him news of Manet and Degas, as well as of Hals, El Greco, Velázquez, and Goya. He directed the search of Glackens, Luks, and Bellows toward a new realism, which he practiced himself in portraits such as that of "Miss Violet Organ."

William J. Glackens and George Luks applied Henri's dexterous technique to subjects drawn from the tenements, the saloons, the cafés, the streets and parks of New York. They established what their enemies called "the Ash-can School of Painting."

The revolt of these painters against the pretty, the idealistic, the sentimental, had a salutary effect on art and revivified the realistic tradition in this country. Glackens in his early work illustrated American life with the colloquial vigor of Ring Lardner as can be seen in the scene in a restaurant entitled "Chez Mouquin."

George Luks's paintings had the same racy, native character. The battered, sometimes vicious faces of old people, like Mrs. Gamley, who have had to fight for existence, the ebullient vitality of poor children dancing in the slums, playing make-believe, undismayed by poverty, these are the subjects he interpreted with brush strokes that are at times sharp and trenchant, at times delicate and feathery.

George W. Bellows, the most famous of the Henri pupils, was a less instinctive painter than Luks. He leaned heavily on El Greco and Manet, on the dynamic symmetry of Jay Hambidge, on the color theories of H. G. Maratta. But in spite of these influences, he maintained the integrity of his own style and remained an American realist, painting such superb pictures of American life as "Stag at Sharkey's."

It is significant that Bellows was the first painter of importance to spend his entire life in this country. He enjoyed advantages in America that earlier artists lacked. He had the opportunity of studying and of measuring his work beside the great paintings of the past, paintings other generations had had to go abroad to see.

Except for a few unfortunate attempts at imaginative illustration, Bellows' paintings are shafts of light irradiating the American scene. After Homer and Eakins he was the first American realist with the broadest scope, the widest variety of interests. But Bellows' realism differs from that of the earlier painters. It is more self-conscious, more aware of its subject matter, more concerned with what America really is, as is evident in the picture of our slums entitled "Cliff Dwellers." Just as his designs have a recondite, studied quality even when they seem, on the surface, immediate and spontaneous, so his treatment of the American scene suggests that the artist had begun to think of himself as an interpreter and had lost something of the innocence of that tradition of realism which began with the colonial portraitists, was continued by the genre painters of the middle of the last century, and culminated in Homer and Eakins.

Thus far we have traced two currents in American style, one realistic, the other imaginative. For the most part they run in distinct channels, but there is still a third stream, a stream which appears where the channels of the other two, of the realistic and the imaginative, seem to come together. This, judging by its effect on contemporary painting, is in some ways the most powerful of all. One might roughly term this third current the stream of primitive painting. Naïveté is, as Henry James said, like a cipher. Its value depends on how many numbers precede it. And in the case of some of our primitive painters one must recognize that there is very little in front of their naïveté. But there are others who reveal ability of a high order directing their expression. The "Buffalo Hunt" by an anonymous artist of the middle of the nineteenth century, though lacking all plastic values, shows a subtly balanced rhythmic pattern suggestive of Persian miniature painting. The "Runaway Horse," on the other hand, evokes those idyllic scenes one finds in the early masters of landscape, artists of the seventeenth century like Annibale Carracci, and Domenichino. "Meditation by the Sea," like the other two by an unknown artist, suggests no painter of the past; rather it leaps forward in time to the primitive painting of our own day. The smallness of the human figure, the vastness of nature, and the sense of a moment of thought held and made permanent, give this little canvas a strangely moving quality. And yet mingling with its mood of wistful sadness, there is a strong element of the ridiculous, something of the quality of these lines from T. S. Eliot, "I shall wear white flannel trousers and walk upon the beach. I have heard the mermaids singing, each to each. I do not think that they will sing to me." The verses from Prufrock are among the most sophisticated expressions of modern poetry, and yet they seem to catch the mood of the painting perfectly. It is curious how the naïve and the sophisticated complete the cycle of taste and meet so often during those periods of apparent decline, such as we are living in today.

This meeting of the extremes, the primitive and the ultra-refined, partially explains the popularity of artists like John Kane. Kane was a realist, working in the tradition of Copley and Eakins, but seeing the world more naïvely. Yet in his case I think you will agree that naïveté is a cipher that counts on the positive side, and gives to his self-portrait an added expressive force: in this case a sense of physical strength, which is conveyed not only by the meticulous rendering of the muscular arms, but also by the triad of bent bars, which thrust against the top and sides of the painting.

I have spoken of primitive painting as a mingling of the realistic and the imaginative currents in American style. In the case of John Kane the realistic stream predominates, whereas with Eilshemius, who also died a few years ago, imagination counts no more. This canvas was painted in 1899 and anticipates contemporary Surrealism by almost thirty years. The landscape itself is very beautiful with the greys and muted greens one associates with Corot; but this beauty is enhanced by the strange embodiment of the title, "Afternoon Wind," in the nude figures of women, who glide through the air conveying an ideated sensation of effortless motion, which I find very pleasing.

These three streams in American art, the realistic, the imaginative, and the primitive, have been relatively unaffected by the revolutionary movements which have caused such vast upheavals in European style. The tremors of these distant earthquakes have reached this country, but they have been too faint to change the general direction of American art. When we show our paintings in London this summer I believe that people on the other side of the Atlantic will recognize that America is producing a style of painting that has no exact counterpart in Europe. In fact, the vigor of American art at the present moment has given it an opportunity for leadership in the world, which it has never had before.

The very fact of physical separation from the center of tradition and I might almost say the lack of technical facility, both if you remember I mentioned at the beginning of my lecture as characteristic of American painting, have been in recent years advantages in themselves. For in a sense it is easier for an American artist than for a European artist to realize, as Bernard Berenson once wrote in connection with Italian painting, that "vitality will reappear only when artists recognize that the types, shapes, attitudes and arrangements produced in the course of evolution are no more to be used than spent cartridges, and that the only hope of resurrection lies in the disappearance of that facility, which is in essence an enslaving habit of visualizing conventionally and of excuting by rote." This is the challenge facing the American painter today—to see and communicate the new images of his modern world. If he meets this challenge successfully then the center of gravity in art will gradually be transferred from Europe to the Western hemisphere. It is to aid our artists in this endeavor that art schools and galleries have been established throughout the country. Among these, as I have come to realize today, one of the most progressive and praiseworthy is the Person Hall Art Museum of your University, at whose Sesquicentennial Celebration I have had the privilege of speaking this evening.

RECEPTION AND EXHIBIT OF AMERICAN PAINTING

The concluding part of the program for Friday evening was presented at Person Hall Art Gallery, where the guests of the University were received informally by the University, and witnessed an extensive exhibit of American paintings made possible through the co-operation of the Department of Art and the generosity of Mrs. Katherine Pendleton Arrington, President of the North Carolina State Art Society, and Mr. William F. Davidson, Vice-President of M. Knoedler and Company, Inc., of New York.

ACADEMIC PROCESSION

Glorious April sunshine; trees, shrubs, and grass dressed in varying shades of early spring green; and spirea, iris, and other flowers in full bloom everywhere furnished a setting of unusual loveliness for the brilliant academic procession and the final Sesquicentennial Convocation held in Memorial Hall at 10:30 A.M., Saturday, April 13. Rarely, if ever, has the University witnessed such an imposing spectacle or participated in ceremonies so impressive and inspiring.

The academic procession, led by the University Band under the direction of Professor Earl Slocum, began its march at the South Building with the University Marshal and the President of the University and party. Included in the party were Secretary of State Byrnes and former Secretary of the Navy Josephus Daniels and trustees and alumni. At the Carolina Playmaker Theatre, the procession was joined by the candidates for honorary degrees. At the Graham Memorial Building it was augmented by the delegates from colleges and universities. At Person Hall its ranks were swelled by the delegates from learned societies and foundations and by the University faculty and officers, and a few minutes later it entered Memorial Hall to the accompaniment of Gounod's "March Pontifical," with Dr. Jan Philip Schinhan at the organ.

THE CONVOCATION

The final event of the celebration, the Sesquicentennial Convocation, began at 10:30 in Memorial Hall, with Chancellor House presiding. Seated on the platform were President Graham, Chancellors House, Jackson, and Harrelson; President Poteat, President Day, and Dr. Barnett; the Marshal of the University and the Director of the Sesquicentennial; the Legislative Commission and committees from the trustees and alumni; and the recipients of honorary degrees. The delegates representing other institutions were seated in front of the platform, and the musical clubs in the balcony.

The Invocation was offered by the Reverend Edwin McNeill Poteat, President, Colgate-Rochester Divinity School.

PRESIDENT POTEAT

Eternal Spirit, evermore creating:
Who hast been to us the Word when our lips were dumb,
Power to us when our hands were feeble,
Hope to us when our hearts were faint,
We acknowledge Thee as the Source and Sustainer
Of our lives.
We thank Thee for the sense of fulness that
Has possessed us when we have done Thy will,
And for the shame that has been Thy rebuke
When we have departed from Thy ways.
For all those, valiant-for-truth,
Who have nourished our spirits and
Builded institutions for the nurture of our minds;
For those who seeking the good, the true, the beautiful
Have been undaunted by the blindness of lesser
Minds; For the inheritance of thrice fifty years celebrated here
    today
And the testament of beauty that is this place—We thank Thee,
    O Lord.
  In these grim days when the voice of compassion
Is muted by the shouts of the powerful;
When the aspirations of men for the universal
Fraternity of all are disputed by the
Faithless or the proud,
Give us, we beseech Thee, hearts warmed by Thy
Compassion, minds illumined by Thy truth
And wills nerved by Thine invincible purposes.
    Brighten the light that shines upon our day,
      Gird with Thy love the weakness of our creeds;
    Help us to trust our fellows in the way,
      Give us the faith that conquers and concedes.
And we will give Thee power and dominion and
Glory, in our lives, through Jesus Christ our Lord. Amen.

Introduction of Delegates

The formal introduction of delegates was made by Dr. William Morton Dey, Marshal of the University. Each delegate arose and stood while his name and that of the institution, society, or foundation which he represented was called.*

The introduction of the delegates was followed by the beautiful rendition of the chorus, "Alleluia," by Randall Thompson, by the University Glee Clubs. Chancellor House then introduced Dr. Edmund Day, President, Cornell University, special speaker of the convocation, the title of whose address was "Educational Mobilization in a Free Society."

President Day

Chancellor House, Your Excellency, President Graham, and members, guests, and friends of the University:

May I preface my more formal remarks with an expression of the great satisfaction I have in returning to Chapel Hill and in sharing in the celebration of this significant anniversary in the life of this great University.

It is now about twenty years since I began coming to Chapel Hill. I visited then as an officer of the Rockefeller Foundation and General Education Board. Under those circumstances I was naturally assured of a very warm welcome. But I am confident it was not the reception I had in that period which led me to develop the feelings I have about the University of North Carolina. It was what the University stood for and was in a position to accomplish that won my admiration from the time of my earliest contacts.

The high esteem in which I have held the University has been strongly reinforced by certain personal connections. Your former president, Harry Woodburn Chase, has been a friend of mine ever since the fall of 1901 when we roomed close together as undergraduates at Dartmouth College. Just when I came to know your present distinguished President I cannot now tell. All I can say is that I feel as if I had known him a long while, certainly long enough to add to my high regard for him a sense of genuine affection.

*See Appendix A.

That might seem to be Graham enough for one not of the Carolina company but, as a matter of fact, I put up with a lot more in the person of the Secretary of Cornell University, Dr. Edward Kidder Graham, an alumnus of this institution, a holder of a doctor's degree in history from Cornell, a cousin of the present President and a son of the earlier President Graham, a veritable Carolina Graham, with all that that connotes, who is an invaluable member of our administrative staff. He is a representative of Chapel Hill at Ithaca of whom you can justly be proud.

There has been much of this sort of interchange between North Carolina and Cornell to the advantage of both institutions. If I am not mistaken, some six or eight of your present senior staff here are Cornell degree holders. I recall that one of the most brilliant of the younger surgeons in the clinical faculty of our Medical College in New York City is a North Carolina graduate of the class of 1931. Our recent experience with an extraordinarily able football coach leaves us with the impression that the interchanges of staff are sometimes of the nature of lend-lease. However, even so, we are sure they are mutually profitable.

Even more important than this continuing exchange of personalities is a fundamental congeniality of background and ideal in the two institutions. The spirit of this campus is such as to make a representative of Cornell feel quickly at home. The great tradition of freedom of inquiry and learning, so carefully guarded over the years here, has its parallel at Ithaca; and the battles fought and the victories won have been essentially the same battles and the same victories at both places. Our institutions share a common heritage in the dreams and the ideals of our founders; we share a common responsibility at this challenging point in the history of our country.

It is in the nature of a great liberal institution that freedom of teaching and research must take us occasionally into areas of sharp controversy. This is inevitable especially as we venture along the paths over which the social studies take us. Even at so great a distance as Ithaca, I have been aware that the University of North Carolina has found itself from time to time in troubled waters. What a responsive note that strikes in the heart of the president of a university which only recently has opened a School of Industrial and Labor Relations to a resounding accompaniment of thunder on the "Left" and thunder on the "Right"! Yet this sort of thing is nothing new for Cornell, and nothing new for Carolina. In our formative years, we were both attacked as "godless" institutions because of our freedom from sectarian control—this despite the abiding faith of our founders and the great spiritual strength of those devout men of all creeds who have rallied to our support throughout succeeding generations. The same tradition of freedom and responsibility of which we are so proud at Cornell I have found a living force on this campus. It will remain, I am sure, for all time to the glory of a truly great University which has won and holds the respect and admiration of the whole nation.

One of the most baffling problems now facing the victorious democracies is the re-education of the conquered nations reared in totalitarianism. The most difficult case of all is likely to be that of the Germans. The National Socialist Party under Hitler promptly sought and ultimately obtained the absolute control of the youth of the nation. Nazi indoctrination at all ages was made so pervasive that there was no escaping it. The influences of home and church were largely broken. Every educational means was taken over by the state. The press, the radio, the theater, the motion picture, publications, public exhibitions, large-scale celebrations, the universities, the schools—all were made to serve the Party program. The result was a unity of national thought and feeling, a sense of common conviction and consecration, which has rarely been equaled and probably never surpassed in human history. It is now reliably reported that the youth of these nations show extraordinary resistance to any attempts to change their ideology. Apparently they exhibit in appalling fashion what can be actually accomplished with up-to-date techniques of thorough-going indoctrination. They represent, in terms of the subject I wish to present to you briefly at this time, the end-result of sustained and complete educational mobilization.

There is, of course, a frightful warning in these evidences of mental and spiritual enslavement. Here we have a dramatic demonstration of the power ruthless dictatorships can bring to bear. But there is also in these same evidences a challenge to education in the free societies. Not that these free societies can wisely think in terms of regimentation, but surely they must be concerned with the problem of marshaling the potential forces of education in defense of the essentials of democratic living. If education, fully mobilized, can achieve for the dictator the extraordinary results we have witnessed, cannot education, wisely mobilized, make great contributions too in the perpetuation of freedom—contributions looking toward fundamental unity among people striving to establish the ideals of liberty and justice and peace? This is the question to which I wish to direct your attention. For the future of education in America, no question seems to me more important.

We can best approach this question if we start by examining the state of the public mind in this country with respect to education. With what interests, attitudes, and ideals do the American people view education in this troubled post-war world of ours?

It is clear, in the first place, that we can count on almost universal interest. A host of people like to think they know something about education. Most of them have had at one time or another some first-hand experience with formal education. Consequently, they think they are in position to talk intelligently about it. Moreover, if parents, they are almost certain at some point to acquire a large measure of concern about education. They are likely, in fact, to talk somewhat violently at times about what they think education is doing to or for their offspring. There is, in fact, no subject with respect to which it is as easy to start animated discussion, if not heated argument. Notwithstanding all this, there is little evidence that the subject of education has the kind of sustained lay study of which it is deserving. The extent of interest in education is certainly no measure at all of the extent of understanding. The fact that the subject presents many complex and difficult problems is not generally appreciated. In other words, the approach to the subject of education on the part of the general public, though full of interest, tends to be superficial and neglectful of the complexities which lie in the educative process.

Associated with widespread interest in education is an amazing faith in it. This faith the American people have exhibited for generations past. An extraordinary belief in education is finding an almost overwhelming expression right now in the demand of the veterans for further education under the G I Bill of Rights. Apparently, the prevailing view is that there is no such thing as too much education. On the contrary, it seems to be generally held that the more education any individual can obtain, the better he or she is likely to fare. In fact, it is in terms of these supposed individual benefits that the American faith in education is largely maintained. Thinking runs to earning power and social position rather than to possibilities of public or social significance. Upon the whole, the American people do not appear to have any genuine realization of what education might do for society as a whole. The fact remains that the faith of the American people in education, limited as it is in certain respects, is not only great but shows no sign of diminishing.

In view of the interest and faith which the American people have in education, it is not surprising to find a rather extraordinary readiness to provide financial support. No people have ever poured money into education as have the Americans. True, this generosity has been commonly evidenced most conspicuously in buildings, equipment, and accessory facilities rather than in compensation of staff. Moreover, there is no indication that this readiness to provide financial support carries with it any readiness to grant real social prestige to the teaching profession. By and large, educators as such do not enjoy high social standing in this country. True, educational administrators who direct the affairs of great institutions or public school systems, and hence to some extent resemble successful business executives, are likely to acquire prestige, but this they do not as educators. Upon the whole, it has to be recognized that the profession of education in America at this time does not begin to have the social standing that other professions have, or that the teaching profession itself has in certain other countries.

With respect to professional leadership, the American people seem to be reconciled to the fact that education is a field in which leadership is bound to be rather diffuse and ineffectual. Here and there from time to time, outstanding leaders appear, but the scope of their influence is likely to be limited, and, upon the whole, they do not succeed in establishing themselves in positions from which they can speak with recognized authority. Right now we can say that one of the most serious phases of the current educational situation in America is the absence of an overall direction such as outstanding leadership might be expected to establish.

Finally, partly in consequence of these several phases of the public's attitude toward education in America, there is no semblance of what might be described as genuine national policy in public education. Of course, it has to be granted that there is every disposition to extend free education—universally at the level of the elementary school, very generally at the level of the secondary school, and more and more widely at the level of the college and university. In other words, the ideal of educational opportunity is firmly established. At the same time, there is no general agreement as to the purposes to be served by public education thus widely extended; and certainly there has been as yet no successful attempt to make public education an instrument of national policy. Perhaps it will be argued that the assignment of responsibility for public education in our American system of government to the states rather than to the federal authority precludes any such development of education in terms of overall national policy. It does not seem to me, however, that this conclusion follows. Certainly if it does, there are fundamental weaknesses in our American system of education which may hamper us more and more seriously. My own contention is that it is quite possible to keep the system state-administered and at the same time develop conceptions of national purpose which will permeate the whole educational operation throughout the nation. It is this ideal which I assert must in due course be realized.

If substantial progress along this line is to be made, certain specific problems must be dealt with more successfully than they have been in the past. I venture to list a few of those which would appear to require prompt and effective consideration.

To a considerable extent a measure of agreement has been effected with respect to the fundamental purposes of general education in our democracy. A good illustration of the extent to which this has been accomplished is to be found in the excellent Report of the Harvard Committee on General Education in a Free Society. But the statement of these general purposes, however satisfactorily made, does not give any guarantee that formal education in the classroom and laboratory where such education actually occurs will effectively implement the general findings. One of the pressing needs of American education at the moment is the translation of governing principles, such as those set forth in the Harvard Committee Report, into the specific procedures employed by actual teachers dealing with actual students. Here all sorts of teaching skills and teaching aids have to be brought to bear. A vast deal needs to be done before we can come anywhere near realizing the aims which are now generally accepted in most competent discussions of the purposes of general education in a free society.

Another problem which very much needs attention is that of the sound co-ordination of the aims of general and vocational education. Unfortunately, these two types of education have tended to be in competition, if not in conflict, in our American system, with the result that both have suffered. That vocational education must continue to play an important role in American public education would seem to be self-evident. At the same time, the contributions to be made by general education are fundamental and must not be neglected. What should be sought is an articulation of the interests of vocational and general education so that both may be pursued simultaneously, and so that both may mutually re-enforce their respective objectives. Much needs to be done to devise the ways and means of accomplishing this dual purpose in specific instructional programs.

Another area in which there is pressing need of constructive work is that involving the relationship between public and private education. There is every reason to believe that public education will come to play a more and more important part at those higher levels of education in which private education continues to maintain a relatively strong position. It will be regrettable, however, if the expansion of public education makes it virtually impossible for private education to retain its influence, or to continue to make the contributions which are to some extent peculiar to education conducted under private auspices. What is needed is a more comprehensive and effectively co-ordinated relationship between public and private education. We can get this only as both public and private education recognize the extent to which their interests are joined.

What I have already said in an earlier connection makes it clear that one of our most pressing needs is a more effective over-all organization of the educational forces of the country. At present we suffer all sorts of disabilities for lack of any thorough co-ordination of the large number of independent educational authorities existing locally and at the level of the several states. This disorganization results in obstacles to top leadership which are at the moment well-nigh insurmountable. At all levels and in all areas the relations of the different educational authorities tend to be intensely competitive, with the result that efforts to institute co-operative or unified undertakings rarely meet with real success. No phase of the whole situation in American education would seem to be more demanding that that of improved organization. The success which has been achieved along this line in the present organization of the forces of higher education in North Carolina is an example which should be noted and followed in many other parts of the country.

Perhaps the most challenging of all the problems facing any attempt to mobilize the forces of education in the United States relates to the possibility of joining effectively the activities of formal and informal education. More and more it becomes evident that the attitudes, the habits, the ideals of free people are shaped in large measure by influences which lie outside the sphere of formal education. Thus, over the past generation in this country probably no influences playing upon the mind and heart of the American people have been quite so potent as those exercised by the motion picture. There is every reason to believe that some of the time the entertainment film has actually been making the work of the school more difficult than it would otherwise have been. The growing recognition by the motion picture industry of its educational responsibilities is in this quarter definitely heartening. It is of the utmost importance that other important media for affecting public opinion—e.g., the power periodicals—come promptly to a similar recognition of their social obligations. Education has to be conceived in terms of all of the forces which are brought systematically to bear upon the thinking and feeling of the American people, and hence there must be a fundamental concern with the relationships which exist between the agencies and activities which operate informally and those which function formally in the educational field.

All of this will serve to evidence the complexity of the problem with which we are faced in undertaking to bring about any genuine mobilization of educational forces in a society such as ours. Nevertheless, the importance of concerted action along this line can hardly be questioned. I cite one specific line of evidence.

The fact that it is generally agreed among competent and well-informed observers that the men who fought under the Stars and Stripes in World War II did not, in general, know what they were fighting for is a fact that cannot fail to give us all pause. Unless the democratic leaders of the world are mistaken, these American fighting men had more to fight for than any others. Nevertheless, they lacked any common sense of a commanding cause. Apparently they had no conception of the essentials of democracy, nor any feeling for the fact that these essentials were in dire jeopardy. Can anyone entertain these thoroughly authentic reports from our valiant fighting forces without coming to the conclusion that some basic mobilization of educational forces in America must be effected, and effected without delay?

Unfortunately there is no opportunity on this occasion for charting a program to this critically important end. However, we can cite some of the chief elements of which such a program must be composed.

That a much wider public understanding and appreciation of education is essential is all too evident. Education must be taken much more seriously than it has been. Its specific purposes in twentieth century democracy must be more clearly envisaged. It must be even more generously supported. It certainly must be given an improved status in our democratic organization.

Out of this better understanding and appreciation must come a concrete program for improved organization. We cannot possibly accomplish the purposes which must be served in American education through the kind of setup we now have. The educational forces of the country must be pulled together in more direct and positive relationship to one another and must by all means be provided with stronger leadership.

Clearly enough, if progress is to be made along this line, we must strive to lift public education above the play of partisan interest. Education, like health, is one of the phases of democratic life which must not be victimized politically. Effective education must become a deep and abiding concern of the entire nation, not an interest subject to partisan promotion.

A generation ago H. G. Wells issued one of his arresting pronouncements. He drew from his amazingly wide and penetrating studies and observations this sweeping generalization: "Human history becomes more and more a race between education and catastrophe." If this conclusion was warranted after World War I, how much more is it unescapable following World War II? Now that mankind has in its possession the incredible power of atomic energy, how can anyone believe that physical force can any longer be offset with physical force? If anything ever was clear, it is that the future of mankind lies in the realm of mind and spirit rather than of body and brute power. It is through education in all its varied forms that the mind and spirit of man has to be shaped to meet the requirements of the atomic world into which we have now entered. For the free peoples of this world an effective mobilization of all available educational resources is indispensable. It is toward this end that statesmen, as well as educators, must devote all the resources of thought and courage and vision they can possibly bring to bear.

May I conclude these remarks by what might be called an "editor's note"? I am fully aware that what I have done is little more than to broach a problem. I have tried to indicate its general nature, certain phases of the social milieu in which it lies imbedded, and something of its scope and content. But I certainly have not presented any adequate analysis of the problem, to say nothing of any direct and clear-cut solution. The fact remains that the problem is before us and is certain to assume larger and larger proportions. In a world possessed of atomic power, peace will not be maintained, justice established, and the rights of man protected save as appropriate educational forces are mobilized and given full effect. The problem of how to do this in a free society is a problem we cannot escape. Let us, as educators, make sure that we do not come to the problem with too little or after it is too late.

PRESIDENT GRAHAM

President Frank Porter Graham was then presented by Chancellor House. In an address at the Sesquicentennial luncheon for the Association of American Universities on University Day, October 12, 1945, President Graham had stressed the dynamic relation of machines and society. In his address at the Sesquicentennial Convocation he emphasized the fundamental role of ideas which precede, accompany, and make possible machines as a part of the more general and creative interrelation of ideas and modern society. He declared that "not only does the spread of ideas interfuse a whole society, but the lowering of the level of ideas lowers the level of the life and history of an age. It was not only the disintegration of the Roman Empire and the decline of the ancient learning in the disorder and obscurantism of the times but it was also the lowering of the level of ideas for adaptation to the untutored, though vigorous, minds of the barbarian conquerors which produced the intellectual recession called the Dark Ages. Scholasticism represents the far upward climb of the western mind under the tutelage of the church away from the ideas of the Dark Ages up to the ideas of the great medieval synthesis which found its stronghold in the universities of the later Middle Ages.

"The medieval universities, for all their ecclesiastical limits upon ideas, yet with an inner ferment of ideas and quest for learning, with their revival of Greek philosophy and medicine,

Roman law and Arabic science, along with the rise of towns, trade, and the handicraft arts, prepared the way for the Revival of Learning."

Citing the lessons of history, President Graham said that "before human society could rise to the opportunities of the first scientific revolution and the mighty Industrial Revolution which came out of it, we find ourselves in the midst of the second scientific revolution and the great atomic revolution in the momentous transition of our times loaded with the hopes or the doom of mankind.

"With all its many and vast values, the commercial revolution was misused for the exploitation and subjugation of defenseless peoples overseas, for the slave trade, for colonialism, and commercial works. The Industrial Revolution, which gave new impetus to four of the great humane movements of modern times, the labor movement, the woman's movement, the peace movement, and universal public education, was also misused for competitive exploitation of human beings, for absolute national sovereignty, and imperialistic wars. In these two great economic revolutions mankind somehow assimilated the misuse with the productive use, the evil with the good, and survived. Man as a human being cannot survive the misuse of atomic power. . . .

"The traditions of history impelled by the compass and later by the steam engine were processes of slow centuries and gradual adjustments. Social drift and slow adjustments did not then, on such a scale as now, mean swift and wide social tragedy and involve mayhap the survival of the human species on this earth. The possession of the earth might return to an animal species which has not learned to make mechanisms beyond its mastery. Human society with an atomic bomb in its bosom cannot lag in adjustment to its explosive power.

"As the home of the atomic bomb, America has a great moral responsibility. America, for the sake of her own soul, must take the lead in putting the atomic bomb under the ban and control of world government. America must, with wise safeguards, share the knowledge and use of atomic power, and with all the peoples, for full production and fair distribution within the nations, and for justice and peace among the nations."

The Conferring of Honorary Degrees

The high moment of the Convocation, which throughout its entirety was marked by unusual simplicity, dignity, and beauty, was the conferring of honorary degrees on thirty-nine scholars and leaders who, by reason of their ability and achievement, had attained high distinction in state and nation. The recipients were presented by Dr. William Whatley Pierson, Jr., Dean of the Graduate School. Each recipient stood and was hooded during the citation made by President Graham, and all stood together as President Graham conferred the degrees. Those receiving degrees and the citations were as follows:

JOSEPH QUINCY ADAMS   *Doctor of Letters*
   A.B., Wake Forest College, 1900; A.M., *ibid.*, 1901; Ph.D., Cornell University, 1906
   Director of the Folger Shakespeare Library, Washington, D. C.

As student, teacher, biographer, and librarian, he has become one of the most authentic and eminent Shakespearean scholars in the English-speaking world.

EUGENE EPPERSON BARNETT   *Doctor of Laws*
   A.B., Emory University, 1907; Vanderbilt University, University of North Carolina, and Columbia University, graduate study, 1907-1910, 1923
   General Secretary of the National Council of the Young Men's Christian Association

A religious leader whose resources of the spirit, insights of mind, and sweep of sympathies have made him a spiritual leader of the students of this University, of the youth of China, and the Christian youth movement of the world.

MAURICE VICTOR BARNHILL   *Doctor of Laws*
   University of North Carolina Law School, 1907-1909; Judge of the Superior Court of the State of North Carolina, 1924-1937
   Associate Justice of the Supreme Court of the State of North Carolina

First honor law student of this University, for twenty-two years distinguished as a trial and appellate judge, courageous in defense of the civil liberties of all citizens regardless of race, color, or creed.

JESSE WAKEFIELD BEAMS   *Doctor of Science*
A.B., Fairmount College, 1921; M.A., University of Wisconsin, 1922;
Ph.D., University of Virginia, 1925
Professor of Physics, University of Virginia

A teacher and experimentalist whose researches and teaching have
blazed trails in molecular physics and made contributions to research in chemistry, biology, and medicine.

JAMES FRANCIS BYRNES   *Doctor of Laws*
Associate Justice of the Supreme Court of the United States, 1941-
1942; Director of War Mobilization, 1943-1945
Secretary of State of the United States of America

The strong right arm of two presidents of the United States and
valiant champion of the United Nations at a post strategic among
the nations and at a time critical yet hopeful for the peace of the
world.

WILLIAM DONALD CARMICHAEL   *Doctor of Laws*
Ph.B., University of North Carolina, 1897
Vice-President (Retired) of Liggett and Myers Tobacco Company

Pioneering leader in public education in North Carolina and widely
respected and beloved industrial leader in the nation, now returned
to the scenes of his youth with a gracious benediction to the fresh
hopes of Alma Mater.

ROBERT GREGG CHERRY   *Doctor of Laws*
A.B., Trinity College (Duke University), 1912; Trinity Law School,
1913-1914
Governor of the State of North Carolina

Able lawyer, courageous soldier, successful legislator, popular all-
out war governor, and farsighted champion of a humanitarian
statewide medical care and hospital program for all the people of
North Carolina.

FRANCIS WILLIAM COKER   *Doctor of Laws*
A.B., University of North Carolina, 1899; A.B., Harvard University,
1902; Ph.D., Columbia University, 1910
Cowles Professor of Government, Yale University

Brilliant son of this University, distinguished professor at Yale,
and one of the foremost political scientists of our time.

NORMAN CHESHIRE CORDON, JR.   *Doctor of Music*
University of North Carolina, 1922-1924
Soloist of the Metropolitan Opera Company

With the high endowment of a God-given voice and by dint of
incessant work he has reached the musical heights to the joy and
inspiration of the people in many lands.

WILLIAM WALTER CORT   *Doctor of Science*
A.B., Colorado College, 1909; A.M., University of Illinois, 1911; Ph.D.,
ibid., 1914
Professor of Parasitology, The Johns Hopkins University

A scientist and teacher, whose researches in parasitology and epi-
demiology and whose students of public health have lifted the level
and extended the power of preventive medicine in peace and war
in both hemispheres.

PRESTON DAVIE   *Doctor of Laws*
A.B., Harvard University, 1904; Harvard Law School, 1904-1907
Lawyer and business executive

Lawyer, soldier, historical collector, and industrialist who served
his country as lieutenant colonel, winning the Distinguished Service Medal, in the First World War, and as an enterprising ship-
builder in the Second World War.

EDMUND EZRA DAY   *Doctor of Laws*
S.B., Dartmouth College, 1905; A.M., *ibid.*, 1906; Ph.D., Harvard Uni-
versity, 1909
President of Cornell University

Pioneering president of a pioneering university, he was the staunch
spokesman for American higher education in the war and is a
forward-minded national leader of cultural and humane causes
in the peace.

EMERY BYRD DENNY   *Doctor of Laws*
University of North Carolina Law School, 1916-1917
Associate Justice of the Supreme Court of the State of North Carolina

An able lawyer, soldier, civic and political leader, and Associate
Justice of the Supreme Court where for four years he has served
our state with integrity and distinction.

HAROLD WILLIS DODDS   *Doctor of Laws*
    A.B., Grove City College, 1909; A.M., Princeton University, 1914;
    Ph.D., University of Pennsylvania, 1917
    President of Princeton University

    Preëminent political scientist, expert in inter-American relations,
    and progressive president of a historic university whose cultural
    and spiritual light shines far across our modern world.

CLARENCE ADDISON DYKSTRA   *Doctor of Laws*
    A.B., University of Iowa, 1903; University of Chicago, graduate study,
    1903-1904, 1906-1908
    Provost of the University of California at Los Angeles

    National authority on municipal government, able administrator
    of state and national responsibilities in critical times, and eloquent
    champion of the university of the people.

EDWIN BROUN FRED   *Doctor of Science*
    B.S., Virginia Polytechnic Institute, 1907; M.S., *ibid.*, 1908; Ph.D., Uni-
    versity of Göttingen, 1911
    President of the University of Wisconsin

    Scientist and executive who has made fundamental contributions
    to the rebuilding and maintenance of the fertility of soils and to
    the administrative leadership of a great state university as a center
    of freedom and a source of democracy.

META GLASS   *Doctor of Laws*
    A.M., Randolph-Macon Woman's College, 1899; Ph.D., Columbia Uni-
    versity, 1913
    President of Sweet Briar College

    For twenty-one years the creative president of a distinguished col-
    lege of liberal arts for women, effective exponent of classical and
    humane studies, and a leader of the university women of America
    for the organization of peace in the world.

LUTHER HARTWELL HODGES   *Doctor of Laws*
    A.B., University of North Carolina, 1919
    Vice-President of Marshall Field and Company

    Beloved leader of the students of this University, respected leader
    of humane causes in North Carolina and in the American metrop-
    olis, and administrator of a great national industrial and com-
    mercial enterprise.

ISAAC LEON KANDEL *Doctor of Laws*
B.A., University of Manchester, 1902; M.A., *ibid.*, 1906; Ph.D., Columbia University, 1910
Professor of Education, Teachers College, Columbia University

Teacher and historian of education, editor of the monumental *Cyclopedia of Education*, he is an international authority on comparative education, whose researches and publications have won high awards on three continents.

WALDO GIFFORD LELAND *Doctor of Laws*
A.B., Brown University, 1900; A.M., Harvard University, 1901
Director of the American Council of Learned Societies

An archivist and historian, who has become a national and international leader in the integration of the humanistic studies, in inter-American intellectual relations, and of the humanistic academies of Europe and America.

ELIAS AVERY LOWE *Doctor of Laws*
A.B., Cornell University, 1902; Ph.D., University of Munich, 1907
Professor of Paleography, Institute for Advanced Study, Princeton, New Jersey

One of the foremost paleographers in the world whose profound humanism includes the cultural interests of people everywhere.

HARRY McMULLAN *Doctor of Laws*
LL.B., University of North Carolina, 1905
Attorney General of the State of North Carolina

A lawyer with a high conception of the law, a legislator devoted to the public welfare, and a public administrator who has served his state in many positions of high trust.

HARRY ALVIN MILLIS *Doctor of Laws*
A.B., Indiana University, 1895; A.M., *ibid.*, 1896; Ph.D., University of Chicago, 1899
Professor Emeritus of Economics, University of Chicago

A labor economist, whose host of devoted students, monumental studies, and national services in labor relations constitute a significant chapter in the history of American industrial relations.

HUGH JACKSON MORGAN *Doctor of Science*
B.S., Vanderbilt University, 1914; M.D., The Johns Hopkins University, 1918; Distinguished Service Medal
Brigadier General, Medical Corps, United States Army

A physician and professor whose varied researches and manifold publications have made notable contributions to the science and teaching of medicine and whose services as Chief Consultant in Medicine for the Army have reached around the earth.

EDWARD R. MURROW   *Doctor of Laws*
A.B., Washington State College, 1930
Vice-President of the Columbia Broadcasting System in charge of correspondents

From the furrowed rows of Guilford County to the air waves of the world, by clear analysis of the news and humane good will, he has become an intellectual and moral force toward international understanding and peace in the world.

WILLIAM FIELDING OGBURN   *Doctor of Laws*
B.S., Mercer University, 1905; A.M., Columbia University, 1909; Ph.D., *ibid.*, 1912
Sewell L. Avery Distinguished Service Professor of Sociology, University of Chicago

An author, professor, and public administrator sharing with another native Georgian preëminence among American sociologists, his authentic scholarship, publications, and teaching have made distinguished contributions to American understanding of social lags and social trends.

GEORGE BRAXTON PEGRAM   *Doctor of Science*
A.B., Trinity College (Duke University), 1895; Ph.D., Columbia University, 1903
Professor of Physics, and Dean of the Graduate Faculties, Columbia University

A distinguished university professor of physics and wise administrator of graduate teaching and research, whose investigations and supervision played a notable part in the capture of atomic power.

EDWIN McNEILL POTEAT   *Doctor of Divinity*
A.B., Furman University, 1912; A.M., *ibid.*, 1913; Th.M., Southern Baptist Theological Seminary, 1916
President of Colgate-Rochester Divinity School

One of the most courageous, dedicated, and prophetic spiritual leaders of our generation.

JULIAN PRICE   *Doctor of Laws*
Past President and Chairman of the Board of Directors, Jefferson Standard Life Insurance Company

Insurance executive and community builder, who has had a creative part in many business enterprises and philanthropic causes and who has developed one of the largest life insurance companies in the southern states.

D. HIDEN RAMSEY *Doctor of Laws*
A.B., University of Virginia, 1912; A.M., *ibid.*, 1913
General Manager of the *Asheville Citizen and Times*

An able journalist, one of the foremost citizens of the North Carolina mountains whence cometh his strength, a public servant whose clear fiscal analysis saved his city from bankruptcy and whose voice is lifted with eloquent power for humane causes in our state and beyond.

ARCHIBALD RUTLEDGE *Doctor of Letters*
B.S., Union College, New York, 1904; A.M., *ibid.*, 1907
Essayist, poet, and short story writer

A naturalist, whose prose and poetry have made the animals and the people of the South Carolina low country charmingly real to the vivid interest and delight of millions of Americans.

JAMES STEVENS SIMMONS *Doctor of Science*
B.S., Davidson College, 1911; University of North Carolina School of Medicine, 1911-1913; M.D., University of Pennsylvania, 1915; Ph.D., George Washington University Medical School, 1934; D.P.H., Harvard School of Public Health, 1939; Distinguished Service Medal, United States Army Typhus Commission Medal
Brigadier General, Medical Corps, United States Army

The Chief of the Preventive Medicine Division of the United States Army, whose researches and publications have helped to make the tropics safer for human habitation and whose far-flung administration has helped to save the lives and health of American soldiers all over the world.

WILLIAM HAY TALIAFERRO *Doctor of Science*
B.S., University of Virginia, 1915; Ph.D., The Johns Hopkins University, 1918
Chairman of the Department of Bacteriology and Parasitology, and Dean of the Division of Biological Sciences, University of Chicago

Distinguished professor of parasitology, author of standard works based on his fundamental researches in protozoölogy, genetics, and immunology, he is one of the most able administrators and nobly useful biological scientists of our times.

STITH THOMPSON   *Doctor of Letters*
B.A., University of Wisconsin, 1909; M.A., University of California, 1912; Ph.D., Harvard University, 1914
Professor of English and Folklore, Indiana Univeristy

Recognized leader of the American Folklore Society, the International Association of Ethnology, and the International Folklore Congress, and author of the definitive six-volume *Motif-Index of Folk Literature*, he stands forth as one of the greatest folklore scholars in the world.

ALLEN HAL TURNAGE   *Doctor of Laws*
University of North Carolina, 1908-1911; Navy Cross, Distinguished Service Medal
Major General and Assistant Commandant, United States Marine Corps

Able and brave commander of the United States Marines in North China, at Camp Lejeune, and of the Third Marine Division which, in brilliant campaigns, captured Guam, the first American soil retaken from the Japanese in the Second World War, and Bougainville.

LINDSAY CARTER WARREN   *Doctor of Laws*
University of North Carolina, 1906-1908; University of North Carolina Law School, 1911-1912
Comptroller General of the United States

Able lawyer, skillful parliamentarian, twice Speaker pro tem of the national House of Representatives, several times serving as majority leader, he piloted through the House many of the most important pieces of Congressional legislation in our times.

ARCHIBALD LEE MANNING WIGGINS   *Doctor of Laws*
A.B., University of North Carolina, 1913
President of the Bank of Hartsville, Hartsville, South Carolina, and Past President of the American Bankers Association

Breeder of pedigreed seeds, merchant, banker, and publisher, whose grasp of affairs, liberal mind, restless imagination, and administrative capacity, in the wake of a great pioneer, have helped to enlarge the enterprises of a small town in the service of the region and the nation.

JOHN WALLACE WINBORNE   *Doctor of Laws*
A.B., University of North Carolina, 1906
Associate Justice of the Supreme Court of the State of North Carolina

Devoted student and interpreter of the law as the way of justice and orderly progress among men, he has, for nine years, been an able and tirelessly industrious Associate Justice of the Supreme Court of North Carolina.

ROBERT SESSIONS WOODWORTH *Doctor of Science*
A.B., Amherst College, 1891; A.M., Harvard University, 1897; Ph.D., Columbia University, 1899
Professor Emeritus of Psychology, Columbia University

Widely recognized for his original work in physiological and experimental psychology, and one-time president of the American Psychological Association and of the Social Science Research Council, his scientific accomplishments, together with his two-score years of distinguished teaching, acclaim him the dean of American psychologists.

The Close of the Sesquicentennial

After the conferring of honorary degrees, the audience and Glee Clubs sang the hymn, "A Mighty Fortress Is Our God," and the Benediction was pronounced by Dr. Eugene Epperson Barnett, General Secretary, National Council of the Young Men's Christian Association.

A delicious buffet luncheon at Lenoir Hall followed the morning convocation and brought the Sesquicentennial, which was begun at Fayetteville on November 21, 1939, to a happy close.

XI

OTHER CELEBRATIONS DURING THE SESQUICENTENNIAL YEARS

D URING the Sesquicentennial period a number of celebrations were held by organizations within the University. Since they were directly related to the general celebration, a record of them is included in these *Chronicles*.

THE CENTENNIAL OF THE CAROLINA MAGAZINE

In April, 1943, the *Carolina Magazine* celebrated its one hundredth anniversary with a forty-four page issue in a special colored cover. The leading article, "Century in Review," by H. C. Cranford, sets forth the history of the publication, in part, as follows:

Buffeted by strong and never ceasing gales of criticism and impeded by a long chain of ill luck, the *Carolina Magazine* has run the full gamut of literary hardships since its shaky debut ninety-nine years ago.

The first issue of the *Carolina Magazine* (known then as the *North Carolina University Magazine*) was distributed on a cold March morning in 1844 and was received by the two hundred students at the University with mingled feelings of pride and disappointment.

Forty-eight pages had been promised in the first issue and when a last-minute check revealed insufficient copy, Printer Loring filled in with a number of news items "suitable for a weekly newspaper," but not, the mortified editors said later, "consistent with the dignity of a literary magazine."

Publication continued without hitch until July when the first board of editors took leave of their duties expressing fears for the future. A goal of 500 subscriptions had been only half realized, and few students made contributions.

During the next eight years, a bold and rugged period in

American history, the *Magazine* slept. Gold was discovered in California and hardy adventurers pushed past the Mississippi River frontier, across sun-baked plains and through Indian-infested territory, on to California and fortunes of gold.

While the Union rocked along from one startling event to another, and the *Carolina Magazine* dozed in temporary retirement, the University maintained a steady growth.

In February, 1852, one J. J. Slade, realizing that North Carolina had not a single sheet that "comes within the proper province of literature," suggested the re-establishment of the *University Magazine*. A mass meeting of students was held and a prospectus was sent out. On February 1, 1852, the first issue of the second series appeared.

There were 376 matriculates in 1860-1861. Then came the Civil War and the following year scarcely a hundred returned. It was decided that continuance of the magazine during the war would be impracticable and publication was halted for a second time.

The death of the ante-bellum *Magazine* had notched the close of an important era in the life of the periodical. The sentiment at the time was that there would be no second resurrection. But in March, 1878, the knowing ones blushed and stepped aside to admit an anaemic sheet of thirty-two pages which listed the title *The North Carolina University Magazine.*

In March-April, 1894, the *Magazine* published its Golden Jubilee number, the largest and most attractive single issue published up until that time, and one of the best all-round numbers ever. As is this one hundredth anniversary effort, the Golden Jubilee issue was a "turning back" number.

Some twenty-five hundred copies of the Golden Jubilee edition were printed and distributed. The editors were still basking in the praise of the issue when, in 1895, President Winston let it be known that he was of the opinion that the *Magazine* had been sustained by the societies and supervised by the faculty to such an extent as to "destroy initiative and discourage literary emulation on the part of the student body."

And so it was in December of 1897 that a new and last series began its climb for a place in the life of the University.

Meanwhile, war drums were beating louder in Europe. In 1914 the Germans invaded Belgium.

The *University Magazine*, thanks to a dependable editor and an alert staff, managed to stay alive throughout the war. In fact, the issues of 1917-1918 were all excellent ones.

Thomas Wolfe, later to become the University's most celebrated son, was "breaking in" on the *Magazine*, doing bits of verse and short stories.

In October, 1920, the *New Carolina Magazine* made its bow. Printed on slick paper and twice the size of its predecessors, the *New Magazine* was without question the best in the history of the publication up until that time.

Since 1923 the *Magazine* has been published as a member of the Publications Union of the University and, during the period of World War II, many of its editorial staff, including the editor-in-chief, have been drawn from the ranks of women students.

Adding to the distinction of the Centennial Number were articles reprinted from earlier volumes, among which were the following: "The Governor's Bourbon," by Zebulon B. Vance; "Streets of Durham," by Thomas Wolfe; "Land of Shadow," by Hatcher Hughes; "The South" and "Other Judases," by Paul Green; "Invisible Empire," by Francis Bradshaw; and "Football Ramble," by F. P. Graham.

The founding of the *Magazine* in 1843-1844 was important not only because it marked the beginning of student publication at the University, but because its beginning was contemporaneous with the organization of the North Carolina Historical Society at Chapel Hill and with the establishment of the Alumni Association of the University. It became the regular medium through which many articles and records dealing with the history of North Carolina appeared and its columns carried many contributions by alumni and notices concerning alumni activities.

THE CENTENNIAL OF THE ALUMNI ASSOCIATION

The celebration of the one hundredth anniversary of the Alumni Association of the University was observed at Commencement in 1943. The following account of the notable event is taken from *The Alumni Review* for May, 1943:

The Alumni Association of the University of North Carolina became a centenarian on May 31. At the University's forty-ninth Commencement a hundred years ago, thirty-one graduates gathered in Chapel Hill and voted to establish an alumni association. The date was May 31, 1843.

At the University's one hundred and forty-ninth Commencement, which was held May 30, 31, and June 1, the centennial birthday of the Alumni Association was celebrated at an alumni dinner on Monday evening, May 31. During the centennial year local clubs of the University Alumni Association will be asked to emphasize the theme of "activated alumni loyalty" as the organization enters upon another hundred years.

John Motley Morehead, then Governor of the State and called by historians "father of modern North Carolina," headed the distinguished company of thirty-one graduates who established the University Alumni Association. A graduate of 1817, Governor Morehead had been a tutor at the University before entering upon a career of law and politics. He was elected Governor of North Carolina in 1840 on the Whig ticket and was re-elected in 1842. Morehead identified himself with a progressive program in state affairs as a recognized leader of an upsurge emphasizing education and internal improvements.

The custom of some years' standing had been an address at Commencement by a distinguished alumnus. The two literary societies, then powerful campus agencies, to one of which every student was required to belong, frequently invited these speakers from among the alumni ranks. Later speakers were invited to address the alumni.

It was at such a meeting on May 31, 1843, that the Alumni Association came into being. Governor Morehead was "called to the chair" as presiding officer. A committee was appointed to draw up a constitution to be reported at the Commencement of 1844. To the committee were appointed William A. Graham of Hillsboro, John D. Hawkins of Franklin, John Hill of Wilmington, Charles Manly of Raleigh, and William M. Green and William H. Battle of Chapel Hill.

The prestige of University alumni in that early period of the state's life is suggested by the fact that the thirty-one alumni present included, in addition to Governor Morehead, two other men soon to become governors of the state, Graham and Manly.

The Alumni Association constitution adopted in 1844 declared the purpose of the organization to be: "to perpetuate the friendships formed in the collegiate course," "to promote the welfare" of Alma Mater, and to promote the "cause of educational generally." Governor Morehead was elected president, and Charles Phillips, a member of the University faculty, was elected secretary. Other officers elected included six vice presidents, a treasurer, and an executive committee.

The Alumni Association's activities in the early years were confined largely to the annual meeting at Commencement. Class reunions were added as a feature about 1855.

Morehead was re-elected president of the Alumni Association at each Commencement gathering of the alumni through 1849. The meeting of 1847 was made particularly noteworthy by the presence of President James Knox Polk, a University graduate of 1818, together with his Secretary of Navy, John Young Mason, an 1816 graduate.

Other prominent alumni attending included two graduates who also occupied cabinet posts as Secretaries of the Navy, John Branch and William A. Graham.

At the 1847 Commencement, the alumni, upon motion of Secretary Mason and President Polk, launched a movement to erect a suitable memorial to Joseph Caldwell, the University's first President. The Caldwell monument still stands at the center of the old campus near the Davie Poplar.

Other presidents of the Alumni Association who served prior to the Civil War included Charles Manly, John Hawkins, James Mebane, Paul C. Cameron, Charles L. Hinton, and Bartholomew F. Moore.

Charles Phillips continued to serve as secretary from 1844 until after the University was closed in 1870-75 during Reconstruction days. Graduate of the University in 1841, he was the son of Dr. James Phillips, who had moved to Chapel Hill with his family in 1826 to join the University faculty. His sister was Cornelia Phillips, who later married James Munroe Spencer, an 1853 University graduate of Clinton, Miss.

The Civil War brought hard days to the University. The institution kept open its doors during the actual years of the war itself, holding Commencement exercises annually. But the darker days of Reconstruction forced the University to close its doors. Its faculty sought positions elsewhere. Professor Phillips accepted a position at Davidson College, where he continued a wide correspondence and acquaintance with University alumni.

Mrs. Cornelia Phillips Spencer, widowed by the death of her husband in 1861, moved back to Chapel Hill in that year from her home in Mississippi. She, too, continued to correspond with old students of the University during the war and during Reconstruction. Continually and constantly she wrote to the public press of the state concerning the affairs of the University. When the University closed, she redoubled her efforts, pleading with alumni to see that the institution was opened again. A series of her articles, which was put together as *Pen and Ink Sketches of the University*, closed with this charge: "To the Alumni must the University look for her restoration. To the Alumni have I addressed these desultory papers, in the hope of kindling their attachment, and awakening their interest."

Following meetings of the alumni, called for the purpose of reviving the institution, former students took leading roles in the enactment of legislation in the General Assembly on March 20, 1875 to reopen the University. Students again came to Chapel Hill in the fall of 1875, and the job of rebuilding was under way.

In 1880, President Kemp P. Battle urged upon a few alumni gathered at Commencement the need for activating the Alumni Association. Some activity ensued, but it was not until the Charter Centennial celebration of 1889 in Chapel Hill that this activity began to assume proportions. The annual alumni dinner, instituted in 1889, has continued to be a Commencement feature. And "branch alumni associations" were subsequently organized at points throughout the state. An *Alumni Quarterly* made its appearance in the fall of 1894 to stimulate the revitalized alumni movement. Later, in 1896, appeared the *University Record*, which included in its scope both University and alumni affairs.

Thomas Stephen Kenan, a graduate of 1867, became president of the Alumni Association in 1892 and served until 1912. General Julian S. Carr served as president in 1912-17.

At the Commencement of 1917, R. D. W. Connor, a graduate of 1899 and then secretary of the State Historical Commission, was elected president, and under him the Alumni Association went through the days of World War I. He laid plans for the organization of a Central Alumni Office, a change which became a reality at the University in 1922.

Beginning with the Charter Centennial celebration of the University in 1889, and until 1922, the Alumni Association went through several stages of organization and reorganization. Under the leadership of such men as President George T. Winston, Walter Murphy, President E. K. Graham, Dr. Louis R. Wilson, Professor W. S. Bernard, Frank P. Graham, E. R. Rankin, and others, both in Chapel Hill and elsewhere, alumni activities were advanced along many lines.

In 1912 *The Alumni Review* was established with Dr. Wilson as editor. With Walter Murphy and E. R. Rankin as secretaries, alumni work during the ensuing decade was stimulated by renewed emphasis upon class reunions, University Day celebrations, and in other ways. *The Alumni Review* continued during the period to be a vehicle for keeping alumni acquainted with affairs of the University and chronicling their own alumni activities.

In 1922 a full-time secretary of the Alumni Association was employed and a Central Alumni Office launched in Chapel Hill. Daniel L. Grant was elected secretary, and among the first projects undertaken was a compiling of adequate alumni records and the publication of an alumni biographical directory. In 1924 the *Alumni History*, a directory of more than 1,000 pages and containing 15,000 names of alumni who had been students since 1795, was published.

Soon an annual business meeting of the Alumni Association with regularly elected representatives from the alumni clubs and organized classes was instituted for the annual election of officers. The Alumni Association was becoming a full-grown organization with representative machinery and with an employed staff to advance its program.

Presidents of the Alumni Association who have served in the period since World War I include Dr. Connor '99, Albert L. Cox '04, Walter Murphy '92, W. N. Everett '86 (deceased), Walter P. Stacy '08, A. M. Scales '92 (deceased), A. B. Andrews '93, W. T. Shore '05, C. Felix Harvey '92 (deceased), K. P. Lewis '00, John J. Parker '07, Dr. Hubert B. Haywood '05, Dr. Howard E. Rondthaler '93, George Stephens '96, J. C. B. Ehringhaus '01, C. W. Tillett '09, Fred I. Sutton '08, W. A. Dees '11, L. P. McLendon '12, and now John Motley Morehead '91.

Succeeding Grant as executive secretary in 1927 was J. Maryon Saunders, who since that time has been secretary and editor of *The Alumni Review*. A graduate of the University in 1925, Saunders has seen the Central Alumni Office moved from South Building, the University administration building, to the Carolina Inn, which was built as a University and alumni hostelry in 1924 by John Sprunt Hill of Durham and given to the University by him and his family in 1935. In the Carolina Inn the Alumni Offices now occupy spacious headquarters on the first floor, and serve as a reception center for alumni visitors to the campus.

In its records department the Alumni Office maintains permanent biographical folders of more than 38,000 former and present students of the University. These folders constitute a veritable genealogical history of University graduates, ranging from Hinton James, the first student in 1795, down to the last freshman to register at the University. All matriculates, whether or not they remain to graduate, are placed upon the University's alumni rolls.

The Alumni Office also maintains in its records department address stencils, arranged so that a mailing machine can quickly provide lists of alumni wherever they now live, for more than 30,000 former students. Changes of address occasioned by the war have become increasingly numerous among University alumni. Addresses and information are on record that 3,327 former students now are in the armed services, and conservative estimates of the alumni in uniform exceed 4,000.

In addition to lists of former students maintained by communities and the master list arranged alphabetically, the Alumni Office is now maintaining a special section devoted to war records of alumni. It also keeps lists by classes, professions, graduates, non-graduating matriculates, and various student organizations.

Today, with the nation at war, University alumni are making significant and vital contributions to state and nation. Alongside the 4,000 younger alumni in uniform and the others who are joining them daily, alumni of the University are occupying important roles in war industries, government posts, and in all walks of life.

THE CENTENNIAL OF THE LAW SCHOOL

No formal exercises were held to commemorate the establishment of the Law School of the University, which occurred in the autumn of 1845. The event, however, was celebrated through the publication of *A Century of Legal Education*, which first appeared as the June, 1946, issue of the *North Carolina Law Review*, and was republished as one of the bound volumes of the Sesquicentennial publications. A special feature of the issue is a history of the Law School, an extended article prepared by Professor Albert Coates, of the faculty of the School, which sets forth the development of the School from its beginning in 1845 under Judge William H. Battle, of the class of 1820, to the present.

Other articles in the issue are: "Salutation," by Walter P. Stacy, Chief Justice of the Supreme Court of North Carolina; "Foreword," by Robert H. Wettach, Dean of the Law School; "History of the Law Library," by Lucile Elliott, Librarian of the Law School; "Early Days of the Law School—Reminiscences," by Thomas Ruffin, of Washington, D. C.; "Teaching Theory and Practice in the New Day," by Merton LeRoy Ferson, Dean of the University of Cincinnati Law School; "Legal Education after the War," by Leon Green, Dean of Northwestern University Law School; "The Place and Future of the State University Law School," by Charles Tilford McCormick, Dean of the University of Texas Law School.

THE FIFTIETH ANNIVERSARY OF THE PHILOLOGICAL CLUB

The celebration of the fiftieth anniversary of the Philological Club was held in the east parlor of the Carolina Inn on the evening of January 20, 1943, with Dr. W. M. Dey, Kenan Professor of Romance Languages, presenting a history of the Club before a large gathering of members of the faculty from the departments of language and literature and friends.

The Club, as described by Professor Dey, was founded Friday, January 20, 1893, by five members of the faculty: Thomas Hume, Professor of English; Eben Alexander, Professor of Greek; Walter D. Toy, Professor of Modern Languages (later Professor of Germanic Languages); Karl P. Harrington, Professor of Latin; and Henry J. Stockard, poet and instructor in English.

At the first meeting, after informal general discussion, the following decisions were reached by the group concerning the future of the organization:

1. That all present approved of the formation of such a Philological Club.
2. That the meetings should be held once a month at the offices of the members in rotation.
3. That a Secretary should be at first the only permanent officer of the Club, while the members should preside in rotation.
4. That each member have the privilege of presenting such long or short original notes or papers as he should desire; or of presenting none, if preferred.
5. That the work of keeping the Club informed of the contents of the various philological journals and other publications accessible should be divided among the members who should report at each meeting.
6. That students especially interested in any line of work being discussed, or such students as may have original work worthy to present before the Club may be invited to be present at any meeting at the pleasure of any member.

Professor Harrington was elected secretary, and the work of reviewing periodicals was assigned to the several members: Professor Alexander—*The American Journal of Philology;* Dr. Hume—*Shaksperiana;* Professor Toy, Dr. Hume, and Mr. Stockard—*Modern Language Notes;* Professor Harrington—*The Classical Review* and the *Berliner philologische Wochenschrift;* Mr. Stockard—*Educational Review* and "similar things"; Professor Alexander—occasional other articles; Professor Alexander also consented to tender information concerning new books.

In accord with these decisions, the Club began formal meetings on February 10, 1893, which have been held monthly during the regular sessions of the University since that date. During the academic year 1893-94, the programs of the meetings assumed a somewhat different character and became more like those of present meetings. Linguistic and literary topics were about equally divided.

Following the formal establishment of the Graduate Department of the University in 1903, the Club became interested in the publication of a journal in its field and in 1906, under the deanship of Dr. C. Alphonso Smith, the publication of *Studies in Philology* was begun. Volume I of *Studies* was issued by Dr. Louis R. Wilson. There was no mention of an editor. Volumes II and III appeared under the editorship of Dr. C. Alphonso Smith, first dean of the Graduate School. From 1909 until 1915, when Dr. Edwin Greenlaw became editor, volumes IV to XI were published under an editorial committee of which Dr. James F. Royster was chairman and Louis R. Wilson and W. M. Dey were members. All of these volumes were published under the auspices of the Club.

Since 1915 the publication has been issued as a quarterly, and its issue for July, 1945 (Vol. XLIII), to which many members of the Club contributed important articles, has been reissued as *Studies in Language and Literature* in the Sesquicentennial publications.

THE FIFTIETH ANNIVERSARY OF THE "TAR HEEL"

The *Tar Heel,* which began publication as the organ of the Athletic Association on February 23, 1893, celebrated its fiftieth anniversary on February 23, 1943.

Because of the shortage of paper and the exigencies of war, the anniversary issue did not run to the length previously contemplated by the editors, but was strictly limited to four pages. On the first of these, the first page of the first issue in 1893 was reproduced. This, an editorial, and the following historical article, by Sam Whitehall, constituted the features of the special issue:

WAR RESTRICTS CELEBRATION OF ANNIVERSARY

The end of one half-century in student journalism here is marked today as the *Daily Tar Heel* briefly pauses in its coverage of the news to celebrate its fiftieth birthday "without pomp and ceremony."

Extensive celebration plans were cancelled as the noted leaders in the field of journalism, several who were former editors, had to decline invitations to attend because of pressing work occasioned by the war. Paper and labor shortages caused the absence of the multi-page special issue in commemoration of the anniversary usual in former years as "the oldest college daily in the South" today observes its "proudest day" with slight reflection and little fanfare in wartime fashion.

Rising from February 23, 1893, when the first *Tar Heel* hit the streets of Chapel Hill, the exclusive publication with its jealously guarded freedom has become a small replica of a metropolitan newspaper.

First begun as a publication of the Athletic Association, the campus organ has included in its masthead as editor the names of University President Frank P. Graham, Thomas Wolfe, famed author, Jonathan Daniels, former editor of the *Raleigh News and Observer* and now on special duty to the president in Washington, Lenoir Chambers, associate editor of the *Norfolk Virginian-Pilot*, Thomas C. Lynn, Near Eastern expert for the *New York Times*, R. D. W. Connor, former National Archivist and at present a professor here, and Jake Wade, sports editor of the *Charlotte Observer*.

Its beginning as a sports page with its major story printed twenty days after the event was in a dilapidated storeroom next to the old Methodist church. Founded by Charles Baskerville and Walter "Pete" Murphy, the paper started as a weekly, stepped up to bi-weekly in 1920 and entered the daily field in 1928. Since, editors have steadily organized and modernized the format and content to fit present newspaper standards.

The proud nomen "only college daily in the South" was altered to that of "the oldest" in 1941 on the forty-eighth birthday in deference to Texas.

Coverage of news was expanded in 1940 to that of the international sphere with the addition of the United Press briefs secured nightly by wire from the Raleigh bureau. Several scoops on state and Southern commercial papers have been registered as in 1941 the *DTH* was the only paper South of Washington to carry complete election returns and in 1939 was the only paper in the state to carry the flash of the German invasion of Belgium.

THE TWENTY-FIFTH ANNIVERSARY OF THE CAROLINA PLAYMAKERS

In spite of the fact that 1943 found the country in the midst of a gigantic world conflict with attendant disruption and change not only in the University, but in the nation, the occasion of the completion of the first quarter-century of progress and achievement in the life of The Carolina Playmakers as a dynamic force in the development of the American Drama was given special recognition. A Twenty-Fifth Anniversary Conference, whose theme was Drama as a Wartime Job, was arranged to coincide with the annual Spring Festival of the Carolina Dramatic Association so that its attending members might have the opportunity of participating. Invitations were sent to a long list of Playmaker alumni scattered throughout the country and in the armed forces and to a host of friends in the field of drama and the theatre. The response was gratifying, for letters came from every quarter, all of which were full of the warmest congratulations and commendations for Professor Koch and The Carolina Playmakers.

The celebration opened on the evening of March 25, 1943, with an Anniversary Dinner Conference in the ballroom of the Carolina Inn attended by some two hundred guests who had gathered from all over the state. Dr. R. B. House, Dean of Administration of the University, presided at the speaker's table, and, after a short, graceful speech commemorating the occasion, introduced Dr. Archibald Henderson, who read a special "Salutation" from Paul Green, who could not be present. The Playmakers' founder and director, Professor Koch, then rose and delivered the following response:

PROFESSOR KOCH

Against the backdrop of blossoming cherry trees and the shimmering mists of the redbud in bloom, again the stage is set for our Carolina Festival. Paul Green has expressed in eloquent phrase something of the thing that brings us together tonight. Spring again! And twenty-five years! We are thankful for this festival in the time of war. I speak for you all, I believe, when I say that each of us feels the need of the creative arts in the life of man. We need it today as never before. At first we felt we must abandon our plans for an Anniversary Festival. Now we feel that our foregathering is more important because of the war. We meet not simply to commemorate twenty-five productive and happy years, but rather to reaffirm our continuing faith in the more abundant life of the human spirit.

Our Playmakers have dedicated themselves to expressing America. From the first our theatre has had an active part in the making of a new drama, in creating a theatre of all the children of all the people. From the first our theatre has been not merely a re-producing but a producing theatre—a creative theatre. Our young playwrights have found fresh fields in the lives of the common people everywhere. It has been a great adventure— this folk playmaking—and a happy one! We thank you all for remembering—and for looking ahead to a brave new world in the making.

We are striving as Thomas Jefferson did "to avail the State of those talents which Nature has sown as liberally among the poor as the rich, but which perish without use unless sought for and cultivated." Of such is our "institution of the dear love of comrades."

Our Playmakers tonight are playing their parts on the far-flung battlelines around the world—in Australia, in Alaska, in

Africa. We are thinking *nearly* of them tonight, for we know they are with us too. Many letters have come to tell us so. One writes, "I think it is grand the way you are keeping things going" in this distressful war. And another: "Above all keep the torch burning!" With Walt Whitman we are "expecting the main things from those that come after. . . ."

Dean House then read brief selections from some of the greetings from various Playmaker alumni: from George Denny, Founder and Director of "Town Hall of the Air"; from Kay Kyser, eminent impresario; Hubert Heffner, Head of the Drama Department at Stanford University; William Woods, novelist —among others. Following this, Dean House introduced Mr. Barrett Clark, distinguished dramatic critic and author, who delivered the principal address. Mr. Clark spoke on "Drama in a Democracy" from which the following excerpt is taken:

Mr. Clark

One of the most striking changes in American life during the past thirty or forty years, so far as the arts are concerned, is in the attitude of the common man toward the artist and his functions. When I was a youngster in the Middle West the artist, generally speaking, was looked upon as something of a freak and his products, usually, as luxury articles. All the arts were thought of as the exclusive concern of the well-to-do and were judged to be superfluities in a world dedicated largely to material success.

The theatre, except perhaps the routine professional theatre, was quite properly not looked upon as an art at all, but simply as entertainment. Then came the day of the so-called Little or Experimental Theatre, which rather intensified the public's attitude toward the artist as a strange and odd social outcast. In spite of this, the torch-bearers of the early years of the present century did manage to make it clear to many of us that the theatre might be richer and more interesting and more full of meaning than it had been, and in spite of affectation and a good deal of faddism, the torch-bearers became as the years advanced a little more realistic and intelligent.

Then, because our directors had received training, both abroad and in the American schools, a new generation of directors came into being who somehow realized that the theatre was something not apart *from* life but literally a part *of* life. That is the point at which Koch with his Playmakers Theatre appeared on the scene and, by working from the inside out, helped make the theatre a function of life and a means of interpretation, rather than an addition to life.

The theatre outside Broadway, despite its technical shortcomings and despite a good deal of bungling, is no longer something for the privileged few but a necessity for the many. Briefly, art in America has taken its place with the other functions of a great democracy.

At the conclusion of Mr. Clark's address the Conference adjourned to the Playmakers Theatre for the experimental production of three new one-act plays by students from the class in Playwriting. The first was a charming comedy of Syrian folk of the Lebanon Mountains by Mary-Averett Seelye entitled *Fleas and Figs*. This was followed by a thoughtful drama of youth and the problems of war by Walter Carroll entitled *My World to Grieve*. The evening came to a close with the presentation of Marcelle Clark's amusing blackout skit for Army Camp entertainment, *The Right and the Left*.

The Anniversary Conference was continued on the following morning at the theatre when Lieutenant Brace Conning of Camp Lee, Virginia, spoke on "Show Business in Uncle Sam's Army," and Fred Crofts, New York publisher, spoke on "Teaching Drama in Wartime." Dr. Koch followed with a talk on "The Theatre in War," and Mr. Clark spoke again on the subject of "The Theatre as a Function of Life."

Both the Anniversary Conference and the Festival bore convincing testimony to the dynamic role of the Carolina Playmakers in the creation and expression of beauty through the dramatic arts and to the vitality of American drama in war as well as in peace.

XII

THE SESQUICENTENNIAL PUBLICATIONS

S INCE 1844, when the *University of North Carolina Magazine* began publication, the University has maintained a
cumulative record of distinctive publication an account of
which is briefly set forth in the volumes in this series entitled *The
Graduate School: Research and Publications* and *Books from
Chapel Hill: A Complete Catalogue, 1923-1945.* Notable events
in the record include among others the establishment of the *Journal of the Elisha Mitchell Scientific Society* in 1884, *The James
Sprunt Historical Monographs* in 1900, *Studies in Philology* in
1906, *The Journal of Social Forces* in 1922, and the founding of
the University of North Carolina Press in 1922. Altogether there
are at present nine publications regularly issued by the University, several others receive editorial and financial assistance from
it, and approximately 500 volumes described in *Books from
Chapel Hill* have been published by the Press since its establishment in 1922.

Because of this record, and on account of war conditions and
the general ban by the Office of Defense Transportation on the
holding of meetings involving a large number of visitors, it was
found desirable to emphasize publication as a principal feature
of the Sesquicentennial. Accordingly, under the general editorship of Professor Wilson, an extensive series of Sesquicentennial
Publications was projected which featured particularly the journals regularly maintained by the University and issued through
the University of North Carolina Press. The journals provided
regular media for publication, and, of special importance, on account of priority limitations, they had paper quotas.

Consequently, nine of the regular publications were requested
to plan special double, treble, or quadruple numbers, which,
with appropriate titles and forewords, could be bound in a general series under the title *The University of North Carolina Sesquicentennial Publications.*

Specific titles were planned by the editorial boards or by

special editors of the journals as follows, and have already been published or will appear soon: *Studies in Science*, edited by W. C. Coker, Kenan Professor of Botany, for the *Journal of the Elisha Mitchell Scientific Society; Studies in Language and Literature*, edited by George R. Coffman, Kenan Professor of English, for *Studies in Philology; Studies in History and Political Science*, edited by A. R. Newsome, '15, Professor of History, for *The Sprunt Studies in History and Political Science; In Search of the Regional Balance of America*, edited by Howard W. Odum, Kenan Professor of Sociology and Katharine Jocher, Ph.D. '29, Professor of Sociology and Assistant Director of the Institute for Research in Social Science, for *Social Forces; Pioneering a People's Theatre*, edited by Archibald Henderson, '98, Kenan Professor of Mathematics, for *The Carolina Play-Book; The Graduate School: Research and Publications*, edited by E. W. Knight, Kenan Professor of Education, and Agatha Boyd Adams, Associate Director of Library Extension, and *The Graduate School: Dissertations and Theses*, edited by James L. Godfrey, Assistant Professor of History, Fletcher M. Green, Kenan Professor of History, and W. W. Pierson, Professor of History and Political Science and Dean of the Graduate School, for *Research in Progress; A Century of Legal Education*, edited by R. H. Wettach, Professor of Law and Dean of the School of Law, for the *North Carolina Law Review; Secondary Education in the South*, edited by W. Carson Ryan, Kenan Profesor of Education, J. Minor Gwynn, '18, Associate Professor of Education, and A. K. King, '25, Professor of Education, for *The High School Journal;* and *University Extension in Action*, edited by Russell M. Grumman, Director of the University Extension Division, for the *University Extension Bulletin.*

In addition to these titles, the following have been prepared or are in preparation as separate volumes: *The Chronicles of the Sesquicentennial*, edited by Louis R. Wilson, '99, Professor of Library Science and Director of the Sesquicentennial; *The University of North Carolina, 1789-1835: A Documentary History*, compiled and edited by R. D. W. Connor, '99, Craige Professor of Jurisprudence and History; *The Campus of the First State University: Its History and Physical Development*, by Archibald Henderson; *A State University Surveys the Humanities*, edited for the Division of Humanities by Loren C. MacKinney, Professor of Medieval History, Nicholson B. Adams, Professor of Spanish, and Harry K. Russell, Ph.D., '31, Associate Professor of English; *Library Resources of the University of North Carolina: A Summary of Facilities for Study and Research*, edited by Charles E. Rush, Director of Libraries; and *Books from Chapel Hill: A Complete Catalogue, 1923-1945*, edited by W. T. Couch, '26, Director of the University of North Carolina Press.

While no specific pattern was followed in the preparation of the volumes, some effort was made, particularly in the publications issued by the journals, to summarize their historical development, to indicate what their general policies and objectives had been, and to forecast as far as possible the interests and problems to which the University would devote itself through them in the future.

As a supplement to these publications, the Faculty Committee on the Sesquicentennial Celebration urged the Administration to provide for the publication of a popularly written, attractively illustrated booklet dealing with the history and the buildings and grounds of the University and Chapel Hill for the use of visitors and the public generally, and an attractively designed brochure through which the needs of the University for scholarships, fellowships, professorships, research, special collections of library materials, and other purposes might be set forth.

APPENDICES

APPENDIX A

SESQUICENTENNIAL COMMITTEES

FACULTY COMMITTEE

Francis F. Bradshaw, *Chairman*

H. G. Baity
Dr. W. R. Berryhill
R. E. Coker
R. D. W. Connor
W. M. Dey
S. T. Emory
R. M. Grumman
D. S. Klaiss
E. L. Mackie
Dr. W. deB. MacNider

R. W. Madry
A. R. Newsome
W. D. Perry
H. K. Russell
Phillips Russell
J. M. Saunders
Sherman Smith
C. P. Spruill
C. E. Teague
Louis R. Wilson

Members ex Officio

F. P. Graham, President
R. B. House, Chancellor
W. D. Carmichael, Jr., Controller

LEGISLATIVE COMMISSION

Victor S. Bryant, *Chairman*

Marsden Bellamy
H. Galt Braxton
Gordon Gray

John L. Morehead
D. Hiden Ramsey
Capus M. Waynick

TRUSTEE COMMITTEE

J. C. B. Ehringhaus, *Chairman*

Mrs. Katherine P. Arrington
Sam M. Blount
Charles Cannon
Mrs. Julius Cone
Burton Craige
Josephus Daniels
James S. Ficklen
Frank W. Hancock

John Sprunt Hill
L. P. McLendon
Kemp B. Nixon
John J. Parker
Thomas J. Pearsall
Dr. Foy Roberson
George Stephens
John W. Umstead

ALUMNI COMMITTEE

Kemp D. Battle, *Chairman*

Lenoir Chambers
Ceasar Cone
Dr. Hubert B. Haywood
Howard Holderness

Henry B. Marrow
C. W. Rankin
Charles G. Rose
Lawrence Watt

307

STUDENT COMMITTEE

C. F. Benbow, Jr., *Chairman*

Donald Bishop   Catherine P. Kelly
Mitchell Britt   Lucy Lee Kennedy
Chauncey Broome   P. Alston Lewis
Robert W. Carr   Mary C. Marett
W. T. Crisp   Turk Newsome
Betty Lou Cypert   W. J. Tripp
Shirley Hartsell   Jack Vernier
A. A. Hodd   Harvey White
Douglass Hunt   Wynette B. White
Joseph S. Huske, Jr.   Charles Wickenberg
Louise Jordan   Elizabeth P. Wiggins
James M. Joyner   Richard B. Willingham
              Mary Wood Winslow

COMMITTEE ON ART EXHIBIT

Mrs. Katherine P. Arrington, *Chairman*
J. V. Allcott   W. F. Davidson

COMMITTEE ON RECEPTION

J. V. Allcott   Mrs. W. D. Carmichael, Jr.
Roy Armstrong   Mrs. F. H. Edmister
              Mrs. M. H. Stacy

COMMITTEE ON ENTERTAINMENT OF GUESTS

Mrs. W. R. Berryhill   Mrs. R. J. M. Hobbs
              Mrs. R. H. Wettach

SESQUICENTENNIAL STAFF

Louis R. Wilson, *Director of the Sesquicentennial Celebration
and Publications*
Russell M. Grumman, *In Charge of Information and Lodging*
J. M. Saunders and H. F. Comer, *In Charge of Public Arrangements*
R. W. Madry, *In Charge of Publicity*
L. H. Gooch, *In Charge of Dining Service*
C. E. Teague, *In Charge of Transportation of Guests*
W. T. Couch, T. J. Wilson, and Miss Porter Cowles, *In Charge
of Printing the Sesquicentennial Publications and
Programs of the Final Convocation*
Mrs. C. D. Beers, *In Charge of Decorations in Memorial Hall*
Mrs. S. M. Shiver, *Secretary*

University Marshal and Aids

University Marshal

W. M. Dey

Aids

Richmond P. Bond

S. H. Hobbs, Jr.

U. T. Holmes, Jr.

J. M. Lear

J. Coriden Lyons

Loren C. MacKinney

William A. Olsen

Sterling A. Stoudemire

William S. Wells

W. Leon Wiley

APPENDIX B

The following delegates were introduced by Dr. William Morton Dey, Marshal of the University, at the Sesquicentennial Convocation on Saturday, April 13, 1946:

DELEGATES FROM UNIVERSITIES AND COLLEGES

DATE OF
FOUNDING

1583	University of Edinburgh . .	Dr. Warren C. Vosburgh
1636	Harvard University . . .	Dr. David Edward Owen
1693	College of William and Mary .	Dean James Wilkinson Miller
1701	Yale University	Dean William Clyde De Vane
1740	University of Pennsylvania . .	Provost Paul Howard Mussey
1746	Princeton University . . .	President Harold W. Dodds
1749	Washington and Lee University	Dr. William Webb Pusey, III
1754	Columbia University . . .	Dean George B. Pegram
1764	Brown University	Vice-President Bruce MacMillan Bigelow
1766	Rutgers University	Dr. Richard Lionel Predmore
1769	Dartmouth College	Dr. Maurice Whittinghill
1770	College of Charleston . . .	President George Daniel Grice Dr. Earle DeWitt Jennings
1772	Salem College	President Howard E. Rondthaler
1776	Hampden-Sydney College . .	President Edgar G. Gammon
1780	Transylvania College . . .	Professor Gwynn McPeck
1782	Washington College . . .	Dr. Charles B. Clark
1783	Dickinson College	Dr. Andrew Blair
1785	University of Georgia . .	Dr. E. Merton Coulter
1787	Franklin and Marshall College .	Dr. Bruce A. Wentz
1787	University of Pittsburgh . .	Chancellor R. H. Fitzgerald
1789	Georgetown University . . .	The Reverend Paul A. McNally, S.J.
1789	Louisburg College	President Walter Patten
1791	University of Vermont . . .	President John S. Millis
1794	Bowdoin College	Dr. Sturgis E. Leavitt
1794	University of Tennessee . .	Dean N. W. Dougherty
1800	Middlebury College . . .	President Samuel S. Stratton
1801	University of South Carolina .	Dr. George Coffin Taylor
1802	United States Military Academy	Colonel Robert F. Sink
1804	Ohio University	Dr. Edna Arundel
1807	Moravian College and Theological Seminary	President Raymond S. Haupert

DATE OF
FOUNDING

1809	Miami University	Mrs. Ernestine C. Milner
1812	Hamilton College	Dr. Paull F. Baum
1812	Princeton Theological Seminary	The Reverend William M. Boyce
1812	Union Theological Seminary in Virginia	Dr. John Sprunt Hill
1813	Colby College	President Julius Seelye Bixler
1815	Allegheny College	Dr. William A. Brownell
1817	Colgate-Rochester Divinity School	Dr. Kenneth Willis Clark
1817	University of Michigan . .	Herman Charles Kleene, Esq.
1819	Colgate University	President Emeritus George Barton Cutten
1819	Maryville College . . .	Miss Laura J. Silsby
1819	University of Virginia . . .	Dean Ivey Foreman Lewis
1820	Indiana University	Dr. Henry M. Burlage Judge Ora L. Wildermuth
1821	Amherst College	The Reverend James T. Cleland
1821	George Washington University	Dr. William Carson Ryan
1822	Hobart College	Dr. Paul W. Wager
1823	Protestant Episcopal Theological Seminary in Virginia . . .	The Reverend David W. Yates
1823	Trinity College	Dr. Frederick A. G. Cowper
1824	Rensselaer Polytechnic Institute	Dr. John E. Dykstra
1826	Furman University	Dean Hobert Norman Daniell
1826	Lafayette College	Dr. William McK. Piatt
1826	Mississippi College	The Reverend A. L. O'Briant
1826	Western Reserve University .	Dr. David Olson
1830	Randolph-Macon College for Men	Dr. J. Paul McConnell
1831	University of Alabama . . .	Dr. William Whatley Pierson, Jr.
1831	Denison University	Theodore S. Johnson, Esq.
1831	LaGrange College	Dr. W. L. Murray
1831	New York University . . .	Vice-Chancellor Harold O. Voorhis
1831	Wesleyan University . . .	Professor Homer E. Woodbridge
1832	Gettysburg College	President William Andrew Hanson
1832	University of Richmond . .	Dean George M. Modlin
1832	Wabash College	President Frank Hugh Sparks

1833	Haverford College	Dr. Allan Wilson Hobbs
1833	Mercer University . . .	President Spright Dowell
1833	Oberlin College	Dr. Hornell Norris Hart
1834	University of Delaware . . .	Dean J. F. Daugherty
1834	Hartford Seminary	Dr. Clyde A. Milner
1834	Tulane University . . .	Dr. H. Clyde Horack
1834	Wake Forest College . . .	President Thurman D. Kitchin
1835	Marietta College	Harry W. Fogle, Esq.
1836	Alfred University	Dr. Arthur F. Greaves-Walker
1836	Emory University	President Goodrich Cook White
1836	Union Theological Seminary .	The Reverend James T. Cleland
1836	Wesleyan College	Dean Samuel L. Akers
1837	Colby Junior College . . .	Miss Katharine A. Bonney
1837	Davidson College	President John R. Cunningham
1837	DePauw University . . .	Dr. Franklin S. Hickman
1837	Guilford College	President Clyde A. Milner
1837	Knox College	Professor Vera Largent
1837	Mount Holyoke College . .	Dr. Helen C. Monchow
1838	Duke University	Dean Calvin B. Hoover
1838	Greensboro College	President Luther L. Gobbel
1839	Boston University	Dr. Franklin S. Hickman
1839	University of Missouri . . .	Vice-President Thomas A. Brady
1840	Carroll College	Mrs. W. M. Foley
1840	Southwestern University . .	Dr. Wilfred Hardy Callcott
1841	Fordham University . . .	Dean Lawrence A. Walsh
1842	The Citadel	Dr. R. C. Smith
1842	Hollins College	President Bessie Carter Randolph
1842	Mary Baldwin College . . .	Miss Catharine Mims
1842	Roanoke College . . .	Dean Edward D. Myers
1842	St. Mary's School and Junior College	The Rev. I. Harding Hughes
1842	Willamette University . . .	Mrs. Eva Miles Newlin
1845	Mary Hardin-Baylor College .	President Gordon G. Singleton
1845	United States Naval Academy .	Captain Rupert M. Zimmerli
1845	Wittenberg College	Dr. Franklin H. McNutt
1846	Baylor University	Mayes Behrman, Esq.
1846	Beloit College	Dr. Raymond Adams
1846	University of Buffalo . . .	Dean Claude E. Puffer
1846	MacMurray College for Women	Miss Margaret Kinsman
1847	Earlham College	Dean Emeritus Elbert Russell
1847	Otterbein College	Dr. Albert S. Kiester

DATE OF
FOUNDING

1847	State University of Iowa . .	Dean H. Claude Horack
1847	College of the City of New York	Dr. Paul Gross
1848	Muhlenberg College	President Levering Tyson
1848	Southwestern College . . .	Dr. John A. Redhead
1848	University of Wisconsin . .	Dr. Norman Foerster
1850	Capital University	Edward S. Schenk, Jr., Esq.
1850	Heidelberg College	Dr. Clement Vollmer
1850	Hiram College	Orris J. Miller, Esq.
1850	University of Rochester . .	Dr. Clarence Heer
1851	University of Minnesota . .	Dr. Walter McKinley Neilsen
1851	Northwestern University . .	Dean Thomas Moody Campbell
1852	Stratford College	President John C. Simpson
1852	Tufts College	Professor Robert B. Rice
1853	Louisville Presbyterian Theological Seminary	Dr. Kelsey Regen
1853	Monmouth College . . .	Dr. Calvin B. Hoover
1853	Western College for Women .	Mrs. Margaret Goldthwaite Dilts
1854	Columbia College	President J. Caldwell Guilds
1854	Hamline University . . .	Dr. Raymond P. Kaighn
1854	Huntingdon College . . .	Dr. Hubert Searcy
1854	Wofford College	Dr. Oscar W. Lever
1855	Berea College	Dean Louis Smith
1855	Elmira College	Mrs. Paul Sutton
1855	Pennsylvania State College .	Dr. Earl H. Newcomer
1856	Birmingham-Southern College .	Professor Keener C. Frazer
1856	Mitchell College	Miss Nancy Blair Eliason
1856	Newberry College	Dr. Ralph Walton Bost
1856	Universty of the South . . .	The Reverend Emmet Gribbin
1857	Peace College	President William C. Pressly
1857	Queens College, Charlotte, North Carolina	President Hunter B. Blakely
1859	Averett College	President Curtis Bishop
1859	Lake Erie College	Dr. Chester Townsend Ruddick
1859	Southern Baptist Theological Seminary	Dr. J. Winston Pearce
1859	Whitman College	Miss Lucille Kelling
1860	Louisiana State University . .	Dr. Archibald Henderson
1860	Wheaton College	Robert H. Spiro, Esq.
1861	Massachusetts Institute of Technology	Beaumert H. Whitton, Esq.
1861	Vassar College	Mrs. Lionne A. Rush
1863	Bates College	Dr. Norman Francis Conant

DATE OF
FOUNDING

1863	Kansas State College . . .	Dr. H. Arlo Stewart
1863	Massachusetts State College .	Dr. Walter Kulash
1864	University of Denver . . .	Dr. Lillian Parker Wallace
1864	Swarthmore College . . .	Mrs. Isabel Van Dewater Ryan
1865	Cornell University	President Edmund Ezra Day
1865	University of Kentucky . .	Professor Albert Dennis Kirwan
1865	University of Maine . . .	Frank B. Hanson, Esq.
1865	Purdue University	Dr. Henry M. Burlage
1865	Worcester Polytechnic Institute	Richard M. Mitchell, Esq.
1866	Carleton College	Professor Elizabeth Cowling
1866	Hope College	William Alan Wichers, Esq.
1866	University of Kansas . . .	Dr. Milton S. Heath
1866	University of New Hampshire	Harold W. Whitcomb, Esq.
1867	Western Maryland College .	Dr. George Stockton Wills
1868	University of California . .	Dr. William Ray Dennes
1868	University of Illinois . . .	Dr. Rex S. Winslow
1868	Iowa State College	Professor Gertrude M. Cox
1868	Southern Seminary and Junior College	President Margaret Durham Robey
1869	University of Nebraska . . .	Dr. Arthur S. Pearse
1869	Pennsylvania College for Women	Mrs. C. Spears Hicks
1869	Southern Illinois Normal University	Dr. Charles D. Tenney
1869	Wilson College	Miss Agnes L. Patterson
1870	Loyola University	Dr. George Penn Dillard
1870	Ohio State University . . .	Dean L. D. Baver
1870	Syracuse University . . .	Dr. William F. Prouty
1870	Wellesley College	Dr. Helen Somersby French
1871	Smith College	Miss Elizabeth H. Thompson
1872	Alabama Polytechnic Institute	Dr. Russel Spurgeon Poor
1872	Doane College	Mrs. Catherine D. Korstian
1872	University of Oregon . . .	Edwin C. Bryson, Esq.
1872	Vanderbilt University . . .	Dr. Hugh J. Morgan
1872	Virginia Polytechnic Institute .	Professor Landon E. Fuller
1873	Texas Christian University .	The Reverend Newton J. Robison
1874	Colorado College	Dr. Arthur Steadman Roe
1876	Agricultural and Mechanical College of Texas . . .	Professor J. E. Lear
1876	Johns Hopkins University . .	Dean J. Harold Lampe
1878	Belmont Abbey College . .	The Reverend Cuthbert Allen, O.S.B.
		Dr. Araceli Astorga

DATE OF
FOUNDING

1879	Radcliffe College	Mrs. Richard S. Lyman
1880	Bridgewater College . . .	Raymond N. Andes, Esq.
1880	Bryn Mawr College . . .	Mrs. Atala Scudder Davison
1880	Case School of Applied Science	Professor Ernest Stephen Theiss
1881	University of California at Los Angeles	Provost Clarence Addison Dykstra
1882	Hastings College	President William Marshall French
1883	John B. Stetson University . .	President William Sims Allen
1883	University of North Dakota .	Dr. Mowat C. Fraser
1884	Farmville State Teachers College	Dr. Sibyl Henry
1884	Temple University	Dr. Gilbert T. Rowe
1885	University of Arizona . . .	Dr. F. E. Coenen
1885	Georgia School of Technology	President Blake R. Van Leer
1885	Goucher College	Mrs. Leonard E. Fields
1885	International Young Men's Christian Association College . .	President Emeritus Laurence L. Doggett
1885	Rollins College	President Hamilton Holt
1886	University of Chattanooga . .	President David A. Lockmiller
1886	Winthrop College	Professor W. W. Rogers
1887	Campbell College	President Leslie Hartwell Campbell
1887	Clark University	Major Wallace W. Atwood, Jr.
1887	Nebraska Wesleyan University	Dr. Ivan D. Jones
1887	Pomona College	Dr. Ruth M. Collings
1888	Teachers College, Columbia University	Dr. Edgar W. Knight
1888	Utah State Agricultural College	Dr. Clyde Fuhriman Smith
1889	Agnes Scott College	Miss Lila Peck Walker
1889	Barnard College, Columbia University	Mrs. Dudley De Witt Carroll
1889	Catholic University of America	Dean Martin R. P. McGuire
1889	Clemson Agricultural College .	President Robert Franklin Poole
1889	Converse College	Mrs. Gordon Blackwell
1889	East Texas State Teachers College	Mrs. Sam Hobgood
1889	Elon College	President Leon Edgar Smith
1889	Georgia State College for Women	President Guy Herbert Wells
1889	Manchester College	Dr. Ray Petry
1889	North Carolina State College of The University of North Carolina	Chancellor John William Harrelson

1889	Western Carolina Teachers College	Professor Anthony Keith Hinds
1890	Colorado State College of Education	Edward C. Beauvais, Esq.
1890	George Williams College	Fred Fletcher, Esq.
1890	North Dakota Agricultural College	Dr. Frederick Harold McCutcheon
1891	California Institute of Technology	Dr. W. Dougald MacMillan
1891	University of Chicago	Dean Emeritus Louis Round Wilson
1891	Drexel Institute of Technology	President James Creese
1891	Lenoir Rhyne College	President P. E. Monroe
1891	Meredith College	President Carlyle Campbell
1891	Stanford University	Dr. Lon L. Fuller
1891	Woman's College of The University of North Carolina	Chancellor Walter Clinton Jackson
1892	Blackstone College for Girls	President John D. Riddick
1892	Illinois Institute of Technology	Vice-President Linton E. Grinter
1892	Millsaps College	Dr. Vernon Lane Wharton
1892	Rhode Island State College	President Carl Raymond Woodward
1892	Scarritt College	Miss Sarah McCracken
1893	Hood College	President Henry Irvin Stahr
1893	Montana School of Mines	Dr. William A. White
1893	Montana State University	Dr. Eston Everett Ericson
1893	Randolph-Macon Woman's College	President Theodore Jack
1894	University of New Mexico	Mrs. Jessie McMillan Stroup
1894	Warren Wilson College	Miss Mary Carola MacLeod
1895	London School of Economics and Political Science	Dr. F. A. von Hayek
1896	Alabama College	Dr. M. L. Orr
1896	Flora Macdonald College	President Henry G. Bedinger
1900	Carnegie Institute of Technology	Eugene Dowling, Esq.
1900	Southwestern Louisiana Institute	President Joel Lafayette Fletcher
1901	Sweet Briar College	President Meta Glass
1901	Texas State College for Women	Mrs. H. G. Baity
1901	Whittier College	Horace S. Haworth, Esq.
1902	Atlantic Christian College	President H. S. Hilley
1903	Lynchburg College	Dr. Gordon W. Lovejoy
1903	Pfeiffer Junior College	President Chi M. Waggoner

DATE OF
FOUNDING

1905	Gardner-Webb Junior College	President P. L. Elliott
1907	East Carolina Teachers College	Acting President Howard J. McGinnis
1908	Coker College	President Donald C. Agnew
1908	Oklahoma College for Women	Dean Howard Taylor
1908	William Smith College . . .	Dr. Paul W. Wager
1909	Middle Tennessee State College	Dr. Philip Macon Cheek
1909	University of Redlands . . .	Dr. J. Russell Andrus
1910	Radford College	President David W. Peters
1911	Connecticut College . . .	Mrs. Walter J. Seeley
1911	Pine Manor Junior College . .	Miss Harriet Valk
1911	Southern Methodist University	Dr. Olin Terrill Mouzon
1912	Rice Institute	President Emeritus Edgar Odell Lovett
1914	Pineland College	Vice-President G. N. Ashley
1918	New Jersey College for Women	Dr. Hulda Magalhaes
1918	Seton Hill College	Captain Jeanne Staunton Smith
1922	Murray State Teachers College	Mrs. Martha Kelly Gardner
1924	High Point College	Dr. N. M. Harrison
1925	Junior College of Augusta . .	Dr. David F. McDowell
1926	Sarah Lawrence College . .	Mrs. Julian S. Stein, Jr.
1928	Presbyterian Junior College .	President Louis C. La Motte
1930	Institute for Advanced Study .	Dr. Elias A. Lowe
1934	Brevard College	President E. J. Coltrane
1935	Edwards Military Institute .	President W. J. Jones
1935	Sacred Heart Junior College .	Miss Ann Bennett Mrs. J. P. Smith
1937	Queens College, Flushing, New York	Dean Margaret Kiely

DELEGATES FROM SOCIETIES AND FOUNDATIONS

1727	American Philosophical Society	Dr. Guy Stanton Ford
1776	United Chapters of Phi Beta Kappa	Dr. Theodore H. Jack
1780	American Academy of Arts and Sciences	Dr. William de Berniere MacNider
1800	Library of Congress	Dr. Lewis Hanke
1812	American Antiquarian Society .	Dr. Archibald Henderson
1837	American Chemical Society .	Dr. Paul Gross
1839	American Statistical Association	Miss Gertrude M. Cox

DATE OF
FOUNDING

1845	New England Historic Genealogical Society	Edward Hudson Young, Esq.
1846	Smithsonian Institution . . .	Dr. Frank H. H. Roberts, Jr.
1847	American Medical Association	Dr. Charles Wesley Roberts
1848	American Association for the Advancement of Science .	Dr. Samuel Alfred Mitchell
1849	North Carolina Medical Society	Dr. Henry L. Sloane
1852	American Geographical Society	Dr. Samuel T. Emory
1852	American Pharmaceutical Association	Harmon C. McAllister, Esq.
1859	American Dental Association .	Dr. H. O. Lineberger
1859	American Entomological Society	Dr. Zeno Payne Metcalf
1863	National Academy of Sciences	Dr. Samuel Alfred Mitchell
1865	American Association of School Administrators	Vice-President W. Frank Warren
1869	American Philological Association	Dr. Charles W. Peppler
1876	American Library Association	Charles M. Adams, Esq.
1878	American Bar Association . .	Francis E. Winslow, Esq.
1879	Archaeological Institute of America	Dr. J. Penrose Harland
1880	American Society of Mechanical Engineers	Edward E. Williams, Esq.
1880	North Carolina Pharmaceutical Association	Ira W. Rose, Esq.
1881	American School of Classical Studies at Athens	Dr. Charles W. Peppler
1882	American Association of University Women . . .	Dr. Meta Glass
1883	Modern Language Association of America	Dr. Jay B. Hubbell
1884	American Historical Association	Dr. William T. Laprade
1884	North Carolina Education Association	John C. Lockhart, Esq.
1885	American Economic Association	Dr. John B. Woosley
1886	Association of American Physicians	Dr. William de Berniere MacNider
1886	Society of the Sigma Xi . .	Dr. Samuel Alfred Mitchell
1887	American Institute of Accountants	George E. Perrin, Esq.
1888	American Association of Anatomists	Dr. J. E. Markee
1888	American Folklore Society . .	President Joseph M. Carrière

DATE OF
FOUNDING

1888	American Mathematical Society	Dr. Joseph Miller Thomas
1888	Geological Society of America	Dr. Jasper L. Stuckey
1889	American Academy of Political and Social Science . . .	Dr. Katharine Jocher
1889	Association of College and Reference Libraries	Olan Victor Cook, Esq.
1890	American Society of Zoologists	Dr. Irving E. Gray
1892	American Psychological Association	Dr. Karl E. Zener
1893	Society for the Promotion of Engineering Education . . .	N. W. Dougherty, Esq.
1894	American Academy in Rome .	Dr. B. L. Ullman
1895	National Association of State Universities	Dr. Harmon W. Caldwell
1898	American Society for Testing Materials	Dr. William B. Hodge
1900	American Association of Colleges of Pharmacy	Dr. Henry M. Burlage
1900	American Philosophical Association	Dr. Louis O. Kattsoff
1900	Association of American Universities	Dr. William Whatley Pierson, Jr.
1900	State Literary and Historical Association	Dr. Robert Burton House
1901	American Association of Pathologists and Bacteriologists .	Dr. Wiley D. Forbus
1901	National Society for the Study of Education	Dr. A. M. Proctor
1901	North Carolina Academy of Science	Dr. Archie Davis Shaftsbury
1901	Rockefeller Institute for Medical Research	Dr. James Bumgardner Murphy
1902	American Anthropological Association	Dr. John Gillin
1902	Carnegie Institution of Washington	Frederick G. Fassett, Jr., Esq.
1902	North Carolina Federation of Women's Clubs . . .	Mrs. Karl Bishopric
1903	American Political Science Association	Dr. Charles B. Robson
1903	North Carolina State Department of Archives and History . .	Dr. William T. Laprade

DATE OF
FOUNDING

1904 Association of American
Geographers . . . . . Dr. Franklin C. Erickson

1904 Bibliographical Society of
America . . . . Charles E. Rush, Esq.

1904 Classical Association of the
Middle West and South . . Dr. B. L. Ullman

1904 National Catholic Educational The Reverend Edward T.
Association . . . . . Gilbert

1904 North Carolina Library Association . . . . President Susan Grey Akers

1906 Botanical Society of America . Dr. William Chambers Coker

1907 American Society of Agronomy Dr. R. W. Cummings

1907 American Society of International Law . . . . . Dr. William Marion Gibson

1907 Mississippi Valley Historical Association . . . . . . Dr. Fletcher M. Green

1909 North Carolina Library Commission . . . . Miss Marjorie Beal

1910 American Association of Col-
legiate Registrars . . . . Miss Mary Taylor Moore

1911 College Art Association of
America . . . . . Dr. Florence H. Robinson

1911 North Carolina Forestry Association . . . . . . Dr. Edward Willard Berry

1913 American Alumni Council . . President J. Maryon Saunders

1913 American College of Surgeons . Dr. Hubert A. Royster

1913 National Vocational Guidance
Association . . . . . Edward W. Boshart, Esq.

1914 American Association of Uni-
versity Professors . . . . Dr. Benjamin U. Ratchford

1914 American Social Hygiene Association . . . . . . Dr. W. Carson Ryan

1915 American College of Physicians Dr. J. B. Bullitt

1915 Association of American Colleges . . . . Dr. Edmund Ezra Day

1915 Mayo Foundation . . . . Dr. Russel Osborne Lyday

1915 National University Extension
Association . . . . . George B. Zehmer, Esq.

1916 Mathematical Association of
America . . . . . . Dr. J. M. Thomas

1916 National Association of Deans of
Women . . . . Dr. Alice M. Baldwin

1916 National Research Council . Dr. Wilburt C. Davison
1918 American Council on Education Dr. John E. Ivey, Jr.
1919 American Catholic Historical As-
      sociation . . . . . . The Rev. Francis J. Morissey
1919 American Classical League . . Dr. B. L. Ullman
1919 American Council of Learned
      Societies . . . . . . Dr. Waldo Gifford Leland
1919 Henry E. Huntington Library
      and Art Gallery . . . . Dr. W. Dougald MacMillan
1919 North Carolina Congress of Par-
      ents and Teachers . . . . Mrs. E. N. Howell
1920 American Association of Junior
      Colleges . . . . . . Dr. Curtis Bishop
1920 Association of Governing Boards
      of State Universities and Allied
      Institutions . . . . . Secretary Ora L. Wildermuth
1920 National Bureau of Economic
      Research . . . . . . Dr. Milton S. Heath
1920 Soil Science Society of America Dr. J. F. Lutz
1920 Southeastern Library Associa-
      tion . . . . Miss Clyde Smith
1922 American Association of Social
      Workers . . . . . . Mrs. Jean Heer
1922 American Horticultural Society William Lanier Hunt, Esq.
1923 Social Science Research Council Dr. Calvin B. Hoover
1924 Trustees of the Duke Endow-
      ment . . . . William S. O'Brien Robinson,
                             Jr., Esq.
1924 Linguistic Society of America . Dr. George Sherman Lane
1925 Mediaeval Academy of America Dr. George R. Coffman
1927 North Carolina State Art Society President Katherine Pendleton
                             Arrington
1927 Southern Political Science Asso-
      ciation . . . . . . Dr. R. Taylor Cole
1928 South Atlantic Modern Language
      Association . . . . . Dr. Sturgis E. Leavitt
1932 Archaelogical Society of North
      Carolina . . . . . . Dr. Raymond Adams
1932 Association of Research Libra-
      ries . . . . Dr. Harry Clemons
1932 National Theatre Conference . Sawyer Falk, Esq.
1934 American Musicological Society Dr. Glen Haydon
1934 National Archives . . . . Thad Page, Esq.

DATE OF
FOUNDING
1934 Southern Historical Association   Dr. James W. Patton
1935 North Carolina Philosophical So-
        ciety . . . .   Alban G. Widgery, Esq.
1935 Southern University Conference   Dr. Harvie Branscomb
1936 American Sociological Society .   Dr. Charles A. Ellwood
1937 North Carolina Geological So-
        ciety . . . .   Dr. Edward Willard Berry
1939 Southeastern Association for
        Adult Education . . . .   Russell M. Grumman, Esq.

APPENDIX C

On the following pages, the first, third, fourth, and nineteenth pages of the official program of the Sesquicentennial Convocation are reproduced in reduced format.

THE UNIVERSITY OF NORTH CAROLINA

THE SESQUICENTENNIAL

CONVOCATION

MEMORIAL HALL
APRIL THE THIRTEENTH
NINETEEN HUNDRED AND FORTY-SIX

THE UNIVERSITY OF NORTH CAROLINA

The Sesquicentennial Convocation

PROGRAM

Ten O'clock

I THE SESQUICENTENNIAL PROCESSION

The Processional March   The University Band
Professor Earl Slocum, Director

The University Marshal

The President of the University and Party

The Trustees, Legislative Commission,
and Alumni Committee

The Candidates for Honorary Degrees

The Delegates from Colleges and Universities

The Delegates from Learned Societies and
Foundations

The University Faculty and Officers

Ten-thirty O'clock

II THE SESQUICENTENNIAL EXERCISES

CHANCELLOR ROBERT BURTON HOUSE, Presiding

Processional: *March Pontifical*, Gounod
Dr. Jan Philip Schinhan, Organist

The Invocation Reverend Edwin McNeill Poteat
President, Colgate-Rochester Divinity School

Hymn: *Holy, Holy, Holy*
The University Glee Clubs and Audience
Professor Paul Young, Director

Holy, Holy, Holy, Lord God Almighty!
Early in the morning our song shall rise to Thee;
Holy, Holy, Holy, merciful and mighty!
God in three persons, blessed Trinity!

Holy, Holy, Holy, all the saints adore Thee,
Casting down their golden crowns around the glassy sea;
Cherubim and seraphim falling down before Thee,
Which wert, and art, and evermore shall be.

Holy, Holy, Holy, Lord God Almighty!
All Thy works shall praise Thy name, in earth, and sky,
and sea;
Holy, Holy, Holy, merciful and mighty!
God in three persons, blessed Trinity!

The Introduction of Delegates Dr. William Morton Dey
Marshal of the University
(For the names of delegates and institutions, see later pages)

Chorus: *Alleluia*, Randall Thompson
The University Glee Clubs

Address: *Educational Mobilization in a Free Society*
Edmund Ezra Day
President, Cornell University

Address: *A Look Ahead* Frank Porter Graham
President, University of North Carolina

The Conferring of Honorary Degrees
(For the names of candidates, see later pages)
Candidates presented by William Whatley Pierson, Jr.
Dean of the Graduate School

Hymn: *A Mighty Fortress Is Our God*

The University Glee Clubs and Audience

A mighty fortress is our God, A bulwark never failing;
Our helper He, amid the flood Of mortal ills prevailing.
For still our ancient foe Doth seek to work us woe;
    His craft and power are great,
And, armed with cruel hate, On earth is not His equal.

And though this world, with demons filled, Should threaten
    to undo us,
We will not fear, for God hath willed His truth to triumph
    through us,
The Prince of darkness grim, We tremble not for him;
    His rage we can endure,
For lo, his doom is sure, One little word shall fell him.

That word above all earthly powers, No thanks to them,
    abideth;
The Spirit and the gifts are ours Through Him who with
    us sideth.
Let goods and kindred go, This mortal life also;
    The body they may kill;
God's truth abideth still, His kingdom is forever. Amen.

The Benediction   Eugene Epperson Barnett
                      General Secretary, National Council of the
                               Young Men's Christian Association

Organ Postlude

THE HALIFAX RESOLUTION OF APRIL 12, 1776

The University of North Carolina is the child of revolution and freedom. Article XLI of the State Constitution of 1776 required the Legislature to establish a system of public education "for the convenient Instruction of Youth," coupled with an injunction that "all useful Learning shall be duly encouraged and promoted in one or more Universities." The Constitution itself stems from a resolution adopted by the Provincial Congress at Halifax on April 12, 1776, that gave expression to the spirit of political and intellectual freedom which inspired the General Assembly in 1789 to pass "An Act to establish a University in this State."

On April 8, the Congress appointed a committee "to take into consideration the usurpations and violences attempted and committed by the King and Parliament of Britain against America, and the further measure to be taken for frustrating the same, and for the better defence of this Province." Four days later, on April 12, this committee made its report, reproduced below, which the Congress unanimously adopted. Thirteen years later, on December 11, 1789, the university was chartered. On October 12, 1793, the cornerstone of Old East Building was laid, and on January 15, 1795, the doors of the university were formally opened.

* * *

It appears to your committee, that pursuant to the plan concerted by the British Ministry for subjugating America, the King and Parliament of Great Britain have usurped a power over the persons and properties of the people unlimited and uncontrouled; and disregarding their humble petitions for peace, liberty and safety, have made divers legislative acts, denouncing war, famine, and every species of calamity, against the Continent in general. The British fleets and armies have been, and still are daily employed in destroying the people, and committing the most horrid devastations on the country. That Governors in different Colonies have declared protection to slaves, who should imbrue their hands in the blood of their masters. That Ships belonging to America are declared prizes of war, and many of them have been violently seized and confiscated. In consequence of all which multitudes of people have been destroyed, or from easy circumstances reduced to the most lamentable distress.

And whereas the moderation hitherto manifested by the United Colonies and their sincere desire to be reconciled to the mother country on constitutional principles, have procured no mitigation of the aforesaid wrongs and usurpations, and no hopes remain of obtaining redress by those means alone which have been hitherto tried, your committee are of opinions that the House should enter into the following resolve, to wit:

Resolved, That the delegates for this Colony in the Continental Con-

gress be impowered to concur with the delegates of the other Colonies in declaring Independency, and forming foreign alliances, reserving to this Colony the sole and exclusive right of forming a Constitution and laws for this Colony, and appointing delegates from time to time (under the direction of a general representation thereof), to meet the delegates of the other Colonies for such purposes as shall be hereafter pointed out.
—*Colonial Records of North Carolina*, X, 512.

INDEX

INDEX